Freeing
The Dead Sea
Scrolls

and Other

Adventures of

an Archaeology

Outsider

BOOKS BY HERSHEL SHANKS

Jerusalem's Temple Mount: From Solomon to the Golden Dome

The Copper Scroll and the Search for the Temple Treasure

Jerusalem: An Archaeological Biography

The Mystery and Meaning of the Dead Sea Scrolls

The City of David: A Guide to Biblical Jerusalem

Judaism in Stone: The Archaeology of Ancient Synagogues

The Dead Sea Scrolls After Forty Years (with James C. VanderKam, P. Kyle McCarter, Jr., and James A. Sanders)

The Rise of Ancient Israel (with William G. Dever, Baruch Halpern, P. Kyle McCarter, Jr.)

The Brother of Jesus (with Ben Witherington III)

BOOKS EDITED BY HERSHEL SHANKS

The Art and Craft of Judging: The Opinions of Judge Learned Hand

Scholars on the Record: Insightful Interviews on Bible and Archaeology

Ancient Israel: From Abraham to the Roman Destruction of Jerusalem

Christianity and Rabbinic Judaism: A Parallel History of Their Origins and Early Development

Understanding the Dead Sea Scrolls

Archaeology and the Bible: The Best of BAR, 2 vols. (with Dan P. Cole)

Feminist Approaches to the Bible (with Phyllis Trible, Tivka Frymer-Kensky, Pamela J. Milne, Jane Schaberg)

Recent Archaeology in the Land of Israel (with Benjamin Mazar)

The Search for Jesus (with Stephen J. Patterson, Marcus J. Borg, John Dominic Crossan)

Frank Moore Cross: Conversations with a Bible Scholar

Abraham & Family: New Insights into the Patriarchal Narratives

Freeing The Dead Sea Scrolls

and Other Adventures of an Archaeology Outsider

HERSHEL SHANKS

continuum

Published by the Continuum International Publishing Group

The Tower Building	80 Maiden Lane
11 York Road	Suite 704
London SE1 7NX	New York, NY 10038

www.continuumbooks.com

First published 2010

British Library Cataloguing-in-Publication Data
A catalogue record for this book is available from the British Library.

ISBN: 978-1441-15217-6

Designed and typeset by Newgen Imaging Systems Pvt Ltd, Chennai, India
Printed and bound in the United States of America

CONTENTS

To JUDITH

my wife of 43 years, the mother of my children
Elizabeth and Julia and the grandmother of my
grandchildren Charlie and Nancy, to whom, then Judy,
my first book was dedicated in 1968

Acknowledgments

I SHOULD LIKE TO BEGIN THESE ACKNOWLEDGMENTS by venting my anger at the contractor I hired to build my treadmill room in the basement. He left a pile of sawdust overnight near an outside drain; a heavy rain that night swept the sawdust over the drain and blocked it. The result was a flooded basement that destroyed, among much else, my family photos. I am grateful to my sister Leah Gordon for supplying the family pictures in this volume.

Three excellent editors reviewed my text and each made a significant contribution to it. I thank Steven Feldman, G. Joseph Corbett and John Loudon for their help.

Most important was the staff of the Biblical Archaeology Society— my longtime colleague, BAS president and *Biblical Archaeology Review* publisher Susan Laden; BAR administrative editor Bonnie Mullin; production manager Heather Metzger; and Janet Bowman who does everything.

The inside of the book was designed by graphic designer Rob Sugar, with whom I have worked happily for more than 30 years, and his assistant Jinna Hagerty of Auras Design.

Hershel Shanks
WASHINGTON, D.C.

NOVEMBER 2009

Preface

I AM SITTING IN AN UNFAMILIAR COURTROOM in Jerusalem.

In general, I am accustomed to courtrooms. For years, I represented the United States of America in courtrooms all over the country when I was a lawyer with the Department of Justice. I know how to question my witnesses on direct and how to examine the other guy's witnesses on cross.

But this is different. I am here not as a lawyer representing someone. I am the defendant!

The testimony is in Hebrew, which I do not understand. My daughter, who is fluent in Hebrew, sits beside me to provide the gist of the testimony against me.

The plaintiff is a distinguished Israeli scholar named Elisha Qimron, a professor at Ben-Gurion University of the Negev in Beer-Sheba. I had published without permission Professor Qimron's one-page Hebrew reconstruction of a fragmentary Dead Sea Scroll known as MMT, in an effort to break the scroll monopoly. Although the reconstruction had circulated widely in samizdat copies, it had not been officially published by Qimron and Harvard professor John Strugnell to whom it had been officially assigned. Moreover, I had not mentioned Qimron's name in my publication; Qimron was anonymous.

I listen as Qimron testifies: For 11 consecutive years, he had worked on the reconstruction I had published. "During the years I worked on it, I did almost no other work." During this time, he says, his "whole family lived very frugally ... When my wife complained, I would tell her, 'Look, this is our life; we will achieve fame.'"

When I published his reconstruction, he was "shocked ... I can't describe the feeling ... It's as if someone came and took away the thing I had made by force, telling me: 'Go away! This belongs to me!'"

I watch the judge and see those tell-tale half-expressions that reveal her sympathy for the plaintiff, as she indeed turned out to have, ultimately awarding Qimron 100,000 shekels in damages (about $40,000). She was not alone in her sympathies. Both the Israeli academic community and the Israeli press considered me a thief. The unbreakable academic convention was that a scholar assigned the publication of an ancient text had exclusive right to it until it was published, even if that took more than a generation.

As I sit in the courtroom listening to Hebrew testimony I cannot understand, my mind wanders. I am no longer the Harvard-trained lawyer. I am back in the little town in western Pennsylvania where I grew up, the son of parents who had never been to college, of a father who sold shoes for a living, the kid who always seemed to be getting into trouble. How did I get here?

Today the angst I felt in that courtroom has passed. Everyone—scholars as well as the press—is happy that the scrolls have been freed. The scholars who once reviled me are now my friends (all except Qimron who is still bitter).

I think of this now as I am involved in another scholarly battle: I am almost the sole public voice defending the authenticity of a first-century bone box inscribed "James, son of Joseph, brother of Jesus" and a small ivory pomegranate that, if authentic, is probably the only relic to have survived from Solomon's Temple. Both are enormously important— if real. However, two committees of the Israel Antiquities Authority (IAA) have, supposedly unanimously, judged both these ancient inscriptions to be modern forgeries. In what has been dubbed "the forgery trial of the century," a criminal indictment likewise alleges that these inscriptions are forgeries. The trial against the two remaining defendants (the others have been dismissed) is now in its fourth year. The defendants deny the charges. In light of the findings of the IAA committees and the indictment charging that the inscriptions are forgeries, the press—from *60 Minutes* to the BBC—has almost unanimously agreed (and assumed) that the inscriptions are forgeries.

That too will change—perhaps by the time these words appear in print. Perhaps in time for my 80th birthday in 2010. Or perhaps not for a generation.

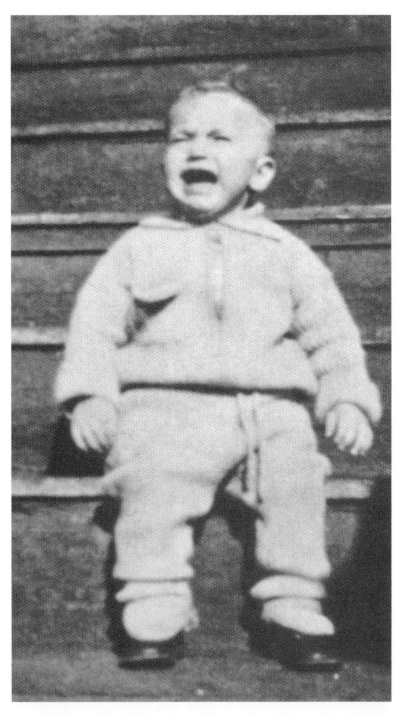

A PORTENT OF THINGS TO COME. Even at the age of two, I was already doing my best to let the world know how I felt about things.

CHAPTER I

In the Beginning

I GUESS I BETTER EXPLAIN AT THE start. This autobiography is not about my sex life. And it is not about my wife Judith to whom I've been happily married for 43 years, nor my daughters Elizabeth and Julia. Nor is it about my lifelong efforts to play the piano. All these things have humbled me, each in its own way. But that is not what this book is about. It is about other things.

I was born on March 8, 1930, in Sharon, Pennsylvania, a small mill town of 15,000 people on the Ohio border and home of the Sharon Steel Corporation. My father sold shoes in a store across from the steel mills. When the store went bankrupt in the Depression, my father and Chubby Rome, a *cheder* buddy (a *cheder* is a young boys' Hebrew school taught after regular school), acquired the store at the bankruptcy sale. But Chubby (actually Ben, but nobody knew that was his name) had to keep working in the mill. The store could not provide an income for both of them. Eventually, the partners acquired another store for Chubby in Warren, Ohio, about 20 miles away.

One of the finest things I can say about my father is that he and Chubby remained partners until Chubby was an old man and retired. And they never had a disagreement. My father was rather humorless and impatient, all business. Chubby was just the opposite—full of jokes and laughter, never in a hurry. But they got along famously. They talked every day after the stores closed, gossiping like fishwives. My father did most of the work. He believed in work. He kept the books. His store, unlike Chubby's, was immaculate. He dusted every shoebox in the store every week. That included the boxes of rubber goulashes in summer.

A FAMILY PORTRAIT taken when I was in high school. By then, my
father Martin, who had been born in Kiev and immigrated with his
family to the United States at six years old, owned a shoe store in Sharon,
Pennsylvania, on the Ohio border. My mother Mildred, with occasional
help from my father, raised me and my sister Leah there.

My mother, on the other hand, was young and beautiful and charm-
ing. She never went to college, but she was the smartest woman I have
ever known.

But that is getting ahead of the story. My story really begins several
thousands of years ago in that little patch of land called Israel. (I've been
learning the details of that fascinating story for the past 35 years as the
editor of *Biblical Archaeology Review*.) But the last couple of generations
are more personal. It starts in Russia at the beginning of the 20th century.

My father's name was originally Sushansky—or perhaps Shushansky.
We're not sure which. My mother thought that if the name were Shushansky
then perhaps our family came from Shushan, where the biblical Mordecai
and his foster daughter Esther came from. Shushan (Susa) was the capital of

ancient Elam in what is now southwestern Iran. There sat King Ahasuerus who made Esther his queen and she saved all the Jews. We read their story at Purim. Perhaps that's where we came from, my mother thought. The etymology, almost surely fanciful, gave us a little *yichus* (pedigree), at least in our own eyes.

In fact, my father was born in Kiev, in the Ukraine. His father was a tailor who made uniforms for the soldiers of the czar, which apparently was something to be proud of. At one point the family moved to Odessa, a port city on the Black Sea. When my father was six years old, there was a pogrom. The Jews in the neighborhood fled to the basement of a friendly Christian neighbor. The Cossacks came into the house looking for Jews. An infant in the basement began to cry and a pillow was pressed on the baby's face so the crying wouldn't be heard upstairs. When the Cossacks left, the pillow was removed. The Jews had been saved, but the baby was dead. That was the incident that caused the family to leave for America.

The story has the ring of truth. The infamous Kishinev pogroms occurred in 1903 and 1905. Kishinev is a bare hundred miles northwest of Odessa. More than 7,000 of Kishinev's 60,000 Jews left between the first and second pogroms, "many emigrating to the United States ..., while many more left after the second [1905] attack."[1] A number of pogroms also occurred in Odessa over the years. "The severest pogroms occurred [there] in 1905 ... Over 300 [Odessa] Jews lost their lives, whilst thousands of families were injured."[2] These facts could not have been known by my father from literary sources. His stories of pogroms (which we got via my mother) must have been based on stories handed down and on dim memories.

According to immigration records, my grandfather Chane (Chunyeh), his wife Lane (Laneh) and four children, one of whom is listed as Abram, six years old, sailed on the *SS Marion* from Liverpool on March 28, 1906, and docked in Philadelphia on April 9, 1906. The immigration manifest lists them as Hebrews who last resided in Odessa. Their passage was paid for by Chane himself. They were bound for Youngstown, Ohio, where a brother Haim and his son Joseph had lived for three years.

The family name is written twice on the manifest, once in connection with Chane and once in connection with Haim. In both cases it is spelled Susanschky. But that is not conclusive. That is just how the immigration officer spelled it.

In any event, the family went to Youngstown, Ohio, where they made their home. The little boy who would become my father had a paper route that he remembered with some pride. He knew just who paid him more than the minimum amount. He eventually forgot his Russian (but not his Yiddish) and spoke English without an accent. He graduated from Rayen High School in Youngstown. Shortly before, however, his father died of cancer. Instead of going to college and medical school as he had intended, he became the breadwinner of the family. He got a job in a steel factory in Youngstown. After a short time, he got a job as a shoe salesman at Reed's Shoe Store in Farrell, Pennsylvania, a small town about 15 miles from Youngstown. He took a street car to work.

Reed's Shoe Store was located on Broadway, just over the state line. The little town was called South Sharon at the time. It was the poor neighbor to Sharon, which was an adjacent town not much larger. One side of the street—the better side—was Sharon; the other, Farrell.

Stores lined only one side of Broadway. On the other side, in the near distance, were the steel mills that provided the customers to the stores.

It was while he was working at Reed's that my father became a citizen. On April 14, 1921, he signed under oath his declaration of intention to become a citizen. This declaration confirms much of his personal history: He was born in Kiev; his last foreign residence was Odessa; he arrived in Philadelphia on the *SS Marion* on April 9, 1906. According to this declaration, however, he sailed from Rotterdam, not Liverpool. Apparently, Rotterdam was the previous port of embarkation; the ship then sailed to Liverpool. I suspect that the family traveled by land from Ukraine to Hamburg, Germany, and that the ship sailed first to Rotterdam and then to Liverpool before landing at Philadelphia.

He gives his birth date as December 10, 1899. In the family, he always gave his birth year as 1900. We could always tell his age by the year. In 1950 he was 50, and so on. Was he lying when he swore he was born in 1899?

DRESSED FOR SUCCESS. An early photo of me with my sister Leah.

Perhaps. He may have lied in order to swear he was 21. He was actually 20. On the other hand, the immigration manifest shows his age as six in April 1906, a date consistent with his birth in 1899.

From the Declaration of Intention to become a citizen, we also get a picture of what he looked like in 1921—five-feet, four-inches; 145 pounds. "Color: White; Complexion: Light; Eyes: Gray; Color of Hair: Brown [his hair must have already changed; as a boy it had a reddish cast and he was called "Red"]; Other Visible Distinctive Marks: None." He lists his occupation as "salesman."

He also swore, as required, that he was not an anarchist, nor a polygamist, "nor a believer in the practice of polygamy."

His name is listed as Martin Shanks, and he signed his name Martin A. Shanks. His petition to become a citizen was granted three years later—on June 27, 1924. In the oath of allegiance and in the order of court granting the petition, however, his name is listed, and written in his own handwriting, as Martin Abraham Sushansky (a third spelling). He had apparently already adopted the name Shanks but only informally.

In 1995, I traveled with my long-time colleague Suzanne Singer to the former Soviet Union in search of stories on Jewish life for *Moment*, a magazine of Jewish cultural affairs of which we were serving as editor and managing editor. (I wrote a lengthy report in the February 1996 issue entitled "Can Jewish Life Be Restored in the Former Soviet Union?") In preparation for the trip I decided to do a little genealogical research.

On the assumption that the name had been spelled correctly by my father on his citizenship application as Sushansky, I speculated as to where it might have come from. The suffix "...sky," of course, is common. It means "person of." In the early 19th century, people in Russia didn't have last names. When this was required, many people took as their last name the place where they were from. The "Sushansky" family would have been "People of Sushan."

I began looking at books with Jewish *shtetl* lists for a *shtetl* (a small Jewish village) with a name close to "Sushan." No candidates. So at the Library of Congress I started looking at old maps of the area that included Kiev for a possible name. I noticed that almost all the little villages included the feminine suffix "...ka." Then I came upon it: Sushanka. Take off the suffix and you have Sushan, the same name you get when you take off the suffix "...sky."

Sushanka was about 10 miles from the center of the city of Kiev. Kiev, where my father was born, designated an area, not just the city itself. Maybe my father's family came from Sushanka. True, Sushanka was not listed as a Jewish *shtetl*, but the books could easily have missed some. I decided to try to visit Sushanka.

Inside the FSU (Former Soviet Union) we were supported by the Joint Distribution Committee, a Jewish relief agency. On our visit to the city of Kiev (where we saw the Great Gate immortalized in Moussorgsky's "Pictures at an Exhibition"), we were supplied with a car and driver to take us to Zhitomir, an important Hasidic center in the 19th century. At the turn of the 20th century, the town had about 60,000 residents, nearly half of whom were Jewish. Then the old story—pogroms, emigration mostly to the United States, the disintegration of Jewish life under the Soviets, the flight of the town's remaining Jews from the Nazis—and now it was attempting a revival led by a Lubavitcher (Hasidic) rabbi. Zhitomir lies about 75 miles west of Kiev. After a day meeting with the Jews of Zhitomir, we headed back to Kiev along a road that on the map looked as if it almost passed through Sushanka.

I asked the driver (through our interpreter) if he could go there on the way. He had never heard of the place but he was glad to comply. I showed him my copies of the ancient maps, and he thought he could get us there. He continually asked people from the area where it was supposed to be, and they kept pointing. We ended up driving through a forest, not even on a path. I was afraid: If we broke down, we would be in the forest for the night. The car was what my father would have called a *tradikeh* (a tin-lizzie in 1930s Yiddish jargon) and the area was, at least in my mind, lawless. But the driver had no such fear (nor did anyone else in the car), and we just proceeded through the route, confirming with an occasional woodsman that indeed Sushanka was on the other side.

We emerged from the forest in a field, drove down the hill, crossed a stream and soon came upon Sushanka. A herd of cows was passing through the center of the village, but stopped us only momentarily. We inquired whether there were any Jews in the town. The reply was no. We then asked whether there had been any in the past. Our friendly respondents replied no, but directed us to the town's only old people, a couple who lived down the road.

"Down the road" we found the couple, who invited us into their poor but neat home. They confirmed that there were no Jews in town, nor had there been before the Second World War, but the wife recalled that when she was a little girl, someone mentioned that there had been some Jews there, and there were knives. That is all she knew. Were the Jews driven away with knives? She didn't know.

She wouldn't allow us to leave without a gift: a handful of small gnarled apples that grew in their yard. We graciously thanked them and returned to Kiev. Had I been to the village where my father's family came from? I will never know for sure.

My mother's family also had a name change—from Jacobovitch to Jacoby, when my mother's grandparents opened up a little confectionery shop next to the bank in Farrell, Pennsylvania. The Jacoby's had five beautiful daughters who reached adulthood, one of whom, Fannie, became my mother's mother. The other four girls—Sarah, Rosie, Sophie and Mary—made excellent marriages to men who earned a living that ranged from adequate to wealthy. They lived with their husbands in Philadelphia (Rose Klein), Cleveland (Mary Lurie and Sarah Gross) and Sharon (Sophie Horowitz). Fannie alone had trouble finding a husband—or more precisely, they had trouble finding a husband for her. Although she too was a beautiful girl, she had had smallpox as a child that left her face pockmarked and bumpy. The disease also left her cross-eyed, which had to be corrected with glasses. So a marriage was arranged with David Freedman, a strapping six-footer from Hungary who was living with relatives in Wilkes Barre, Pennsylvania, several hundred miles from Farrell. David was 18 at the time and had a job carrying bricks upstairs for the construction of a building several stories high.

David was brought to Farrell. Early efforts at introducing him to the world of business failed. He soon got a job in the steel mills and worked there for the rest of his working life, except for a short period when he opened a grocery store with his son Phillip that failed. At the mill, he was known as Big Dave and ultimately rose to the position of millwright.

I never knew my paternal grandparents. They died before I was born. But I remember both my maternal grandparents clearly. The account I have just written of Dave Freedman gives a wholly one-sided picture. He was a man of character and quality. And so far as I ever saw, he was uncomplaining, despite his difficult life. In those days, men worked six days a week. But in the mills, the day off varied; the furnaces had to be kept going 24 hours a day, seven days a week. Men worked in three shifts—a morning shift from eight to four; an afternoon shift from four to midnight; and a midnight shift from midnight to eight. The shift changed every two weeks—I can't imagine that, working a different shift every two weeks. But that's what my grandfather did all his life. As a boy and a young man, I remember so many family gatherings in Sharon when one of "the boys"—his sons Phil and Hersh—would have to drive "Papa" to work at 2:30 on a Sunday afternoon. (Papa never had a car of his own.) They would drive Papa to the mill entrance on Broadway, which had an open steel arch that in retrospect looked much like the steel arch at the entrance to Auschwitz. There they would drop Papa off. Papa had to walk another half-mile to get to the mill from the entrance. Private cars were not allowed inside the gate. But worst of all, as I remember it, Papa had to miss the rest of the Sunday party.

When Dave's father-in-law died, his mother-in-law, Lena Jacoby, moved in not with her wealthy daughters, but with her poorest daughter, Fannie. Lena was a difficult woman and, I am told, the source of much friction between Dave and Fannie. On one occasion, according to my mother, Dave almost killed her with a knife. But I never saw this side of him. I remember his lumbering gait and his powerful hands tightly closing the jar lids on the delicious fruit and vegetables that Grandma canned and lined up on the kitchen table for him to give the final touch to the warm jars. When his corncob pipe wasn't lit, he was chewing Weyman's Cut & Dried Tobacco, which we always gave him for Father's Day and his birthday. I recall his racing through the Passover *haggadah* in his heavily Hungarian-accented Hebrew (no English) as we all urged him (especially

Phil and Hersh whom I imitated) to go faster so we could get to the dinner. I remember his taking me by the hand as we walked together to *shul* (synagogue). That is my earliest recollection of *shul*—sitting next to my grandfather in his regular place on the bench, to the right of the raised *bima* in the center of the prayer hall. My grandfather sat next to Litvak Rosenblum. There were several Rosenblums in Farrell and Sharon, but he was different; he came from Lithuania. So he was known as Litvak Rosenblum. I don't know if anyone knew his real name. Litvak Rosenblum would pinch my cheek—hard, so hard it would sting for a few minutes. But I liked it—and him.

Lena Jacoby was the source of friction not only between my grandparents, but also with my mother. My mother was an identical twin. Her sister Jeanette was the weaker, more sickly one who, my mother felt, was favored. In fact, Jeanette died at 52 from breast cancer. When the twins graduated from high school, it was decided that Jeanette should go to what was then called normal school, a two-year college that qualified graduates to teach in public schools. To afford it, Grandpa could provide part of the money and Mildred could get a job and supply the rest. That is what happened. My mother got a job in the high school where they had graduated and soon was tapped as secretary to the principal, Mr. Stillings. My mother always spoke adoringly of Mr. Stillings. She desperately wanted to go to college, however. The opportunity came: Mr. Stillings was to have a sabbatical which he planned to spend at Slippery Rock State Teachers College, and he offered my mother lodging in his house down there so she could go to college despite her limited means. With her meager savings, she would still have enough to get her through the year. At this point, enter Lena Jacoby. She would not permit Mildred to live in the same house with a married man. Mildred was defiant. She would go anyway. The day before she was ready to leave, she packed her bags and went to sleep. In the night, her father, doubtless at Lena Jacoby's instructions, hid her bags in the rafters under the roof. In tears, Mildred surrendered. This created a permanent psychic wound. Mildred still speaks of the two years she worked for Mr. Stillings as the happiest years of her life.

Yet there is another side. Gossip had it that she had been seen at Levine's men's store buying a man's collar. Yes, Mildred had done this. Mr. Stillings had an event to attend and had a dirty collar, so he asked if Mildred would go down to Levine's and buy him a fresh one. All very innocent. But was it? When she was in her 90s, she told me that Mr. Stillings had been divorced. We will never know the truth. I'm not sure I want to.

It was while my mother was working for Mr. Stillings that she met my father. His friend Irv Barker had a date with Jeanette, and she asked him to get a date for her sister. So Irv asked Martin. Not long after, they married. In our family lore, it was a legendary wedding. Held at Aunt Sophie's home in Sharon, the crowds were so thick the police had to come out to direct traffic.

I spent a lot of time with my grandparents. Once, at my insistence, Papa gave me his lit pipe to draw on. One draw and I got sick—vomited. Then my grandfather took me by the hand and we had a nice walk outside in the cool breeze.

On New Year's Eve, my parents would deposit me and my sister Leah at Grandma and Papa's and we would play casino (a card game) with them until ten or eleven at night.

I also had friends in my grandparents' neighborhood. I recall digging out the tar from between the bricks with which the streets were paved and chewing it like gum, just as the rest of the kids did. When I got a penny or two, we would buy candy at Pasconi's, next to Magnatto's gas station, where my dad always filled up his Pontiac. If I were a poet I would lyricize about the delights of Pasconi's. Since I am not, I will say that only now do I realize from the names that there was a large Italian population in Farrell. (Two doors down from my father's Reed Shoe Store was Marino's Hardware Store.) Farrell was a town of mixed immigrant communities—Italians, Poles, Czechs, Hungarians, Lithuanians, Jews, each with its own "Home." For the Jews, it was the *shul*. I'm sure there were some conflicts between these ethnic communities, but I don't remember any and I never heard of any.

On one July Fourth, I had enough money to buy some firecrackers at Pasconi's. These included some Roman candles, which didn't make noise but sent beautiful sparks into the air. Sammy Schermer, who lived across the street from my grandparents, was with me. Sammy was considerably older than I—perhaps by as much as three years—but I had the money and they were my firecrackers. I was young enough that I was not yet able to light matches, however. Sammy could. That is an important part of the story. Impatient for the evening, we sought a dark place in the afternoon where we could light the Roman candles. We found it in the Solomon's garage, next door to my grandparents. It was a dilapidated wooden structure, an ideal place to light Roman candles in the afternoon. Sammy lit the match. We lit—or rather he lit—the Roman candles, and they were beautiful. We then went out to play, entirely forgetting about what we had done. A half-hour later, there were shouts in the neighborhood. We ran back to my grandparent's house and there saw the most beautiful fire that I have ever seen: The Solomon garage was all ablaze, every bit of it. It was not long before the sirens of the fire truck announced its arrival, and the whole neighborhood watched as water doused the flames. But, alas, nothing was left of the garage. It was never rebuilt, just cleared away. Mr. Solomon didn't need it anyway because he sold vegetables from a horse-drawn cart and didn't have a car. Because the firecrackers were mine, however, I was blamed. But, as I said, it was really Sammy who lit the match. Later that summer, I saw Sammy at the Buhl Farm swimming pool and told him that he had lit the match. He just ignored me and jumped into the water.

My grandparents died within three days of each other in 1955 when I was in law school in Cambridge, Massachusetts. My parents called to tell me my grandmother had died. But it was too expensive for me to come home for the funeral. The same conversation was repeated three days later when my grandfather died. I have always been sorry that I didn't come home for their funerals. I had nothing to mark their passing. For years when I would come home, I would think about visiting Grandma and Papa, forgetting that they were no longer there.

CHAPTER II

The Sharon Years

AS I TRY TO CALL UP MEMORIES of my childhood and the small western Pennsylvania town where I was raised, I have no memories of being happy—or unhappy. I just was. I didn't think in those terms—even of being satisfied or unsatisfied. I am told that when my sister Leah arrived (I was four), I tried to sell her.

I recall one supper (which is what we called it, not dinner) that affected me for years. I must have been eight or nine at the time. My mother never liked to get up once supper was served. "Once I sit down, I'm not getting up," she would say, so if there was something you wanted, ask for it now. We sat at a kind of picnic table in a dining nook in the kitchen.

So that she wouldn't have to get up even for dessert, she would put the four desserts on plates at the end of the table, near the wall where I sat, opposite my sister. On this particular occasion, it was cheesecake. I accidentally spilled my water into one of the plates of cheesecake. I quickly finished my meal and ate one of the other plates of cheesecake. When my parents, sitting on the outside, finished their meal, I passed them each an unwatered plate of cheesecake. When Leah finally finished eating, she took the remaining plate of cheesecake—it was full of water! She began to cry and it was apparent to everyone what had happened. My mother yelled at me and pronounced the punishment: I would have to eat the watered cheesecake. That couldn't have been so bad, but I remember that it tasted terrible and I was full besides. I had to stuff myself with this terrible cheesecake. For years after that—I think until I went to college—I would not eat cheesecake, even the unwatered kind. I had no taste for it.

I suppose this sounds like a kid's prank. And it was. But there is perhaps something deeper in it. For better or worse, in some ways it presaged the man.

I had a happy, normal childhood. I suppose I occasionally wished I had other parents, but only fleetingly. When I would get mad at my parents, I would "get even" with them by sleeping on the wooden hall floor using the throw rugs for covers. It was quite comfortable, they would feel sorry for me I thought, and I knew I would awaken in the morning comfortably ensconced in my own bed with the covers carefully folded under my chin.

I never thought about living in New York, or even Youngstown, Ohio, the big, sophisticated city about 15 miles from Sharon. Sharon simply was. That was the only world I knew. In my mind, it had no description. Of course it was where I lived, but that was all.

A recurring theme in this tale is a certain rebelliousness, an unwillingness to follow the accepted rules. But there was also something else: An inability to appreciate or even realize that there was a world beyond— indeed, that there were other worlds. It was only years later, when I had somehow miraculously escaped from Sharon that I appreciated that there were other possibilities. As I did not think about this as a little child, so I did not think about it until I went to college.

* * * *

I still remember the names of my grade school teachers, from grades one to six, all unmarried ladies of a certain age: Miss Franey, Miss Gaines, Miss Elliot, Miss Ague, Miss Hoagland and Miss Evans. Each of these teachers had her own reputation. Miss Franey was nice; Miss Gaines was mean; Miss Elliot had a stiff leg and limped, and she was strict; Miss Ague was not nice; but Miss Hoagland was very nice—couldn't wait to get to fifth grade. Miss Evans was old and fat. She became the principal when I reached sixth grade so we changed teachers in the middle. I don't remember the name of the other one.

I was a bright, but not brilliant student—A's and B's. My only bad subject was "Deportment"—usually D; sometimes I would get up to a C.

My mother would have to make her annual trip to school to discuss my behavior with the teacher. I don't remember what I did wrong. I couldn't understand rules that didn't make sense.

In second grade, Miss Gaines told me in front of the class that I had a button unbuttoned. I looked at the line of buttons down the front of my shirt; they were all buttoned. So I denied it, but she insisted. Perhaps she meant the buttons on my cuffs, so on the second round I looked there as well, but they too were buttoned. I didn't know what to do except deny it. She told me to leave the room and not come back until I found the unbuttoned button. So I retreated to the big hall outside "Miss Gaines's room." Again I looked but didn't find it. Then it occurred to me: my fly. I looked down. Those were the days before zippers. Sure enough, a button was unbuttoned. I buttoned it and, mortified, had to return to my seat while the rest of the class silently looked at me.

My best friend was Joe Ellovich, who lived in a fine house across the street from me. Although he was born only five months before me (on October 29 to my March 8), he was a grade ahead of me. Second grade is nothing, he would tell me. It's easy. Wait until you get to third grade. Of course when I got to third grade, thinking I had finally arrived, he would tell me the same thing about third grade, and so on for several years. Finally, it didn't bother me. I showed myself I could make it.

Until the war (World War II), we had a middle-aged live-in maid named Monica Jurino. Monica was always threatening to quit because of my behavior. I never really believed those threats, but my mother took them seriously. We had only one bathroom, and the rule was that you washed the bathtub as the water ran out, being careful not to leave a black ring. From the sounds emanating from the bathroom, I could tell when Monica was taking a bath. When she got out of the tub, she began washing around the tub, as I could tell by hearing the swishing. On one occasion I quickly went to the landing of the stairs on the other side of the bathtub drain. There was a small wooden door that I quietly opened, exposing the back of the tub and its drain. I carefully moved the drain so that the water was no longer draining out: Monica was swishing a bathtub that was not draining. Finally, she realized the drain was closed and the water was not draining out. She turned it, thinking the mistake was hers. Quietly listening on the balcony, I turned the drain so that it would again not drain. This time, Monica suspected something. With a towel around her, she stuck her head past the door and looked down at the landing. There I was with the plumbing door open—caught red-handed, as they say. Monica again threatened to quit—this time she really meant it—but my mother succeeded in mollifying her. She stayed with us until she got a job in the mill during the war. When the men were away in the army, high-paying manual jobs opened up for women. Besides, it was the patriotic thing to do. I never missed Monica, but my mother did. They remained friends for many years, even writing each other letters when Monica married (for the second time) and moved to Cleveland.

At the end of the school year in sixth grade, report cards were handed out. As usual, mine stated that I had passed to the next grade. But seventh grade was junior high, a different building, downtown, a delightful half-hour's walk each morning with my friends. Best of all, I was no longer under the control or authority—under the jurisdiction, as I might later say—of Jefferson Avenue Elementary School. Free at last. I took my hated sixth-grade geography notebooks and tore them to shreds, strewing them around the schoolhouse yard. Then I proceeded home where I would scream to an adoring mother, "Mom, I passed. I passed."

This time, my mother was waiting for me on the porch, arms folded. My screams did not produce the anticipated response. Miss Evans's telephone call had preceded me. I was instructed to return to school and pick up the torn pieces from my geography notebooks—all of them. So I did. It probably took 20 minutes, but it seemed like 20 hours. Fortunately, Susie Hyde happened along and agreed to help me. But even her assistance could not erase the humiliation. I had obviously misjudged the jurisdictional issue.

In junior high, unlike grade school, we changed classrooms each period, with a different teacher for each subject. My English teacher, whose class I had immediately after lunch, was Miss Kahl. I remember her even now as Patricia Kahl, as if I had risen to a new level of relationship. Miss Kahl was not only young and pretty (all my other teachers had been older), but she wore colorful cashmere sweaters with two rather prominent bulges in front. Each day I would wisecrack or do something like hiding the girls' books (left there during lunch breaks) and she would kick me out of class and send me to the library. This became a habit, and it was fine with me. Not that I minded her class, but the offense gave me a smart-alecky high, which even now I am reluctant to confess to. Apparently, Miss Kahl was a new teacher, although I didn't know it at the time; kicking me out was her way of preventing disruption and controlling the class.

I would usually get to class early, while everyone, including Miss Kahl, was still at lunch. On one occasion, I took a coconut that she kept on her desk that was cut out in the shape of a head with facial features and set it as if it were looking at the figure seated at the desk. I placed her glasses that she had left on the desk on the coconut. In front of it, I opened the Bible (in those days, we still began the school day in "homeroom" with a Bible reading, including the New Testament).

As the students straggled in, they snickered and laughed. Then came Miss Kahl. She knew immediately who had done it. The class had not even started and I was already kicked out, sent to the library. I didn't mind. While I was comfortably ensconced reading, however, six-foot-three Mr. Crowell, the principal, came in, grabbed me by the ear, dragged me to his office and proceeded to kick me out of school. Not just Miss Kahl's class. I was terribly frightened and began to cry. I pleaded with him to allow me to stay in the library until my mother came in for a conference. He agreed. I remember sitting in the library reading a book about baseball, in which I had no interest whatever; it was the first time I had read a complete book in one day. Whether my mother came in later that day or the next morning I do not remember, but we met in Mr. Crowell's office, where she apologized and I was allowed back in class. Thereafter, at least for a time, I was a model of good behavior.

Along with secular school, I went to *chedar* in the afternoon four days a week where I learned to read (but not translate) Hebrew. Then *shul* on Saturday and Sunday School on Sunday. At 13, I had an exemplary Bar Mitzvah: I *davened* (chanted) the Prophetic portion, the *musaf* section of prayers that followed and gave my little speech.

Even before my Bar Mitzvah, I was often in my father's store sell-ing shoes. It is hard to believe that I made my first sale at 11. It was at my insistence, although I later came to hate "the store."

By that time, my father had acquired another store on the main street in Sharon, but I was assigned to Reed's in Farrell where the cus-tomers were more Old World. For lunch I would walk up the hill from Broadway to 614 Wallis Avenue, where my grandparents lived, and my grandmother would give me lunch, just like my mother's brother Hersh, who managed the store. It was a very grown-up feeling.

I worked at the store only sporadically then. I had other obligations. But by the time I got to high school, it had become the primary obliga-tion. It was not only Saturday, but whenever school was out—especially Christmas vacation. "I need you in the store," was my father's constant refrain. And I had to comply. By then I worked in the Sharon store.

I was an active member of AZA, a Jewish boys' club associated with B'nai B'rith with active chapters all along the river valleys south to Pittsburgh and north to Erie. AZA would often bring the chapters together for weekend conventions, but often I could not go because of my obliga-tion to "the store." The store also made my social life difficult: It was open until 9 p.m. on Saturday. I could not leave for my Saturday night date, often with a girl from Youngstown, until we cleaned up the store after it closed. This meant my Saturday night date often began at 10 p.m.

I suppose you could say this hardly mattered because I didn't miss much. Dates were not really very much fun. We hardly knew the girls and what we did together was often boring.

I recently went to the ballet with my wife. In the last third of the program the troupe danced to nine famous old songs of Frank Sinatra, recorded and sung by the crooner himself. The audience loved it. So did the reviewer. So did my wife. I was ready to scream. In fact, I did yell about it in bitter tones on the way home. It made me furious—at the memories it called up. I heard songs like that when I was in high school at nightclubs we went to with our dates on Saturday night. I had worked until nine, then driven to Youngstown to pick up my date whom I had called earlier in the week to see if she wanted to go out on Saturday night and from there to a low one-story wooden building out in the country with a flashing neon sign above the door. Inside was a smoky room with a small combo and a tiny dance floor in front of it. The show consisted of a master of ceremonies who would tell a few jokes and introduce a singer as we sat at a table smoking cigarettes and drinking something like a rum and Coke. The big question was whether you would get a kiss good night, usually signaled by where she sat on the way home on the wide front-seat couch built, in those days, to accommodate three people.

I am not bitter; I didn't know I lived a narrow life. It was a confined world in a way I cannot describe. I only know it because I somehow escaped and now know there is another world.

Although I was not bitter, I was not happy about it either. You really don't think about life with other possibilities. That's the way life is—or was.

At home, my father was active in the Sharon synagogue and the B'nai B'rith chapter, and my mother was active in Hadassah, even traveling around to make speeches to Hadassah chapters. She also taught Sunday School.

Every evening after dinner my father would wash the dishes and I would dry them. Later he would take his bath, emerge in his pajamas and robe and settle in to read the *Sharon Herald*. He was a creature of habit, a trait I may have inherited somewhat from him. But he was not an intellectual, like my mother. He did not read books. After my parents retired to Florida, I saw him reading a book—the first ever. It was a biography of Eddie Cantor.

We had several sets of books in the house. One was the 50-volume set of The Harvard Classics, no doubt acquired by my mother. I now have them, my mother's legacy. Whether she read them, I don't know. Volume 16 is *Grimm's Fairy Tales*. As children Leah and I loved them. It is now the only well-worn volume in the set. We also had a set of the works of Josephus, but I never knew who Josephus was. A copy of Heinrich Graetz's classic, multi-volume, now-outmoded 19th-century *History of the Jews* completed the major part of our home library. I think my mother read these books.

High school brought a sea change to my intellectual life—because of two teachers, Smitty and Mac. Anna Grace Smith and Elizabeth McMullin were the intellectual lights of the Sharon High School faculty.

Both taught English. They reached and inspired students not only through their classes, but even more widely in the extracurricular activities they directed. Smitty was the adviser to the *Sharon High Gazette* and Mac ran the drama department.

Smitty was slightly disabled. She had a stiff leg. Her coupe had special pedals to allow her to drive it despite her disability. She had a wry sense of humor and a sly, twisted smile that often said the precise opposite of her words. She laughed often and even told jokes: What goes 99-klop? Answer: A centipede with a wooden leg.

Smitty was short—about five-feet, three-inches. Mac was tall, about five-feet, eleven-inches. Mac carried herself elegantly. She had a voice to match—smooth and soft and beautifully enunciated. Her large prominent nose gave her an additional air of authority.

Both Smitty and Mac were unmarried, which I think was customary those days for teachers. They lived together at 142 Forker Boulevard, where honored students would be invited to listen to and discuss the radio program "Town Meeting of the Air." (Three decades later, someone in this group reported to the FBI that I had expressed Communist ideas at some of these sessions at Smitty and Mac's. By 1956, however, this kind of report did not prevent me from getting a security clearance at the Department of Justice. This report of 1948 discussions, however, reflects the atmosphere at that time.)

Smitty and Mac made it clear that there was no room for what they called "bathroom humor" at these meetings. And the thought that their relationship was anything other than two single women of like minds sharing living quarters never crossed our minds.

I never had a class with Smitty. I met her because I tried out and worked for the school newspaper, ultimately becoming its editor. Eventually, Smitty kicked me off the paper—a seeming repetition of one facet of my character. Even before that episode, however, Smitty had to defend me. In the entrance hall of the school was a trophy case with all the cups won by teams from the school. In addition to the sports trophies were some equally impressive trophies from the 1930s for our debating and oratory teams. But these stopped in the 1940s. We no longer had a debate or oratory team. I wrote an editorial describing these trophies that stopped in the 1940s and asked why we no longer had a debate or oratory team. The Monday morning after the Friday paper appeared, a messenger brought a copy of the issue to the editorial office. Over my editorial, an orange crayon had scrawled: "Who wrote this and why? CMM." Clem M. Musser had risen to be the superintendent of schools via the usual path: coach of sports teams. I never learned how Smitty handled this. But she did. And I was never taken to task for it. I did not need to be reminded, however, not to pull this kind of thing again.

A second episode involved my social life, which had the usual unsuccessful attempts and the customary adolescent heartbreaks. There was little joy here. To make matters worse, I often had difficulty in getting access the family car to drive to Youngstown and pick up my date after the store closed at nine, especially as my father needed it to get home. To alleviate this matter, I took a piece of school stationery from the newspaper office and wrote a letter to my parents in the name of the guidance director, Mr. Grimes. He was concerned, it said, at my studiousness. I was taking too many courses. I was too occupied with my studies. My parents, he urged, should encourage my social life—more specifically making the family car available to allow me to have a social life. I had no doubt that my parents would get the joke. They would never be fooled by antics like this. And of course they immediately recognized my joke. But one day in the newspaper office, I told a member of my staff about it. She told Smitty. And I was removed as editor and kicked off the paper.

I did have Mac for senior English, but by that time I knew her well, not only from the newspaper office where she often hung out, but from school plays that she produced. The highlight was my senior play. At the tryout I "performed" the climactic paragraph of Patrick Henry's dramatic "Give me liberty or give me death" speech. As I think about it, it is obvious that even prior to the tryout Mac had chosen me as the lead in "Death Takes a Holiday." The play was reviewed on the front page of the *Sharon Herald*. To make sure that my memory had not exaggerated in the eighth decade of my life, after writing this, I decided to check with the newspaper to see if I could get a copy of the review. The newspaper, surprisingly still in business, kept issues only for the last two years; the library, however, had a complete microfiche of issues. So I called the Sharon Public Library. Indeed, they did have it, but it was not searchable; I would have to come in to look for it. However, perhaps a woman from the genealogical society might be able to help, the man said—and she just happened to be in the library at that time. I talked to Toni Sheehan, a grandparent like me, who was willing to look at the issues of April and May 1948. The next day she sent me a photocopy of the front-page story from April 13, 1948, headed "Difficult Play Is Presented by Sharon H.S. Students":

> . . . To Hershel Shanks, tall editor of the school newspaper the past year, goes much of the credit for success of the production. It was his assignment to make convincing the role of Prince Sirki (Death), who came to the castle of an Italian Duke as a weekend guest to learn why men fear him and to feel human emotions. Appearing in black hood and cape and later as a suave nobleman, Hershel turned in a performance quite remarkable for a high school boy. He handled his soliloquies on the meaning of life and death with restraint, in a well-modulated voice.

The review was as wonderful as I had remembered it. That was the highlight of my theatrical career. I knew that it would be all down hill from there. I have never set foot on a theatrical stage again.

I graduated from high school in 1948. In a class of over 500 students, I missed the top 10 percent by a few places; I did not graduate with honors. However, when it came to electing the three best students to compete for the Pepsi Cola scholarships, I was one of them. (None of us won a scholarship.) Apparently I was known to be smart. But that did not translate into grades. In contrast to the usual situation where a student's class standing drops as he climbs the educational ladder and the competition becomes tougher, my class standing continued to rise from high school to college to graduate school to law school.

I have spoken admiringly of Smitty and Mac. It was something else they did for me that changed my life. They told me about two elite Quaker colleges outside Philadelphia—Haverford and Swarthmore. I had never heard of them. Without their guidance, I would probably have ended up at Penn State or, if I decided to reach, at Ohio State.

Somewhere along the line I decided to reach, even if I would almost certainly fail. After all, I was editor of the school paper and star of the senior play and I missed by only a fraction of a point being in the top 10 percent of my graduating class. I applied to Harvard, Yale, Dartmouth (simply because I had heard of it), Haverford and Swarthmore. In addition, I applied to Washington and Jefferson, a small liberal arts college near Pittsburgh, where I had a better chance. This was the fall of 1948 and veterans were flocking back from the war and attending college on the GI Bill of Rights.

I of course had to take the SAT college aptitude test. In those days, however, students were not told how well or poorly they did. It was a deep, dark secret, not to be divulged by the authorities to anyone. I have often wondered how I did. There was certainly a basis to think I did very poorly and that may perhaps account for my rejections. On the other hand, there was reason to think that my natural intellectual vigor would shine through on an aptitude test.

I was rejected at Harvard, Yale, Dartmouth, Haverford and Swarthmore. Fortunately, I was accepted at Washington and Jefferson College in Washington, Pennsylvania, where I matriculated in the fall of 1948.

CHAPTER III

My College Years

FROM THE OUTSET I TOOK TO THE intellectual life of the college experience. I enjoyed studying and I was excited by learning.

Almost all of my professors at Washington and Jefferson loved their subject and communicated this to the students. This was especially true of my English professor, Joe Doyle. That we referred to him as Joe Doyle, not Joseph Doyle or Professor Doyle, says something about his relationship to the students.

I met Ted Friedman in Doyle's class. Ted was from a highly intellectual, New York Zionist family (his full name was Theodore Herzl Friedman) and was far more sophisticated and less wide-eyed than I. At one point in the semester, Ted and I decided on a reading program for ourselves that involved reading a book a day. This lasted for less than a week.

There was another side of college life at W & J (as the school is popularly known), which from my current vantage point I can describe as collegiate silliness. But at the time I wanted very much to fit in. The college year began with six weeks of orientation that required all freshmen to wear silly-looking beanies. This period also involved limited freshman hazing, designed to put freshman in their place. Disobedience to the rules involved punishments such as having to wear long johns all day or singing a phone book to the tune of a popular song. Ted and I seemed to have personalities that more often invoked these penalties.

Social life on campus was dominated by Greek life, the fraternities with their fraternity houses and parties. After the six-week period of freshman indoctrination came the period of "rushing," when the fraternities would invite prospective members to be considered for membership.

There was a strictly limited period for "rushing" and an unstated hierarchy of fraternities, depending on their social status.

Deep into the freshman indoctrination period, I was invited to one of the toniest fraternity houses for a private chat with a fraternity leader, a blatant infraction of the "rushing" rules. There he confided to me that some of my behavior—too frequent infraction of the freshman indoctrination rules—could adversely impact on the invitations I might otherwise receive during the "rushing" period. I expressed my gratitude for this advice and added that I would also tell this to my friend Ted Friedman who was behaving just as badly as I was. "Oh, he doesn't have to worry," he said. "He's Jewish." And so I learned that there were Christian fraternities and Jewish fraternities.

Joe Ellovich, my boyhood friend from Sharon who was a year ahead of me at W & J, had decided not to join a fraternity. I saw this—then and now—as an exhibit of strength of character. I was not so strong. I accepted an invitation to "pledge"—that was the tryout period—to Pi Lamda Phi, an exclusively Jewish fraternity. I quit, however, when I refused to be paddled as part of the initiation process.

Once the freshman indoctrination period was over, I (of course) signed up for the school newspaper and was soon writing a regular column called "Up and Atom." I wrote, naturally, on such controversial subjects as whether beer should be allowed on campus. This brought me in contact with the president, Herbert Case, and the dean, Edward Davison, a Scotsman who had published a number of highly regarded books of poetry. One of them, *Collected Poems 1917–1939*,[3] was the first book I ever owned signed by the author. It was inscribed to me "in the brotherhood of W & J." Neither Case nor Davison were critical of my columns in the paper, apparently recognizing my right to write about whatever I wanted.

After my first-semester grades came in, I decided the advantages of a Haverford education would be so far superior to what I had to look forward to at W & J that I would try for admission to Haverford as a transfer student. I reasoned that my previous rejection at Haverford must have had something to do with my poor performance on the college aptitude test. It was clear that I was near the top of my class at W & J as reflected in my first-semester grades. So Haverford's decision might be different this time. When Haverford asked for a transcript of my first-semester grades, President Case learned of my application. He invited me to his office and sought to dissuade me. Help him, he told me, to make W & J the kind of place we both wanted it to be. I was of course flattered, but I replied that Haverford would give me the tools to do the job even more effectively. This was the time of my life, I told him, when I felt I should be perfecting my skills in order more powerfully to give to society later.

I heard nothing from Haverford. No "yes," "no" or "maybe." I returned to Sharon—to spend the summer selling shoes in my father's store.

Then, by way of the grapevine, I learned the news: Both President Case and Dean Davison had been kicked out! They were too "liberal."

I immediately decided to drive down to W & J to talk to whomever I could. I did not see Case or Davison. Although I did not know it when I left W & J to drive home, the result of my efforts was that the ousted president of W & J (President Case who later became president of Bard College) sent a letter of recommendation on my behalf to Haverford's president, Gilbert Fowler White. I soon received a letter admitting me to Haverford as a transfer student, as a member of the sophomore class.

Like so many turning points in my life, that too seemed to be the result of chance—if the president and dean of W & J had not been kicked out at the end of my freshman year. . .

But it was also a lesson for me: Keep pushing. Keep trying.

My first days at Haverford were not auspicious. I was assigned a room with three other fellows who had formed a friendship the year before. And they clearly did not want a fourth—an unknown quantity who took up intimate space. I watched as one of my new roommates took out of his suitcase a picture of his family's coat of arms and hung it on the wall. This was clearly not a place for me. I asked the administration for a room change. I was reassigned to a single room in the freshman dorm, Barclay Hall. The result was that all my friends at Haverford were a year behind me. I was never integrated into my class, the class of 1952.

I promptly tried out for the school newspaper, but the editor informed me (as he was instructed by the administration) that I could write stories, but not editorials. Apparently my reputation as a trouble maker had preceded me. So I resigned from the paper. I never participated in any of Haverford's extracurricular activities thereafter for fear that I was a marked man.

But all that never bothered me—except deep down. I formed fast friendships with some of the freshmen in my dorm and four of us moved the next year into an apartment dorm—with a living room, a hall and two small bedrooms with bunk beds. Best of all, it had a working fireplace. It was like living in a mansion.

Most importantly, I loved the intellectual life at Haverford. Of course I took a course in Shakespeare as well as the Romantic poets such as Keats and Shelley and Lord Byron. I studied Greek plays—Sophocles, Euripides, Aristophanes and Aeschylus (*pathei mathos:* by suffering, we learn). I learned a bit of French and tried to read Baudelaire, Camus and Sartre in the original. The latter's modish existentialism intersected with my interest in philosophy in general.

I remember one spring vacation during the middle of a philosophy course when I was selling shoes in my father's store. In a lull, I chatted with the long-time manager, Frank Pearce. Pointing to a table full of sale shoes, I asked him: "Frank, how do you know that table of shoes actually exists?" He looked at me quizzically. Was I off my rocker? "How do you know that it's not just an idea in your head?" I was simplistically spouting Bishop Berkeley's idealism. Fortunately, a couple of customers walked in at that point.

Haverford students could also take courses at nearby Bryn Mawr College, so I took Paul Schrecker's course on Immanuel Kant. We spent the entire semester on Kant's *Critique of Pure Reason*. I loved it.

And then there was Ira de Augustine Reid—an African-American professor of sociology. Tall (six-foot, four-inches), handsome and statuesque, he had a broad laugh and laughed often. He dressed immaculately. He was a mesmerizing lecturer and a warm, inspiring teacher. He was the only black man on the faculty. (I cannot remember any African-American students, although there must have been a few.) Ira Reid had attended a historically black undergraduate college (Morehouse College in Atlanta).

I'm sure I did not understand his inner workings—what tensions must have drawn his life, what bitterness he harbored, what humiliations he had suffered. But I never saw it. We never discussed it. He was a senior faculty member. His large home on the best part of faculty drive was always open, and my visits there were always happy ones.

Many years later, I wrote an article in the *University of Pennsylvania Law Review* about a case involving Girard College, which was established by a will creating a fine school for poor, orphan boys. The problem was that Girard's will limited admission to "white" boys. The Pennsylvania Supreme Court had upheld the limitation. I criticized the Pennsylvania court's decision and traced the source of the discrimination to the state (state discrimination), rather than to Mr. Girard's will (private discrimination) which created the school. The United States Supreme Court later reversed the decision of the Pennsylvania Supreme Court, although it is unlikely that they were influenced by my law review article.[4] I like to think that what I wrote, however, was influenced by Ira Reid.

In light of my future career as editor of a biblical archaeology magazine, it seems there is an odd omission in my college curriculum. I never took a course in the Bible or in religion, despite the fact that it was all available at this Quaker college with its required attendance at Fifth-Day meeting. This was not a conscious decision on my part. Those subjects were simply not on my radar screen. I wish I could give a better explanation for this, but I can't. Many years later, after *Biblical Archaeology Review* had become a well-established magazine, I would explain that I had the perfect preparation for the editorship: I never had a course in Bible, I never had a course in archaeology and I knew nothing about publishing.

As I think back on it, perhaps I was a little uncomfortable at Haverford about displaying my Judaism. Today, in 21st-century Washington, D.C., being Jewish is a little like being a member of some elite society. More than a half-century earlier at elite Haverford College, it was by no means so clear.

In my senior year at Haverford, I was elected to Phi Beta Kappa, the honorary fraternity based on intellectual achievement. I also graduated with honors—something I did not achieve at Sharon High School. Nearly half a century later, I was invited back, to give the address at the 100th anniversary of the Haverford Phi Beta Kappa chapter. I began my talk by saying that I was the only person in the room who had been rejected for admission to Haverford. Then I explained how I managed to transfer from W & J after being rejected. I was accepted at Haverford as a result of "pull," rather than my qualifications.

Phi Beta Kappa was my vindication, I told my audience. It was proof that I was up to Haverford's standards. If I can be a bit grandioso here, "The stone that the builders rejected has become the cornerstone" (Psalm 118:22, quoted in all three Synoptic Gospels).

But still, how is it that someone who makes Phi Beta Kappa is rejected? Doesn't this reflect some egregious error in the admission process? I would sometimes look at my classmates, especially the less accomplished ones, and ask myself how it could be that they were admitted and I was rejected.

Of course it occurred to me: Haverford had a quota—a limit on the number of Jewish students who would be admitted. Haverford has not denied this. Was this the reason I was rejected? I will never know.

My mother, father and sister came to my graduation and to take my things back to Sharon. As we drove away from Haverford, I recall my eyes welled up with tears. For all my ambivalence, these were wonderful, exciting and broadening years—and I knew it.

CHAPTER IV

Columbia, Harvard and the Department of Justice

"FILL 'ER UP, SAM," I SAID, DRIVING the family's old Pontiac into Sam Magnato's gas station. It was late summer; the summer "vacation" was ending; and I would be a senior when I returned to Haverford.

As he washed the windshield, he asked me, "What are you studying in college, Hershel?"

"English," I replied.

"What are you going to be?"

"An Englishman." We both laughed.

But the time came when I had to make some move: During the next nine months, I would be deciding what to do after Haverford.

I was indeed an English major, but I was increasingly more inspired by Ira Reid's courses in sociology. I loved studying literature, but I did not want to spend my life teaching it. Perhaps it would be better to be a sociologist.

Law was another possibility—the perennial choice when you didn't know what you wanted to do. So, postponing a decision, I applied for admission to both. I sent applications to Harvard and Yale law schools and to Harvard and Columbia universities in sociology.

Harvard sociology turned me down—as it did when I sought to enter as a freshman. I still remember my interview with Louis Toepfer, however, the admissions officer at Harvard Law School. I had hoped to solve my dilemma—law or sociology—if I could just get him to say that law was really applied sociology. I worked around to it slowly. Finally he said, "Look, we do one thing at Harvard Law School. We train lawyers. If you don't want to be a lawyer, don't come to Harvard Law School."

So I decided to go to Columbia University to study sociology. But something intervened. Yale Law School gave me a full scholarship—$600! Yale Law School was more sociologically oriented anyway. (The same bankruptcy course called "Creditors Rights" at Harvard was called "Debtors Estates" at Yale.) So I told my roommates that I would be going to Yale Law School on a scholarship. Leo Dvorken, who was like a brother to me, was disdainful: "If $600 means that much to you, you are not the man I thought you were." That did it.

I was off to the big city and Columbia University: A year (actually nine months) on the tenth floor of Furnald Hall (the elevator went up to the ninth floor) and some of the most exciting intellectual activity I have ever known. It was the place of giants: mathematical sociologist Paul F. Lazarsfeld, philosopher of science Ernest Nagel, sociologist (and later president of the American Sociological Association) Seymour M. Lipset (Marty, as he was known, and I later became friends), and the theoretical genius Robert King Merton (he invented concepts like the "self-fulfilling prophecy"). I had them all. I took six courses. If I wasn't enrolled in a course, I audited. After nine months, having written my master's thesis, I got my M.A.—Master of Arts. Although I loved the intellectual excitement, I knew, however, I did not want to spend my life doing what sociologists do. So it was back to law.

I again went to see Lou Toepfer at Harvard. I reminded him of our earlier conversation. "Now I want to be a lawyer," I told him.

In the fall of 1953, I enrolled as a first-year student at the Harvard Law School. Everyone there had been smart as an undergraduate; this was a new level of competition. In those days, there was a standard first-year curriculum—property, agency, trusts, legal procedure. The teaching method, known as the Socratic method, was more like structured humiliation. The professor would assign several appellate court opinions and he would then interrogate the class about them. He had a seating chart, so there was no escaping the question even by sitting in the back. He would simply call your name. "State the case, Mr. Shanks." The most humiliating answer was "Unprepared." The truth is I enjoyed it. I never said "Unprepared."

There was one scary part, however: No examinations until the end of the year. The results of these first-year examinations would determine your whole life—or at least so it was thought. The top 25 people were awarded a spot on the *Harvard Law Review* (only in law are the most prestigious journals edited by students). The next eight were assigned to the Board of Student Advisers, which administered the moot court competitions. The next 20 or so became members of Legal Aid. After that, nothing—in a class of over 500.

Classes ended a week before the exams to allow for exam preparation. It was not a question of memorizing answers, however. Your legal conclusion didn't matter. There was no right or wrong answer. It was a question of how you got to the answer, how sophisticated your legal reasoning was. And most important: Did you see the legal issues?

On Saturday night a couple of my roommates (four of us lived in a rented house) decided to "flick out," as it was called in those days, and I joined them. The movie turned out to be a double feature. I really wanted to get back to study. But I waited with my buddies until the end of the second feature. We rushed back to the house after it was over. There, waiting for me, was a girl I had dated sometime back for the wrong reasons.

"I have to take you home," I said. "I'm really sick. I think I have an upset stomach," I lied. She lived in the suburbs and it took me another half hour to drive her home.

The next morning I awoke, suffering from exactly the symptoms I had feigned having the night before. By the end of the day I decided to go to the infirmary, where they examined me and then admitted me.

The general rule was that if you were conscious, you took the exams. I had my own proctor in the infirmary to ensure that I did not cheat. The only concession to my condition was that I was allowed to have a glass of milk during each of the four-hour exams.

After two days of exams in the infirmary, I was released and took the remainder of the exams with everyone else.

I had no idea how I had done. There was certainly no reason to believe that I had done well. I had not been a star in class. And everyone in Harvard Law School was smart.

When the grades came out later in the summer, I learned that I was 32nd in my class, which placed me on the Board of Student Advisers, the honorary organization that administered the moot court in which students wrote briefs and argued appellate cases before a court composed of actual judges and law professors. The competition was stiff and, in the final round, one of the judges was always a United States Supreme Court justice.

Technically, those who sat on the Board of Student Advisers were members of the faculty, entitled, among other things, to join the Faculty Club. But, so far as I know, none of us did. However, I think from that point on, I took a slightly snobbish pride in being a Harvard student. Until then, I was mostly scared. At this point, I had a feeling I had arrived. I remember a *New Yorker* cartoon in which a double-deck tour bus is driving through Cambridge past two students. One of the students pokes the other in the ribs, and says, "Quick, Shapiro, look like a Harvard student." That was me.

In the semifinals of the moot courts, the panel of three judges would include at least one judge from a United States Court of Appeals. When Judge Harry Kalodner of the United States Court of Appeals for the Third Circuit, which includes Pennsylvania, agreed to preside at one of these cases, I was assigned to accompany him on his visit to the school. He was friendly and, not surprisingly, interested in my post-law school plans. I told him that I planned to come back to Pennsylvania to practice—in Philadelphia. A couple of prominent first-rate firms had expressed an interest in me and one—Drinker, Biddle and Reath, founded in 1849—was going to fly me down for an interview. Henry Drinker was perhaps the country's leading authority on legal ethics. He wrote *the* book on the subject and was chairman of the American Bar Association's Standing Committee on Ethics and Professional Responsibility.

When I told Judge Kalodner about my impending interview with Drinker, Biddle and Reath, he stopped as we were walking along and looked at me quizzically. "Aren't you Jewish?" he queried.

And so I learned: There were Jewish firms and there were Christian firms. No mixing allowed.

I went ahead with the interview anyway. It was in very posh surroundings, but finally the subject came up. I explained that I was Jewish. Soon thereafter the interview was very politely and cordially terminated, almost naturally, and I was led to the door and thanked. I never heard from Drinker, Biddle and Reath.

There was another hurdle in gaining admission to the Philadelphia bar. At that time, there was no state-wide admission. You had to be admitted to a county bar, although there was a state-wide bar exam. Each county had its own bar. I wanted to join the Philadelphia bar, but I was from Mercer County, a poor county in the extreme western part of the state. I don't remember the name of the lawyer from Philadelphia who interviewed (or rather interrogated) me concerning my application for admission to the Philadelphia bar, but his name began with Mc. "Did you ever consider going back to Sharon to practice?" he barked at me. "No, not seriously," I replied.

He whipped around in his swivel chair and fairly shouted in his best cross-examiner's voice: "I didn't ask you whether you considered it *seriously*. I asked you whether you *considered* it."

Despite my inexact answer, I was nevertheless admitted to the Philadelphia bar, contingent on my passing the bar examination and, a final qualification at that time, clerking in the office of a Philadelphia lawyer for six months. Neither appeared to be a problem for me.

I passed the Pennsylvania bar exam, but I never did my clerkship, as explained below, so I never became a member of the Pennsylvania bar. My preceptor, the technical name of my legal sponsor, was Robert Wolf, son of the founder of the city's most distinguished Jewish firm: Wolf, Block, Schorr and Solis-Cohen. Bobby was a Haverford graduate, which was how I got to him, and I had worked at his firm the previous summer. I was beginning to learn the importance of "connections."

I remember my first interview with him. He was looking for something good to say about me to the firm's hiring committee. I told him that I had been Phi Beta Kappa at Haverford. He looked up and smiled. Here was an angle, something noteworthy. "Junior year?" he queried. "No", I had to admit; not until my senior year. He looked down dejectedly. Apparently a Phi-Bet not admitted until his senior year was not impressive. But in the end I was given a summer job. I could have had a permanent job after graduation from Harvard, but I decided instead to go to Washington. In those days, it was said that the shortest route to Washington was to go to Harvard Law School and turn left.

I applied for a position in the Honors Program of the Department of Justice. I chose to serve in the Office of Alien Property. This was the division that served as legal counsel to the Alien Property Custodian. A statute vested in him title to all property owned by citizens of alien enemies during the war. As a result, he had all the problems that anyone would have who owned an enormous amount of different kinds of property. I looked forward to a varied experience.

On a trip to Washington, I looked up a Harvard Law School graduate whom I did not know but who worked for the Justice Department. When I told him of my application to the Honors Program and my choice of serving in the office of the Alien Property Custodian, he was quick to tell me this was a terrible choice. The place to be—where he was—was the appellate section of the Civil Division. That section handled appeals of civil cases to United States Court of Appeals, as well as considerable litigation in the Supreme Court. So I changed my application and was accepted. (I was never admitted to the Pennsylvania bar because service with the United States Department of Justice would not qualify for the six-month clerkship.)

I have to say that for a kid just out of law school, working for the appellate section of the Civil Division was heady stuff. I was briefing and arguing cases in federal courts of appeals all over the country and writing briefs in the Supreme Court.

We closely followed decisions of the Supreme Court and I frequently attended oral arguments there. In those days, the court was even more formal than today. We sat in front of the bar—the section reserved for members of the Supreme Court bar—and a marshal would admonish us if our coat jacket was unbuttoned. Quill pens and ink were still placed on counsel's table, although they were rarely used. Government lawyers wore formal morning coats and striped trousers when appearing before the court. The government allowance for transportation was not enough to take a cab, so the Justice Department lawyers would take a street car in their formal attire.

When we had to fly, however, we were entitled to fly first class. On one trip to California, I traded my first-class ticket for an economy-class return via Mexico City, my first trip to our southern neighbor. Our daily allowance in 1956 was twelve dollars—six dollars for the hotel and six dollars for food.

This was more than adequate. In Washington, I lived on two dollars a day for food: 35 cents for breakfast, 65 cents for lunch and a dollar for dinner. I lived in a furnished room above a laundry for ten dollars a week. I did not have a private bath. But it was a handsomer room than the one rented by my Harvard classmate David Rose (the only person I knew when I came to Washington), which cost only eight dollars a week. (However, he had the advantage of having a girlfriend, Annie, living in England for the year from whom he received a letter every day. He later married her.)

My first government paycheck did not come for a month. To tide me over, my mother lent me fifty dollars and I borrowed fifty dollars on a life insurance policy my father had bought for me. My government salary was initially $3,500 a year. Even though I was a graduate lawyer and had passed the District of Columbia bar exam, I was not formally sworn in for several months, so initially my position was a law clerk. When I was finally sworn in, my salary increased to $4,500 a year, which was competitive with what the best law firms in the city were paying.

The atmosphere in the department was collegial, and my fellow lawyers were extremely knowledgeable and sophisticated in the law. My cases were challenging and often involved important principles of law. Even when they didn't, they were interesting.

For decades (before pornography was readily available) you could tell where one of my cases was reported in the official volumes containing opinions and decisions of the Courts of Appeals: Even when closed, the volume would have a dark line on the edge of the pages of my case, it had been consulted so often, especially in law schools. The case is *Boyd v. Folsom*, 257 F.2d 778 (1958).

It involved a widow's entitlement to Social Security benefits based on her husband's earnings. Both had been previously married. She brought two children to the marriage; he, nine. His children did not get along with hers, so he moved down the street with his kids and regularly "visited" with his wife. As a result of these visits they had two children of their own. Then, on one of these visits, at age 59, he had a heart attack while having sex and died. A neighbor woman had to lift him off. (How the neighbor learned of the need for this is unclear in the record.) I call it the case of the virile man.

Under the Social Security statute, a widow is entitled to benefits based on her husband's earnings only if she was "living with" him at the time of his death. My position on the appeal was that she was not living with him at the time of his death even though he had died while having sexual intercourse with her.

Snickers aside, I did have a case. A widow's Social Security benefits were designed to replace the support provided by the deceased husband. The statute had nothing to do with the fact that death occurred in this case while the couple, who were living apart, were having sexual intercourse.

I lost the case. (How many lawyers tell you about cases they lost?) But the court divided: I got a dissent.

After three years at the Department of Justice, some of the glamour wore off. When I finished one brief, I would just reach up on the shelf, so to speak, for a file to write another brief. I decided it was time to move on. But I left with the greatest respect for career government lawyers and especially my colleagues in the Department of Justice. They were as fine a group of lawyers as I have ever worked with.

CHAPTER V

Practicing Law

I JOINED WEAVER AND GLASSIE, AN EIGHT-MAN law firm, mid-sized in those days, as an associate. The firm was actively involved in major real estate transactions in the Washington area and also represented such large companies as Philco. The partners were mostly white-shoe Virginians, some even FFV (First Families of Virginia). This time, however, being Jewish helped me.

Among our clients were large insurance companies whose loans financed a host of multimillion-dollar construction projects. Many of the real estate people Henry Glassie was involved with were Jewish. One of the developers, Herb Blum of Swesnick and Blum, asked Henry why they had no Jews in the firm. "I don't know," Henry replied. "It just happened." "Well, why don't you make it happen to have one," Herb replied. So, I learned much later, I was hired.

Henry Glassie, I hasten to add, was a beautiful soul, thoroughly without bias or prejudice. He lived with his then-wife in an area that had once been full of fine houses, but had deteriorated badly. (He was, ultimately, married five times—to different women. As was said of Justice William Douglas, Henry thought he had to marry every woman he slept with.) Henry was the only white man in the neighborhood. On Sunday morning he would take his wooden Coke case to sit on at the neighborhood gas station where the guys would gather to chat. I worked with Henry happily for more than 25 years—until I left the law.

Hank Weaver, the other name-partner, was another story. But that can wait.

Given my experience, I was naturally assigned to work on the firm's litigation, if only as a subsidiary to the principal attorney on the case.

Some friends who still earn their living as litigation lawyers have admonished me not to yield to the temptation to include here a litany of my own litigation triumphs. There is nothing so boring as a lawyer's recitation of one great victory after another. I will not follow my friends' advice, however, although most of these cases involve some loss as well as some victory. Those who wish to skip this chapter can do so.

I suppose I could explain my rejection of the sage advice I received by saying that these cases are part of my life and this book is about my life. But I think there is another justification for including them. They will take the non-lawyer inside the world of litigation, of lawyering. That is a world I love. It is a world of intensity, complexity, imagination and intellectual challenge. Ultimately, it is a search for justice. And lawyers are an essential element in that search. In addition, these cases will help explain the attitudes I brought with me when I founded a biblical archaeology magazine.

It has become fashionable today to idolize the lawyer who fights for a just cause against all odds. That is not my model. I prefer to think of litigation lawyers as hired guns. They fight for the cause that hires them. And they are (or should be) available to represent either side. Yes, there is a natural tendency to come to believe in the side that hires you, although that is not always the case—and certainly not necessarily the case. But hired guns—and good ones—are essential to that beautiful goal, the pursuit of justice. "Justice, justice shalt thou pursue," saith the Lord (Deuteronomy 16:20). One of the requirements of our marvelous system of justice, which I revere, is that even the worst of us must be well represented. The way our justice system works is that one person (a competent lawyer) is charged with saying all the good things about his or her client and all the bad things about the other fellow's. And the other fellow also has someone like this, to say all the good things about *him* and all the bad things about the first guy. Both representatives are essential. It is only in that way that the person who is supposed to dispense justice—the judge—can in fact do so. The only way the judge can decide justly is when someone from each side tells the judge all the reasons why he or she should decide for one side or the other. That is the only way that we can assure that the field of justice is a level playing field. And that means that the worst imaginable defendant must have a competent lawyer to represent him. Indeed, it is especially important that the worst defendants are competently represented—it is the worst who are most likely to be railroaded in a pretense of justice.

To make the system work, we must respect the lawyer who defends the most heinous defendant. It is that lawyer who should be most honored.

In practice, it is the rare case in which nothing good can be said about a defendant's case. Notice, I said about "the defendant's case," not about the defendant. There is almost always some legally arguable defense. This brings to mind a defendant who wanted to retain me, but told me beforehand that he was guilty.

"Whoa," I shouted. "Who's the lawyer here? You or me?" I went on: "You're not a lawyer. I'm the lawyer. I decide whether you're guilty or not. 'Guilt' is a legal concept." There are many reasons why a defendant may not be legally guilty even though he committed the act.

I get a visceral thrill whenever I walk into a courtroom—even when I have a case I know I may lose (which is almost every case)—as I watch the process of justice. It is a glorious, a precious thing. That is a bit of a grandiose way to characterize some of the cases I will describe, but that kernel of "participation in justice" is always there and borne in mind.

Most of the cases I will tell you about involved elements of both winning and losing—a little like life. In one case, we won but the man we got off was murdered. In another case, we lost, but we sprung the man from jail. The lesson, as with life: Keep fighting. Use your imagination and intellect to find new ways. And winning is often part of losing—and losing part of winning. Perhaps that, in a nutshell, is a theme of this book.

Indeed, that might well be a description of one of the first cases I was involved with in my new firm. Based on his signed confession, John Hodges was convicted of robbery and sentenced to seven years in prison. He failed to appeal his conviction but later alleged that his confession had been coerced from him by the police and that his conviction must therefore be thrown out. The Supreme Court long ago had decided that if a confession has been coerced it cannot be the basis for a conviction. Our firm had been appointed by the court to serve as Hodges's attorney in pressing his claim. We did this by applying to the court for what is known as the Great Writ, the hoary and honored writ of *habeas corpus* (in this case incorporated into a Congressional statute) by which anyone can come into court and contest his (or her) illegal detention.

By the time I got into the case, the federal District Court had denied Hodges's claim to the writ and that decision denying his claim had been affirmed by the Court of Appeals. The question for us as legal counsel was whether we should ask the Supreme Court to hear the case. The Supreme Court's jurisdiction is almost wholly discretionary, and it agrees to take only the most significant cases. Should we ask the high court to hear Hodges's case? As the attorney in our firm with the most Supreme Court experience, I was brought into the case.

When I studied the case, I found what I thought might be another ground on which to claim Hodges's confession had been coerced. This is not unusual when taking a case through the various levels of appeals and rehearings. One of the fascinations of the law is that each time you re-study a case you find something new. I suspect the professional historian might say the same thing. The same is probably true in any intellectual endeavor—re-study brings new insights.

In the law, however, a litigant is barred from raising an argument on appeal that he did not raise before the court below. But I also found what I thought was a good excuse for failing to raise my new issue in the court below.

Appeals to United States Courts of Appeals are usually heard by three-judge panels, which had been true in the Hodges case. My strategy was to ask for a rehearing at which we could reargue the merits of our case and the new issue I had developed, but to seek to present the case not just to the old three-judge panel that had already ruled against us, but to present it to all nine of the judges of the Court of Appeals. This would give us some fresh minds on the case and would also give us a trial run at arguing the case in the Supreme Court if we lost on the rehearing. Rehearings of the full court—rehearings *en banc*, they are called—are extremely rare and discretionary with the court. We nevertheless decided to take the chance. So we applied for a rehearing *en banc*. And it was granted!

That was the good news. The bad news was that when we presented the case to the court *en banc*, we lost. But the good news was that we got the votes of three of the nine judges. On this basis, we decided that we had a good shot at the Supreme Court. We formally asked the Supreme Court to hear our case (that document is called a Petition for Writ of Certiorari).

And the Supreme Court of the United States agreed to hear our case. Another victory.

At this point I had another far-out idea. Why not try to get Hodges out of jail on bail? I don't know whether this had ever been done before— or since—in the circumstances of this case: Hodges had been in jail for years pursuant to a final, unappealed conviction and was attacking the conviction only collaterally by way of a writ of *habeas corpus*. Moreover, the *en banc* court of appeals had heard Hodges's case and rejected it.

On the other hand, the case was iffy enough for the Supreme Court to accept it for review. And if Hodges won in the Supreme Court, the additional time he would have served while the case was being considered by the Supreme Court could not be returned to him.

True, a bail application was a long shot, but it was worth trying; there was no downside to it, except the loss of our time.

I had to start at the bottom of the court system with the bail application, which meant going back to the judge before whom Hodges's application for a writ of *habeas corpus* had been denied. The judge promptly denied the application for bail.

So I took the application to the Court of Appeals. Ditto. Denied.

Undaunted, I made an application for bail to the Chief Justice of the United States. I also pressed my case informally to people in the solicitor general's office of the Justice Department—and they agreed not to oppose my application for bail, which was then an unopposed application. The Chief Justice granted my application for bail!

John Hodges was out of jail. There was now no need to rush the case through the Supreme Court.

It took more than a year for the case to wend its way through the Supreme Court. When the court finally handed down its decision, its nine justices split just as the nine judges of the Court of Appeals had done: six to three. We lost! There was nowhere else we could appeal. The Supreme Court of the United States was the end of the line. Bail would be automatically revoked. Hodges would go back to jail to finish his sentence.

In the year that Hodges was out of jail, however, he had lived an exemplary life. He had a girlfriend, a job and was well adjusted to life on the outside. For me, it was back to the books. I found a statute allowing the sentencing judge to reduce Hodges's sentence to time-served in unusual circumstances. I would argue that it would be a worse crime to return Hodges to jail than the crime he originally committed. I talked to the lawyers at the Justice Department and they agreed to the reduction of the sentence. On this basis, the trial judge reduced the sentence to time-served.

John Hodges was a free man. We lost the case, but we sprung the defendant.

If the Hodges case was one that we lost but won, another case we won but lost—the case of Eddie Dulac.

Eddie had been incarcerated in a jail run by the State of Virginia. One day, when the prisoners were playing horseshoes, a fellow prisoner got angry at Eddie and took the iron pole at which the horseshoes were aimed, raised it over his head and brought it down on Eddie's head, knocking off nearly a quarter of Eddie's skull. Miraculously, Eddie survived. The missing piece of skull had been replaced with a steel plate and Eddie seemed no worse for wear. Our case against the State alleged that Eddie's injury had resulted from the State's negligence and that it must compensate Eddie for his pain and suffering.

To prepare for trial, parties to a lawsuit are permitted to take the oral testimony of potential witnesses to learn all the facts of the case beforehand. These interrogations are called depositions. I took the deposition of Eddie's assailant, who was brought to Richmond in chains. I also took the deposition of one of the guards. From him I elicited testimony that the State had been lax in allowing drugs inside the penitentiary. It was this that induced the State to enter into settlement negotiations.

We finally got the State up to an offer of $100,000. This was an enormous amount at the time. The case was assigned to Judge Robert Merhige, one of Virginia's most distinguished—and courageous—federal judges; he had ordered the desegregation of Virginia's public schools. I vividly remember sitting in Judge Merhige's chambers with its huge oak fireplace in the Richmond federal courthouse, agonizing over whether to accept the State's $100,000 offer. It had many attractive features—most importantly, it was money now. And it was money for sure. Who knows what a jury would award to a convicted felon? The amount was more than enough to give Eddie a fresh start in life. Eddie had a girlfriend who had stuck by him all the time he had been in prison. She had a child whom Eddie loved and regarded as his own. And naturally the settlement included Eddie's release from prison. It was mid-December when I sat in Judge Merhige's chambers. Christmas was in the air. If we accepted the offer, Eddie would be out by Christmas. Eddie had already said he would do whatever we wanted. I pondered out loud, "What would one of the greats do?" Judge Merhige flattered and encouraged me to take it: "You are one of the greats," he said. I accepted the State's offer of $100,000.

We had an excellent relationship with Eddie. We got him out of jail a few days before Christmas. His girlfriend came down to welcome him. My colleague Steve Standiford and I took the happy couple out to lunch at a restaurant of their choice—a steakhouse where the meat was tough, but they loved it. We gave Eddie some cash before departing for Washington.

Eddie agreed to allow us to put his recovery into a trust that we controlled. He decided he wanted to make a living doing minor house repairs, and for this he needed a truck. So we bought him a truck. He now had everything—a girlfriend, a child, a truck and a big bank account that was squander-proof. But that is not the end.

It was not long before Eddie got into a Saturday night brawl and was murdered.

We won the case of *Eddie Dulac v. The Commonwealth of Virginia*, but in the end we lost.

In those days, I also screened cases for the ACLU (American Civil Liberties Union) to decide whether the ACLU should take the case. One of the cases I reviewed involved the conviction of a man named Russell Nesbitt who was going to jail for violating a statute prohibiting the use of a child under 14 years as an acrobat. It seemed like a silly statute. No harm had been done. No money was involved. I recommended that the ACLU take the case. My recommendation was rejected: The case did not involve a civil liberties issue of sufficient significance, I was told.

So I started the HCLU—Hershel's Civil Liberties Union. Not really. I just decided to take on the case myself.

Russell, a wiry, gregarious, affable man, taught acrobatics to street kids as a hobby. Occasionally they would perform as an act titled "The Flying Nesbits." A policewoman observed a tumbling act of "The Flying Nesbits" at 11:30 p.m. on New Year's Eve at Jimmy McPhail's Golden Room. Among the performers were a girl of 13 and a girl of eight. The act lasted 15 minutes and consisted of body-supporting exhibits and human pyramids. No props.

The prosecutor apparently brought the case because he suspected Russell of playing around with the girls. There was no evidence of this and no complaint, however. Russell was black and the girls were white. I didn't like the smell of the case.

As far as I could tell, Russell had been bum's-rushed through the trial by Judge Scalley, one of the worst judges on the local court, with a reputation as lazy, uninformed and injudicious. It was widely known that almost all his work was in fact done by his long-time clerk, Charlie Driscoll.

In those days, the testimony at trials in the lowest District of Columbia courts was not recorded or transcribed. This presented a problem in those rare cases when the judgment was appealed. On an appeal, the appellate judges had to decide whether errors had been committed by the trial court. How could they decide if there was no record of what happened?

The rules provided that the attorneys for the two sides were to get together and create a joint narrative of the testimony and proceedings. But what if they could not agree? Then they were to meet with the trial judge and he would decide.

That is what happened in this case. Based on what Russell told me, I could not agree with the prosecutor on the testimony, so we had a conference with Judge Scalley in his chambers. Like the usual judges' chambers, the walls were lined with bookshelves containing series of volumes with legal opinions from a variety of courts. Judge Scalley was, with all his faults, a jovial man and he had a large collection of funny hats. These he tacked on the wooden shelves holding the volumes of legal opinions. The result was that the books could not be removed unless the hat was removed first!

I was under somewhat of a disability. I had not been at the trial. When the prosecutor and I had a disagreement as to what the testimony had been, Judge Scalley would yell at me, "How do you know; you weren't there?" I could only reply, "That is what my client told me." But I persisted. Then Judge Scalley turned to the prosecutor and yelled, "Ah, give it to him. Maybe he'll shut up!" That, of course, was my signal to keep it up. And the judge kept saying, "Ah, give it to him. Maybe he'll shut up!" That is how we settled the record.

On my way out of his chambers, he growled at me, "Where did you go to law school?" Harvard, I told him. "That's what I thought," he muttered contemptuously.

The record showed that Russell had been teaching acrobatics as a hobby for more than 20 years at places like the YMCA, the Metropolitan Police Boys Club and the Southeast Neighborhood House. His lessons were free and his students had included people of all ages. Children must have their parents' permission. He used no props, just body supporting acts, such as pyramids and what is called risley. In 20 years of teaching, none of his students had suffered injuries.

The statute under which the jury convicted Russell was very explicit. It makes it a crime for "any person ... having in his custody or control a child under the age of fourteen years, who shall in any way dispose of it with a view to its being employed as an acrobat, or a gymnast, or a contortionist, or a circus rider, or a rope-walker, or in any exhibition of like dangerous character."

The statute had been enacted by Congress in 1885, when it was discovered that the District of Columbia had a law outlawing cruelty to dogs and other animals, but not to children. The quoted provision was part of a larger section making cruelty to children a crime. The same paragraph containing the language quoted above also made it a crime to "torture, cruelly beat, abuse, or otherwise mistreat" any child under 18 years.

On appeal I argued that the provision outlawing the use of children as acrobats applied only to "dangerous" acrobatics, as implied by the use of this word later in the statute. The Court of Appeals went even further, however. In a somewhat path-breaking opinion, the court ruled that the statute did not mean the same thing today that it meant in 1885 when it was enacted by Congress. Citing a California ruling, the court found that "new and changed conditions may invalidate or require a reinterpretation of a statute." The court then described the changed conditions: "We note that direct efforts are being made to improve the physical fitness of American youth. Were we to adopt the government's view we would condemn the use of the trampoline on the city playground, the stunts and activities which form a part of track meets, and much of the program specifically prescribed in the physical education curriculum of the District of Columbia public schools. Such a construction would be highly unrealistic and unwarranted." The court even cited the "Presidential Message to the Schools on the Physical Fitness of Youth."

Russell Nesbitt was vindicated. His victory was widely heralded and his acrobatic courses became more popular than ever. For years thereafter, I would get an elaborate Christmas card from Russell full of praise and gratitude.

I enjoyed working with the other associates and with the partners in the firm—all except one. Hank Weaver, the senior name-partner, was a pompous martinet. Too often he interfered in my litigation. Yet I would be responsible if things went awry. I once got the courage to tell him: "I know how to be a subordinate and I know how to be the boss. Just tell me which I am."

My assessment of Hank Weaver was shared by the other associates. In a rare explosion of vulgarity, I told them at lunch: "We all have to eat Hank Weaver's shit. But the difference between you guys and me is that you've developed a taste for it."

Despite the fact that I could reasonably expect to become a partner within a year, I decided to leave the practice and become a law professor. I already had the credentials: I had graduated with honors from Harvard Law School, I was an experienced litigation lawyer both in private practice and at the Department of Justice, I had already published several articles in leading law journals and I had written a book entitled *The Art and Craft of*

Judging: The Opinions of Judge Learned Hand that was chosen as a selection of the Lawyers' Literary Club. Judge Hand sat on the court just below the Supreme Court, the United States Court of Appeals for the Second Circuit, which included New York, so it naturally heard some of the most important cases to come before the courts. Hand's opinions were so frequently quoted by the Supreme Court that the media regularly referred to him as the tenth member of the Supreme Court. His brother Augustus sat on the same Court of Appeals as Learned did. The saying among the bar was, "Cite Gus, but quote Learned."

Once having made the decision to go into teaching law, I contacted Ken Pye, then dean of Georgetown Law School (he later became president of Duke University). I went through the application process and all went well. I was accepted. Even my salary was agreed upon: $14,000 a year. All that remained was a formal faculty vote.

At nine o'clock on the Monday that the vote was to occur, Ken called me at my office. "Hershel," he said, "I'm going to ask you for permission to withdraw your name from consideration." To say I was shocked is to put it mildly. Ken explained that one faculty member, Stanley Metzger, was going to blackball me, and that he had enough influence with other faculty members that I was very likely to be rejected.

I did not immediately recognize the name Metzger, but Ken explained that my name appeared as counsel on a complaint (which is how a lawsuit is begun) in a suit against Metzger that he considered unethical. Then I remembered:

One of the firm's major clients was the Equitable Life Assurance Society, otherwise known as big Equitable, which financed multimillion-dollar real estate developments. The Washington office was headed by Stan Garber. Stan lived in a posh Georgetown neighborhood next to another Stan—Professor Stanley Metzger. And their wives did not get along. Stanley Metzger decided to cut down a large tree in his yard and hired a company in nearby Maryland to do it. It was done negligently and a limb fell on Stan Garber's house, doing substantial damage. Henry Glassie, who was the senior partner on the Equitable account, asked me to research the matter. Garber wanted to sue Metzger.

My advice was that the better course would be to sue the tree surgeon in Maryland. True, Garber had a reasonable case against Metzger on the theory of a nondelegable duty (Metzger could not shunt responsibility to his agent), but if he lost on this issue, it might be too late to sue the tree surgeon in Maryland (the statute of limitations having run). Therefore I suggested that the better course would be to sue the Maryland tree surgeon at the outset.

The only thing wrong with this was that in Maryland, Garber would have to pay a lawyer. In the District of Columbia, we would represent him as a courtesy. Garber decided he wanted to sue in Washington. Henry Glassie instructed me to prepare a complaint based on a nondelegable duty. I did so and it was then filed in the local trial court. At the end of the complaint, Henry's and my name appeared as counsel for the plaintiff.

This was the basis of Stanley Metzger's threatened blackball. I rushed down to see him. This was not an apartment or even a job that he was denying me, I told him; it was my whole career! He was himself a lawyer; he understood the difference between a lawyer and his client: I was just an associate following the instructions of a senior partner. Moreover, Metzger was insured so that the suit was really against the insurance company; Metzger had no financial exposure.

Metzger would not be moved. The faculty vote was postponed and a close friend of mine, Dan Rezneck, a brilliant lawyer who had clerked for Justice William Brennan on the Supreme Court and who was teaching a course at Georgetown, went to see Metzger. Before joining the Georgetown faculty, Metzger had been Assistant Legal Adviser to the State Department. He explained to Dan, "When I was in the State Department after the war and I was told to return property to the Nazis, I refused. Shanks was no mere amanuensis. He should have refused to prepare the complaint."

With this comparison, I knew that there was no chance of changing Metzger's mind. I withdrew my application from consideration.

Stanley Metzger's career at Georgetown ended badly. It was discovered that he plagiarized passages in a book he had written for the Brookings Institution. Brookings described the discovery as a "distressing and unprecedented incident." All copies of the book were recalled and destroyed. Metzger resigned in disgrace.

For me, as I look back on it, I was fortunate that Metzger blackballed me. I would never have started *Biblical Archaeology Review* if it hadn't been for Stanley Metzger's blackball. I would simply have led a life as a law school professor.

In the immediate aftermath, I continued to practice law. Not long thereafter, I was made a partner. The firm was eventually called Glassie, Pewett, Beebe and Shanks. Yes, Hank Weaver, my nemesis, lost his major clients as a result of mergers, and he left the firm to take a corporate job as inside counsel.

I continued to have exciting and stimulating cases of all kinds. We represented the State of Arkansas in a price-fixing case against the oil companies. (My local counsel was "Bix" Shaver, who had represented Governor Orval Faubus when he tried to prevent the integration of Little Rock's Central High School in defiance of a United States Supreme Court order, but Bix—like Faubus—had completely altered his views by this time, and we got along famously.) We also represented the owners of a 7,000-acre farm that was cut in half by the Dulles Airport Access Highway. We represented the makers of "Virginia Gentleman" bourbon against the makers of "Kentucky Gentleman" bourbon. And on and on.

In a way, litigation channeled my rebelliousness and provided an outlet for it. It allowed me to be one kind of person in court, so to speak, and another in my private life. Litigation also challenged me intellectually. The kind of litigation I was involved in at the Department of Justice and in private practice demanded research in new areas, intellectual challenges, creativity, imagination and serious thought. And it was not just a game; it was an attempt to pursue justice. Only just arguments would prevail—at least that is the theory. Of course it doesn't always work that way, but it does most of the time. And when a lawyer's ideas are adopted by a court and become embedded in a judicial opinion, they become a part of the law. In such cases you have literally made law.

After the nation's first state-wide teachers' strike failed, I was sent to Florida by the National Education Association to determine whether there had been any violations of law during the strike. Several important civil rights cases grew out of this, and made law in the way I have just described. One of them ultimately went to the Supreme Court.

Arguing before the Supreme Court is an extraordinary experience—both terrifying and exhilarating. The preparation is intense. I actually moved out of my home a few days before the argument and stayed at a motel so I would have no family distractions. I devoted myself solely to preparation for the oral argument.

The Supreme Court building itself has an imposing majesty about it with its tall white marble columns supporting a Greek pediment. Before it was built, the court met in a room in the Senate Office Building. When the present courthouse was built, Justice Cardozo is said to have remarked that he felt he should be riding to work on an elephant. The courtroom inside is high-ceilinged and crystal-lit. A bar separates the spectators from the forward area reserved for lawyers (members of the bar). Capacious mahogany tables are reserved for counsel in the case being argued. Between the tables is the podium for the lawyer arguing the case. He or she is literally "before the court": Intimately close in front of the lawyer is the raised "bench" at which the nine black-robed justices sit. And behind the bench are the huge drapes of plush maroon that open when the justices enter and leave.

Court sessions begin with the court clerk crying in a loud shrill voice for all who have business before this honorable court to draw near and they will be heard.

I rose and began my argument in *Askew v. Hargrave*. Within seconds I was pummeled with questions from the justices. And so it went for my allotted half-hour. The lectern has a little light on it that flashes red when your time is up. You are permitted only to finish your sentence and then you must sit down. In my case, however, the court kept asking me questions after the red light flashed and I was permitted to go on for another ten minutes. The justices were obviously intrigued with the issue and uncertain as to how they should decide. I should have been flattered that I had interested them sufficiently so that they gave me additional time to argue, but I had no time for such thoughts.

Nor had I time to think about the little boy from Sharon arguing before the Supreme Court of the United States. My parents and family had come down for the event and sat in the special section of the courtroom reserved for them. But I had no time for pride either.

Well, how a lawyer does is not necessarily reflected in the outcome. You can make a beautiful argument and lose the case. And vice versa. I now jocularly maintain that this case made a substantial contribution to healing the well-known rift in the high court between the conservative justices and the liberal justices. I managed to bring them all together: I lost 9–0. The case raised the question of whether the state violated the Constitution because different county school systems within the state spent different amounts per student depending on how wealthy the county's residents were. A wealthy county, even with a low tax rate, would spend more per pupil than a poor county with a high tax rate. It was a difficult issue even for the Supreme Court. In the end, the court avoided the difficult issue by sending the case back to the trial court to develop the record more completely. That was effectively the end of the case. A few years later, in another case in which I was not involved, the court faced the issue and decided for my side.

Unlike most of the other cases I've discussed, some of my cases involved a lot of money. Here is one. It returns ultimately to my lesson in life—of winning and losing, or losing and winning, at the same time.

Jerry Maiatico immigrated to this country from Italy during the Depression of the 1930s. He never really learned English fluently and what English he knew he spoke with a heavy Italian accent. However, he was a good building contractor and his business grew and grew.

George Lemm graduated from law school in the Depression and had a hard time finding paying clients, although he was a good lawyer. He finally fell into representing small contractors in the Italian-American community. Gradually, he confined himself to one—Jerry Maiatico.

As Jerry's business grew, he decided to put up his own buildings, not just build them for others. And when a legal matter too complex for George came up, he would bring the matter to us. One such case involved the Matomic Building, which Jerry built soon after World War II when the attacks on Hiroshima and Nagasaki were still fresh in everyone's mind.

The Matomic Building was Jerry's pride and joy—a huge 11-story office building, a block from the White House. It was built with an enormous amount, really an excessive amount, of steel girders. It was intended to withstand an atomic attack. That is why it was called the Matomic Building—M for Maiatico, plus atomic. Jerry wanted to leave it to his daughters as their legacy, the assurance from their immigrant father that they would never want for money.

Jerry leased the building to the federal government, which filled it with government agencies. One of them was the then-secret Atomic Energy Commission, especially appropriate for the Matomic Building. At the conclusion of the lease term, the government said it wanted to renew the lease. When Jerry gave the government the new lease terms, the government balked. Too much, it said. OK, said Jerry, if you don't want to pay the new rent, you can move out.

The government leasing agents didn't like the way they were treated. They didn't like being pushed around this way. They weren't used to it. The government decided it would take title to the building; it would buy the building, even against Jerry's wishes. They would do this by condemning the property for a public purpose under the laws of eminent domain.

The government filed the condemnation papers with the federal court and deposited what it deemed to be the fair market value of the building—$10 million, an enormous amount in those days, but not close to what the property was worth.

Jerry ran to George, and George ran to us.

The party whose property is taken by eminent domain is constitutionally assured of the right to contest the government's estimate of fair market value of the property. The government must pay whatever the court and jury fix as the fair market value, or "just compensation" in constitutional terms. Rarely, however, may the property owner contest the government's right to take the property. In the thousands of cases in which the federal government has taken title to property by eminent domain, there are not a half dozen in which the owner has successfully contested the government's right to take title to the property.

But in a case involving this amount of money, it was worth trying. I hit the books and soon found an argument that a taking in this area of Washington was not permitted without the permission of two Congressional committees. And the government had not obtained the requisite permissions.

The case was assigned to Judge John Sirica of Watergate fame and an excellent judge. I thought this was fortunate since it would take a good judge to understand my argument. But Judge Sirica simply listened to my argument and denied my motion.

I felt he was wrong. I wanted to appeal his ruling, but there was a problem. A party can appeal only when the case is over—from a final judgment, as the lawyers say—not at an earlier stage involving interlocutory rulings. If this rule were to be applied, I would have to wait until after a major trial to determine the fair market value of the building. That could take years.

There is an exception to this rule against interlocutory appeals, however. If the issue is central to the case and the judge certifies that "there is substantial ground for difference of opinion," an interlocutory appeal is permitted. So I went back to Judge Sirica and asked him to certify the case under this provision of the law (28 U.S.C. 1292(b)). "Mr. Shanks," he told me in open court, "I think your case is frivolous."

I still felt I was right. There was only one thing to do: Sue the judge.

It's called *mandamus*. I brought my case in the United States Court of Appeals, asking that court to issue a writ of *mandamus*, ordering Judge Sirica to certify the case for an interlocutory appeal. As you can imagine, courts are generally reluctant to invoke such a drastic remedy, especially against so distinguished a bench brother. Indeed, the Court of Appeals denied my petition for *mandamus*. But the Court of Appeals opinion made it clear that I seemed to have a pretty good case for an interlocutory appeal, even if this wasn't a case for *mandamus*.

With this opinion in hand, I went back to Judge Sirica and, in effect, said: "See! It's not frivolous." He called the attorneys into his chambers and we had a wonderful discussion, even touching on Watergate. Judge Sirica ended by agreeing to certify my case for an interlocutory appeal.

The case had a bittersweet ending, however. George wanted to do some lobbying at the Department of Justice, which we felt was improper since the case was in court. After my brief on appeal was written and filed, we learned that George was doing just what we had instructed him not to do. We withdrew from the case. George himself argued the case in the Court of Appeals—on my brief. And of course he won.

The government authorities did not give up so easily, however. Acting like the bully in the schoolyard, they inserted a provision in a Congressional bill that would override the court decision and allow the government to condemn the property. In the Senate committee hearing, Senator John Pastore told the government authorities that they were "sneaking in the back door to write language into the bill to try to defeat the Court of Appeals decision." This, the senator said, was "un-American."

The *Washington Post* report the next day began this way:

"In a cross-my-heart, hope-to-die statement, General Services Administrator Barnard L. Boutin promised yesterday that he will not try to take over the Matomic Building by any backdoor methods."

On Jerry's death, the property passed to his daughters, just as Jerry always intended.

So we won. But, as usual, there was a loss, too. By the time we won we were no longer in the case, although it was won on my brief.

I guess I'm litigation-prone, not only professionally but personally. In one case, I personally sued TWA when it lost my luggage on a flight from New York to Tel Aviv. I put in a claim for $1,600, my estimate of the value of my clothes. I was politely told to read my ticket carefully and I would see that the limit of liability on claims on international flights was $750. I looked at my ticket. They were right; that indeed was what it said. That limit on liability, however, was based on an international treaty known as the Warsaw Convention. That treaty did set limits on liability of claims on international flights of air carriers. But the limits were expressed not in dollars but in Poincare francs, a French currency named for the prime minister of France in office in 1934 when the treaty was agreed upon. The nice thing about the Poincare franc was that it had a fixed amount of gold—65.5 milligrams. *That* established the limit of the airlines' liability. But the Warsaw

Convention did not say how the gold was to be valued. TWA had established the value of gold at the last official value when the United States went off the gold standard—$44 an ounce—even though the value of gold on the open market, no longer controlled by an official price, was at the time of my claim in the hundreds of dollars. I argued that the value of the gold that limited the airline's liability (expressed in Poincare francs) should be fixed by the price of gold on the open market. At that point, the airline offered me $4,500 (which included my other incidental damages) to settle the case. I accepted. With the money I informally established the Hershel Shanks Clothing Trust, which would finance my purchase of clothes for the next decade. In a subsequent case brought by other plaintiffs, the Supreme Court later ruled that my argument was correct. This led to a new international convention and the limits on liability of air carriers on international flights is now established by what is known as the Montreal Convention.

Sometimes a lawsuit is even better and more convenient than a telephone call—if you consider litigation easy and fun. It's civilized, rational, no yelling and screaming, no calling names, just reasoning with published rules that are supposed to determine the outcome. On a recent flight from London to Washington, British Airways (BA) damaged my luggage. A pleasant BA agent at Dulles airport called my attention to it, gave me a claim slip with a number on it and told me that BA would contact me shortly to pick up the suitcase, which it would send to somewhere in Texas for repair. When I never heard from them, I dropped them a note, but this produced no answer. So I decided to call them. But nowhere could I find a telephone number for BA that would give me a human being to whom I could explain my problem, and none of the recorded messages seemed to fit my case. The easiest thing to do was to file a suit in Small Claims Court. I asked for $350, my estimate of the replacement value of the suitcase. In short order, I received a very pleasant call from a lawyer in their legal office, saying they would send me a check for $350, which they did. The lawyer and I started chatting and it turned out he had an interest in biblical archaeology, so I sent him a complimentary subscription to BAR—a wholly pleasant experience. This was so much easier than trying to find someone to talk to on the phone.

CHAPTER VI

Our Year in Israel

AT LUNCH WITH MY LAWYER FRIENDS, WE were discussing Newton Frohlich. A prominent divorce lawyer (he had written *Making the Best of It: A Common-Sense Guide to Negotiating a Divorce*), Newton had decided to take some time off from the practice and go to southern France to write a novel. (He ultimately made the trip—and wrote a novel about the life of Christopher Columbus.) I jokingly (and not very tastefully) lamented to my luncheon companions, "My wife would never allow me to do that, after the level of comfort I've accustomed her to."

At dinner that night, I related the story. Judith responded, "Try me!"

That was it. I would take a year's sabbatical from the law. I had always wanted to live for a year in some exciting foreign country. In college, it was the Left Bank of the Seine. Later, it was Florence. During the previous March, Judith and I had taken a trip to Israel and I was becoming increasingly interested in the Bible, so that was now the place.

I was just finishing a major antitrust case (with a very satisfactory settlement from our client's viewpoint). My partners would not get any healthier, I reasoned, only sicker. Our two little girls—Julia three and Elizabeth five—were not yet in school; later it would be difficult taking them out of school for a year. So if we were ever going to do it, now was the time.

But what would be the reaction of my law partners? Would they simply kick me out of the firm? None of them was Jewish and none had ever elicited any special interest in or concern for Israel. I decided that the best thing to do was to announce that I was taking a sabbatical, rather than asking if they would agree to it. That is what I did—one by one I told my partners that I was taking a year off to live in Israel. I was surprised and relieved that even those whom I expected would be most critical could not help responding, "How exciting. Isn't that wonderful?" My partners made it very easy for me. They treated me not only fairly, but generously.

I knew I wanted nothing to do with the law during that year, but what *did* I want to do? Gradually, I developed a list of ten projects, in descending order. At the top of the list was a novel about the complex, tragic figure of Saul, the first king of Israel. I had recently read Thomas Mann's magisterial tetralogy, *Joseph and His Brothers*, the first volume of which was *The Tales of Jacob*. I would begin with the tales of the prophet-priest Samuel.

The next item on my list of projects was less grandiose. On our previous trip to Jerusalem, we had walked through a long, knee-deep water tunnel, known as Hezekiah's Tunnel, underneath the oldest part of Jerusalem. We were able to see our way with the help of a candle given to us (for a couple shekels) by an Arab sitting at the entrance to the winding, third-of-a-mile-long tunnel. While the venture was indeed exciting, there was nothing there to tell a visitor about the tunnel. My idea was that I would write a little pamphlet about Hezekiah's Tunnel and sell it (or have it sold) for 10 or 15 cents at the entrance to the tunnel.

I cannot even recall the rest of the projects on my list. They quickly became irrelevant.

We considered two places to live—Arad in the desert (Ah, the isolation of it all! Besides, that's where the much admired Israeli novelist Amos Oz lived) or Jerusalem. We finally decided on Jerusalem and proceeded to try to locate an apartment, which turned out to be no small problem. We suddenly realized that we did not know a single soul in Israel. We finally learned that an Israeli woman who was teaching in the local Jewish day school had a sister in Jerusalem who was a lawyer and that in Israel apartment rentals were usually handled by lawyers. The place she found us was a walk-up on the third floor, which we rejected on that basis. She then found us another apartment one flight up. We took it. When we arrived, we found that it was indeed one fight up. But to get to the entrance, you had to go 67 steps down from the parking lot of the building! It was a lovely apartment, however, near Hebrew

University overlooking the valley. And we quickly got used to the steps; they kept us healthy. Soon, we didn't even notice.

I spent my days mostly at the Hebrew University library learning more about Samuel and Saul and writing my novel. An early letter home to friends describes my routine and my mood:

> I had thought to wait a bit before writing again, until the initial euphoria had died down, but it hasn't very much. So I will write anyway. In short, having all my time to read and write just what I please has made me manic. I have been reading voraciously—day and night except for the time I write. And I have been wildly happy doing it. I get up about six in the morning and write for a few hours. Then I take a walk in the mid-morning sun up a hill and through a pine wood to the [Hebrew] University library. I have a little lunch about 1:30 in the afternoon, then back to the library for an hour or so. Then I walk back home for an afternoon nap. When I get up, I read until dinnertime, eat and then read again until bedtime. I have literally been in another world—the world of my books. I am unconscious of time passing. By now, I've gotten hold of myself a bit, but I'm still enjoying it immensely.
>
> Of course, the regimen isn't unchanging. Sometimes I stop writing after a few hours. Sometimes I can go on all morning. Sometimes I have my books in the apartment so I don't need to go to the library. I also wash the dishes and give the kids their bath. And we even take off occasionally.
>
> What am I reading? To me, it seems like an enormous variety. But from another viewpoint, I realize it is probably pretty narrow. Of course, there are lots of books on the books of Samuel—studies, commentaries, criticism, etc. Then there are archaeological reports on sites I'm interested in. And I read lots of arcane articles in magazines with magical names, like *Vetus Testamentum*. Other subjects include books on Old Testament theology, the Philistines, biblical warfare, studies in ancient technology and on and on. I also look at more general books like Yehezkel Kaufmann's *The Religion of Israel*, G. Earnest Wright's *Biblical Archaeology*, Kathleen Kenyon's *Royal Cities of the Old Testament*

and Yohanan Aharoni's *Land of the Bible*. I've relaxed with more popular things like Larry Collins and Dominique Lapierre's *O Jerusalem!* which talks about things all around us, so it's exciting to relate to.

After writing nearly 300 pages of my novel, however, I began to have doubts about the project. Writing a novel I knew was not easy. In addition to a lot of *zitsfleish*, it takes a certain imaginative talent that I began to doubt that I had. Writing a legal brief or even a scholarly article I knew how to do, but a novel was something else. I continued to plug away, however, day by day.

Then a chance meeting of my wife's while shopping at Chaim the Butcher's on Aza Street changed my life. This, however, requires some background.

As the reader may have noticed, I have not spoken of my biblical training—because I had none. I had learned to read Hebrew (but not to translate it) at after-school *cheder*. I was bar-mitzvahed. I went to Sunday school. We were kosher at home, but not out. My parents were active in the Jewish community and avid Zionists. But that's it.

When I came to Washington, I heard about a Saturday morning television course in the New Testament taught by a Bible scholar named Edward Bauman who was also the pastor of one of Washington's largest and best-known churches. The New Testament was even further from my ken than the Hebrew Bible. I had never had any contact with the New Testament. There was something *treyf* (unkosher) about it. We certainly had no copy of it in my parental home. Indeed, I had never actually held a copy.

But I took Bauman's course and found it fascinating (alas, this excellent teacher later fell from grace; over an eight-year period, he had had numerous sexual relationships with women in his congregation and was forced to resign). Indeed, I found the subject so fascinating that I decided to learn something about the Hebrew Bible as well. Paradoxically, I came to the Hebrew Bible through the New Testament.

At the time, I was a member of an informal play-reading group that met every other Thursday night—a bunch of young lawyers (all men) and girls (as they were then called) who mostly worked for the

government. We referred to ourselves jokingly as the Thursday Evening
Legal Discussion and Play-Reading Group. When I finished Bauman's
course in the New Testament, I suggested that our play-reading group
form an additional group that soon became known as the Bible Discussion
Group. It continued for many years, even after most of us were married
and had children. Gradually, different members of the group began to
specialize, bringing different perspectives to the discussion. One person
knew Hebrew. Another brought the Talmud. Another brought a Marxist
perspective. It was then that I became interested in archaeology. I brought
the archaeological perspective.

In my background reading, I discovered an interesting, though perhaps minor, difference of views between Solomon Zeitlin, the sage of
Dropsie College in Philadelphia (which gave only Ph.D. degrees), and the
world's most prominent biblical archaeologist, William Foxwell Albright
of The Johns Hopkins University in Baltimore. The dispute concerned the
word "rabbi," a title applied to Jesus in the Gospels of Matthew and John.
Was this title used at the time of Jesus? Or was it used anachronistically in
the Gospels, applied to Jesus by a later writer? The title appears nowhere
else other than the New Testament as early as the time of Jesus. Zeitlin
was of the view that it was anachronistic in the New Testament. Albright
took the opposite view. It was the old puzzle: Is the absence of evidence
evidence of absence? Albright could cite at least some reason to believe
the title was probably used at the time of Jesus even though we have no
examples other than the New Testament.

I saw an opportunity in this difference of scholarly views for my
lawyerly skills. I could not do research either in Greek or Hebrew but, as
a lawyer, I could assess the reasonableness of the arguments. And I agreed
with Albright: The term was used in Jesus' time. I wrote an article on the
subject in the scholarly journal of Dropsie College (*The Jewish Quarterly
Review*) entitled "Is the Title 'Rabbi' Anachronistic in the Gospels?" to
which Professor Zeitlin replied in the same issue, to which I responded
in a subsequent issue, to which he likewise responded. The outcome was
indecisive. But in the course of this dispute, I consulted Albright and
became friendly with him. Perhaps he treated me so warmly because one

of his sons was attending law school and this became a kind of bond between the father and me.

When my acquaintance with Albright came up at a meeting of our Bible Discussion Group, several people asked if I could arrange a session of our group with the great man. We would, of course, go to Baltimore: He was not only distinguished, but in his late 70s. (Yikes! That's my age now.) I contacted Albright and he was most gracious. Yes, he would gladly meet with us. It was an inspiring evening.

My friendship with Albright had reverberations. In 1971 he passed away. And in March 1972, before Judith and I had even thought of going to Israel for a year, we took a trip there, as I mentioned earlier. In Jerusalem we stayed in the National Palace Hotel in the Arab section of the city, opposite the building that housed the so-called "American School," more formally the Jerusalem branch of the American Schools of Oriental Research. Albright had been its early director and guiding light and now its patron saint. The school had been recently renamed The William F. Albright School of Archaeological Research. One afternoon, Judith and I crossed the street from our hotel and knocked on the door of the stately mansion that housed the school. This turned out to be the door to the director's residential quarters in the most luxurious wing of the building. We knew no one at the school or even the current director's name. A man answered our knock and I explained that I had been a friend of Professor Albright's. The man who had answered the door was the then-director, William G. Dever, one of the two or three most prominent and distinguished American archaeologists in the field. No doubt because of my relationship to Professor Albright, Professor Dever invited us into his living room to have a cup of coffee. I don't remember what we talked about, but I do recall being suitably impressed.

And that brings me back to Chaim the Butcher. A month or so after we arrived in Jerusalem for the year, my wife went to Chaim's to pick up something for dinner. There she bumped into someone she thought she knew and who thought he recognized her. It turned out to be Bill Dever. He invited her (and me) to an afternoon gathering at the school a few days hence.

The entire archaeological community turned out for the lecture and reception at the American School. By that time I was thinking about writing my pamphlet on Hezekiah's Tunnel, either in addition to or instead of the novel about Saul. So I asked one of the scholars at the party, "Who knows more about Jerusalem archaeology than anyone?" "Oh, Dani Bahat," he replied. "He's standing right over there." And thus began my 35-year friendship with Dan Bahat (who indeed knows more than anybody about Jerusalem archaeology). That chance meeting at Chaim the Butcher's—which came about only because I knew Albright, whom I knew because I needed help in writing an article about whether the title "rabbi" was anachronistic in the Gospels—may have changed my life. It was a grand party—a wonderful introduction to Israel's foremost archaeological community.

Soon after the party at the American School, we joined a small, informal "pottery group," which met together to study, identify and date ancient pottery. It was led by Gus Van Beek, who directed the archaeological excavations at Tel Jemmeh near Gaza and who was the chief Near Eastern archaeologist at the Smithsonian Institution. We would later see him and his Israeli wife Ora in Washington. The pottery group also included Val and Horatio Vester, proprietors of the famed American Colony Hotel, housed in a pasha's palace. Horatio was a direct descendant of Bertha Spafford Vester, whose family established the American Colony in Jerusalem in the 19th century. Val and Horatio were elegant, gracious and more English than American. Another member of the group was Father Jerome Murphy-O'Connor of the École biblique et archéologique Française in East Jerusalem. The École biblique had been home to Père Roland de Vaux, excavator of Qumran, where the Dead Sea Scrolls had been found. Its faculty was generally thought to be more sympathetic to the Arab viewpoint than to the Zionists, but that was changing. Jerry made his first trip to Jewish Jerusalem, which had become accessible only since 1967, to attend one of the pottery sessions at our apartment. He has since become an authority on both the New Testament and the archaeology of the land, as well as a good friend.

As I became more interested in archaeology, I became less interested in pursuing my novel. Several hundred pages into it, I realized that I was

GETTING MY FEET WET. During my 1972 sabbatical in Israel, I began to explore my burgeoning fascination with biblical archaeology. This photo shows me (yes, that's me with a beard) wading through the thigh-high water of Hezekiah's Tunnel under the City of David.

not a novelist. I didn't need anybody else to tell me that. And nobody did. In fact, the draft has never been read by anyone, including me. I knew it was no good. Since I wanted to be a thorough researcher in writing this autobiography, I decided to look at the draft again after 35 years, confident that my earlier judgment would be confirmed. I thought I knew just where it lay, unread. But it was no longer there. I think I threw it out, not wanting my descendants to form a judgment of me based on it, especially my description of how the priest Eli's sons were screwing around with the women who served at the Tent of Meeting (1 Samuel 2:22).

In the meantime, I was learning more about, and becoming more fascinated with, archaeology, especially as Dani Bahat and I would explore the area around Hezekiah's Tunnel together. (He made some amazing archaeological suggestions that decades later were proved accurate in the course of Yigal Shiloh's excavations.) And every Shabbat, Judith, the kids and I would take a family *tiyul* (excursion), usually to explore some archaeological site.

As Judith had made a critical contact at Chaim the Butcher's, so my daughter Elizabeth (then Elisheva, as Julia was Yael) made a critical discovery at the biblical site of Hazor. The site had been excavated by the most famous and most glamorous archaeologist in Israel, Yigael Yadin. He was the closest thing Israel had to a movie star. He had led the Haganah, Israel's pre-state army, in Israel's War of Independence. He was not only a war hero, he was the excavator of Masada. Atop this mesa in the Judean Desert was King Herod's palace, where according to the ancient Jewish historian Josephus, the rebels in the Great Jewish Revolt against Rome had made their last stand before committing mass suicide.

I had attended two of Yadin's lectures and had been introduced to him by his chief assistant, Amnon Ben-Tor, who lived in the same apartment building as we did. Ben-Tor would eventually succeed Yadin as director of the Hazor excavations and hold the Yigal Yadin Chair of Archaeology at Hebrew University. But that was long in the future. Naturally, lots of amateurs like me sought Yadin's audience. His devoted wife Carmella ran a very effective guard around him. As I became more interested in exploring Hezekiah's Tunnel and the area around it, I knew that a talk with Yadin would be helpful.

I had already learned that the ridge through which Hezekiah's Tunnel ran was the very earliest inhabited part of Jerusalem—the Jerusalem of David and Solomon—even though it was outside and south of the walled Old City. Known as the City of David (or 'ir David, in Hebrew), this ridge has been extensively excavated in the past 35 years, but in 1972 there was not a single sign even to identify it. It was dusty and ignored. And although today there is an enormous literature about the City of David, both popular and scholarly, in 1972 there was very little reliable material about it. The few archaeological excavations that had taken place there had occurred mostly in the early part of the century. The famous British archaeologist Kathleen Kenyon had dug there in the 1960s, but she stopped when control of the area fell to Israel in the 1967 Six-Day War. And in 1972 she had not published the final report on her excavation (that was not to come until long after her death in 1978).

In short, to talk to Yadin about the archaeology of the City of David would give me a perspective that would be hard to get otherwise.

When we decided to drive to Hazor (Yadin's site) with the kids one Shabbat morning, I had no thought that this might lead to a relationship with its famous excavator. Fortified with our usual cardboard carton full of Jericho oranges, we headed north up the Jordan Valley, arriving at the site early enough to visit the small museum of Hazor finds located at the nearby kibbutz. Elisheva, six, and Yael, three, were already old hands at collecting the sherds (pieces of broken pottery) that are strewn all over archaeological sites. We no longer wanted body sherds, which had little to tell us. We were interested only in so-called diagnostic sherds, fragments of a rim, base or handle from an ancient pot. The museum displayed a case of these diagnostic sherds, including handles that had been impressed with inscribed seals. I pointed to the inscribed handles, telling the kids, "See! That's the kind of things we want," in my usual kidding manner.

Then we went out on the *tell*, the mound that comprised strata of one city atop the other in reverse chronological order, the most recent being the highest layer of the mound. It was not long before Elisheva came running to us with a small piece of a clay handle less than an inch-and-a-half long with something incised (or, as we then thought, impressed) into

A LUCKY FIND. On a weekend trip to the mound of Hazor, my six-year-old daughter Elizabeth happened upon this small, inch-and-a-half-long pottery handle, incised with a figure wearing a pointed hat and upturned shoes. The site's excavator, legendary archaeologist Yigael Yadin, identified the image as a Syro-Hittite deity from the Late Bronze Age (13th century B.C.E.).

it. Only the sharp eyes of a child close to the ground would have noticed it. At first, I was not sure there was anything deliberately etched into it. After all, lying around for thousands of years, it would not be unusual for a sherd to be scratched and damaged. As I looked and looked at the fragmentary handle, the figure of a man emerged, however, with a pointed hat and upturned shoes. He seemed to hold a long staff in one hand. In the other hand was something that looked like a mace he was about to hurl.

Suppressing my excitement, I congratulated Elisheva and said, "You better let me hold it."

"No," she screamed. "I found it."

FAIR TRADE. Elizabeth listens intently as Yigael Yadin shows her a picture of a juglet from the excavations at Hazor that he would give her in return for her donation of the incised potsherd to the Hazor Archaeological Expedition.

"OK," I said, "but be careful. It could be valuable."

We proceeded with our exploration of the *tell* until we came to its water tunnel, which descends by steps carved in the rock nearly three thousand years ago. To provide a modicum of safety for visitors, wooden slats were built over the ancient rock steps. As we descended, little light penetrated. All of a sudden Elisheva blurted out, "I dropped it."

"Don't move," I said. I dropped to the ground in the dark, moving my hands lightly and cautiously on the wooden slats around her, fearful that if the little sherd fell between the slats it would be lost forever. Fortunately, I was able to retrieve it.

"Now will you let me hold it," I said sternly. This was not a question. Elisheva, pouting for a moment, accepted my judgment.

When we returned to Jerusalem, I showed the sherd to Amnon Ben-Tor. "I would like to show it to Yadin," I said. After all, it was found on "his" site. Ben-Tor talked to Carmella and, in no time, it was arranged for me to give it to Yadin at his home.

There was no question that we would give the sherd to the Hazor excavation. All I wanted, I told him, was a replica of the sherd, a letter from him to Elisheva thanking her for the gift and a picture of her presenting the gift to Yadin. He readily agreed. I was bowled over, however, when he suggested that I publish an article on the handle for the *Israel Exploration Journal*. "I really don't know if I can," I said. He offered to help me. I said I would be delighted to have him as the senior author. No, he encouraged me; I could do it, he said. I *did* do it, but with considerable help from Yadin. The article appeared shortly after we returned to Washington.[5]

The figure on the handle depicted a Syro-Hittite deity from the Late Bronze Age (13th century B.C.E.) in a pose known as the "smiting god." It demonstrated how far south Syro-Hittite influence had penetrated—into Canaan. In a footnote, I duly acknowledged Yadin's assistance in writing the article and noted that the sherd had been found by six-year-old Elizabeth Shanks, who had donated it to the Hazor Expedition.

At my meeting with Yadin, we also got into a discussion of my City of David project. I had previously sent him a copy of my manuscript, which he had read. He proceeded to give me a nearly two-hour private lecture on the archaeology of Jerusalem. I sat mesmerized. This was one of the highlights of my year in Jerusalem. In a letter home after that visit, I wrote, "I wish I could convey the feeling of being in the presence of this man. He really radiates greatness, and all his ideas seem large and grand. I have talked to a lot of archaeologists since I have been here and there is simply no other one like him. He is a real genius—vast knowledge and great enthusiasm. I came home [from my meeting with him] walking on air." When Judith asked me about him, I pulled from the shelf Larry Collins and Dominique Lapierre's *O Jerusalem!* and opened it to the account of Jerusalem in Israel's War of Independence. Here is how I described it in one of my letters to friends at home, ending by quoting from the book:

The Jews in Jerusalem were under siege. There was no food or water. The Jewish convoys could not get through from the coast. Ben-Gurion knew that if the Jews could take Latrun, they could break the blockade and save Jerusalem.

At this point, I will let Larry Collins and Dominique Lapierre take over:

David Ben-Gurion pondered with distress the pile of cables littering his desk ... The situation in Jerusalem was so alarming that a disaster was inevitable if some way was not found to get help to the city. 'I knew', he would later recall, 'that if ever the people of the country saw Jerusalem fall, they would lose their faith in us and in our hopes of winning.' He had never before directly intervened in a tactical problem of the Haganah. Tonight he was going to. Despite the lateness of the hour, he summoned to his office Yigael Yadin and his senior officers. He then told his Chief of Operations, 'I want you to occupy Latrun and open the road to Jerusalem.'

Yadin stiffened. For the young archaeologist who had overall direction of the Haganah, other fronts that night had priority over Jerusalem. The Egyptians were menacing Tel Aviv ... The Syrians were threatening Galilee ...

Ben-Gurion insisted. Yadin's timetable was not his and their clash was violent and acrimonious. 'By the time we take Latrun under your plan, there won't be any Jerusalem left to save,' said Ben-Gurion.

At these words, Ben-Gurion saw his young subordinate's face pale. Yadin crashed his fist down on the desk, shattering the glass cover. The young man wiped a few flecks of blood from his fist and stared at his leader.

'Listen', Yadin said, his voice low with fury and barely controlled passion. 'I was born in Jerusalem. My wife is in Jerusalem. My father and mother are in Jerusalem. Everybody I love is there. Everything that binds you to Jerusalem binds me even more. I should agree with you to send everything we have to Jerusalem. But I don't because I'm convinced they can hold on with what we've given them and we need our forces for situations even more desperate.'

Shaken by Yadin's unexpected outburst, Ben-Gurion drew his head down into his shoulders like a wrestler, the certain sign of his

ISRAEL'S EQUIVALENT OF A MOVIE STAR. Unlike many scholars who considered me an "outsider," Israeli archaeologist and celebrated war hero Yigael Yadin (shown here surveying the excavations at Hazor), helped me in my early efforts to make biblical archaeology accessible and interesting to a general audience.

unshaken determination. He quietly studied Yadin, then he gave him a straightforward, unequivocal order. 'Take Latrun.'

Yadin was proved right. They tried to take Latrun—three times they tried, with great loss of life. But they could not take Latrun. And Jerusalem's Old City remained in Jordanian hands for 19 years, until the 1967 Six-Day War.

This was the man from whom I had just learned about the archaeology of the oldest part of Jerusalem, the City of David.

The City of David—A Guide to Biblical Jerusalem came out while we were still in Jerusalem. The first tribute in the acknowledgments was of course to Yadin, "whose vast scholarship and perspicacious comments on the entire text have been immeasurably helpful."

It was not only that the book was published while we were still there, it was even reviewed in the *Jerusalem Post*. The reviewer described it as "one of the most fascinating books I have ever read ... fresh, vivid and quite new in its approach." *This Week in Israel* said it "will leave you spellbound by history." *Ha'aretz* called it "fascinating in an armchair; indispensable on the site." *Yediot Achronot* said it "deserves to be in the library of all to whom Jerusalem is close at heart."

During that year, I found that scholars were divided into two camps in their attitude toward me, the outsider. One group was like Yadin, warmly welcoming me and helping me. Then there were others, like the highly regarded archaeologist Ruth Amiram, who was at best dismissive and perhaps even discourteous. Ruth worked at the Israel Museum, and I decided to "do the nice thing" and present her with a copy of my book. I stopped by her office and gave her an inscribed copy. "You've been in Israel five days," she snapped, "and you've written a book!" After many years, I came to appreciate this aspect of Ruth's personality. In a way, it was typically Israeli—rough, blunt, too honest. I took her comment to me as saying I had no right to write a book after only "five days," but maybe she was admiring my achievement after such a brief time in the country. Ruth was of the founding generation. After many years, I believe she came to accept me—the outsider. She ultimately wrote something for BAR about her dig at Arad, and I later attended many Shabbat afternoon soirees with Ruth at the apartment of the elder statesman of Israeli archaeology, Benjamin Mazar. Perhaps to make up for the way she initially treated me, she bent over backward to be pleasant.

In its way, my little book led to the next major excavation of the City of David, led by Hebrew University professor Yigal Shiloh.

Mendel Kaplan was (and is) a wealthy South African businessman, a major Jewish community leader and a devoted Zionist. He read my book and used it to guide prospective United Jewish Appeal donors around the site. He quickly realized the potential for excavation, especially as I had decried in a footnote the dilapidated and ignored condition of the site.

With several wealthy friends whom he assembled, Mendel decided to support a major excavation of the site and took the idea to the legendary Jerusalem mayor, Teddy Kollek. Kollek in turn assembled all the interested archaeological parties at a meeting with Mendel. Instead of grasping the opportunity, the archaeologists, as is their wont, raised all kinds of questions and potential objections. In a recently published *festschrift* in Kollek's honor (he unfortunately passed away before its publication), Mendel describes this meeting:

> There followed a heated discussion about the feasibility of such a project and whether it might not be best to focus attention on a particular area. Teddy lost his patience [as he often did], pounded the table and in Hebrew, thinking that I did not understand, said: 'Listen—you have a South African willing to spend a large amount of money and all you are doing is putting him off.' To me he turned in English and said: 'It is February and before Pesach, in April, you will receive a positive response.' He was true to his word.[6]

And thus the ten-year excavation of the site directed by Yigal Shiloh was born. It ended only with Shiloh's tragic and untimely death in 1987.

The Kollek *festschrift* came out only in 2007. Mendel's appreciation of Teddy, which was written in English, included a generous reference to me and my book on the City of David. As he "walked across the hillside with" my book, he wrote, he was "shocked" at what had been allowed "to become a cesspool and rubbish heap." That was the beginning of the idea of what became Yigal Shiloh's excavation of the site. Mendel's piece was translated into Hebrew and was also printed in the Hebrew section of the *festschrift*. There, however, all references to me and my book were simply deleted. Otherwise, Mendel's piece is translated word for word. I was still the outsider.

Once I turned in my *City of David* manuscript to the publisher, I needed a new project. It grew naturally out of our Shabbat *tiyulim*. Among the sites we explored were some ancient synagogues mostly from the first six centuries of the common era—some excavated, some in ruins, some reconstructed, some evidenced only by a small surviving mosaic or inscribed stone or architectural fragment. Even then, more than a hundred such synagogues were known in the scholarly literature. But there was no popular account.

I decided to write one. Some ancient synagogues I could learn of only from scholarly reports, for example, the extraordinary mid-third-century synagogue at Dura-Europos in Syria, with its remarkable biblical paintings that covered the walls. Others, however, were easily accessible, such as the synagogue in Hammath-Tiberias on the Sea of Galilee, with its handsome mosaic floor featuring depictions of the holy ark flanked by large menorot and, surprisingly, a seemingly pagan zodiac with the Greek god Helios in the center riding his chariot. This strange combination of Jewish and the apparently pagan was repeated in a number of ancient synagogues. By contrast, in a synagogue in Jericho, the mosaic carpet includes an almost artistically modern, stylized ark and a realistic menorah below it with a quotation from Psalm 125: *shalom al yisrael* ("peace unto Israel"). One Shabbat, we devoted the entire day to searching for a fragment from an ancient synagogue. The fragment was inscribed with a menorah and had been reused as a lintel in a church in a small Palestinian village. Learning about ancient synagogues was fun—for the whole family. I decided to write a book on ancient synagogues.

Two small matters presaged my involvement in later disputes. One involved a mosaic found in the ancient synagogue at the hot springs of

THE CLAWS COME OUT. I was initially denied permission to publish this picture of an anatomically-correct lion from the Hammath-Gader synagogue mosaic because the excavation report had never been published, although the excavation itself had ended in the 1930s. Ultimately, I won the right to use the photo, but it wouldn't be the last time I had to stand my ground on this issue.

Gader, east of the Kinneret (the Sea of Galilee). The Hammath-Gader mosaic includes two wonderfully alive lions on either side of a wreath enclosing an inscription to a donor of the synagogue. The lions have heavy manes, hanging tongues and raised tails exposing their very explicit genitals. Going through the slide archives at Hebrew University, I discovered a picture of one of these lions, which I thought to include in my book. However, permission to use the picture was initially denied on the ground that it had not yet been published—*even though the picture was from a 1930s excavation.* I protested audibly and the decision was ultimately reversed. A picture of the lion appears on page 111 of my book, which I was able to finish only after we returned to the States. It was published in 1979 under the title *Judaism in Stone—The Archaeology of Ancient Synagogues*. Yigael Yadin wrote the preface to it. In it, he recounted memories of his father Eleazer Lipa Sukenik who, traveling by horseback, explored the ruins of ancient synagogues in Palestine in the 1920s. In the 1930s, Sukenik was invited to give the Schweich Lectures at the British Academy in London. The lectures were later published as *Ancient Synagogues in Palestine and Greece*. "Except for collections of articles, that book," Yadin wrote in his preface to my book, "was the last to be published which canvasses the subject as a whole—until now ... *Judaism in Stone* by Hershel Shanks brings the subject up to date. It is a fascinating description and interpretation of these ancient synagogue remains."

I devoted one chapter of the book to what it was like to excavate an ancient synagogue. For this purpose I chose the synagogue at Ein Gedi on the shore of the Dead Sea. Among the unusual objects excavated there was not simply a mosaic of a menorah, which was common enough, but an actual bronze menorah found lying on the floor of the synagogue. The excavators also uncovered a charred wooden disc, one of the roller ends from a Torah scroll. A long mosaic inscription in the entrance aisle of the synagogue includes biblical quotations, a literary zodiac and curses on those who would divide the community.

A gorgeous mosaic with peacocks, fruit and geometric designs in the main hall of the synagogue is not surprising. When it was lifted, however, it revealed an earlier plain white mosaic floor decorated only with a large black swastika! The significance of the swastika 1,500 years ago remains a mystery.

The chapter on the Ein Gedi synagogue was particularly difficult to write because excavator Dan Barag had never written a scientific report on the excavation. The old bugaboo raised its head: Could a popular account be published before that scholarly account? But that's not the worst of it. Today, nearly 30 years later, the excavation report has still not been written. Several years ago, thinking that the problem may have been the lack of funds to support the study of the excavation records, I talked to someone about funding the publication of the excavation. The answer was that money would be readily available. I then contacted Barag, but he was less than enthusiastic. When he finally contacted Hebrew University, as he reported to me, all the excavation records had been lost. There is nothing there with which to write an excavation report. The failure of archaeologists to publish the results of their excavations is, unfortunately, not uncommon. The Biblical Archaeology Society, publisher of *Biblical Archaeology Review*, would later become heavily involved in this issue.

One thing that made it easier—and more fun—to write *Judaism in Stone* was that during our year in Israel, from September 1972 through August 1973, the country was entirely peaceful and we could explore the West Bank and the Sinai without security concerns. We spent a week in the Sinai with the SPNI (Society for the Preservation of Nature in Israel). We climbed up to the Egyptian temple at Serabit al-Khadem dedicated to the goddess of turquoise, which Semitic slaves mined in the caves nearby in about 1500 B.C.E. The miners left on the walls of the mine some of the earliest known alphabetic writing. (My photographs of the inscriptions *in situ* are still some of the best.) We clambered up Jebel ed-Deir, opposite Mt. Sinai, so we could look down on the monastery of Saint Catherine from a height. We walked through sculptured rock gorges of Sinai in the moonlight. And, on our own, we regularly drove down the Sinai coast south from Eilat to the then little-known beaches at Zahav and Nuweiba.

We often rode to Jericho for dinner, eating at the town's beautiful outdoor restaurants. If we didn't go to Jericho, it would be the square in Ramallah. Or to East Jerusalem with its numerous Arab restaurants. Or to the Dolphin, a fish restaurant in East Jerusalem famously owned by a Jew and an Arab.

One weekend we went to Gaza with our little girls. We stayed in a small guest house where I saw my first Pleyel piano, the French equivalent of a Steinway. We lolled on the beach and shopped. We bought rugs and some cloth from which Judith would make a dress. And of course we visited the Great Mosque of Gaza. It had been built as a Crusader church that had incorporated pillars in its lofty construction taken from an ancient synagogue. One of the pillars was decorated with a menorah, flanked on one side by the familiar *lulav* (palm frond) and *etrog* (citron) associated with the festival of Sukkot and on the other side with a shofar—not unusual for an ancient synagogue, but, still, a little odd in a Crusader church, now converted into a mosque. (It has now been gouged out.)

One time, after exploring Mt. Ebal and Mt. Gerizim, we stopped for a lunch in the town square at Nablus (ancient Shechem). While we were eating, an argument developed between the restaurant's Arab owner and an Israeli soldier with a gun strapped on his shoulder. It got quite vociferous on both sides. It turned out to be an argument over a bill. But that's all it was—an argument over a bill. It had nothing to do with the fact that the argument was between an Arab and an Israeli soldier.

When I think about how peaceful it was that year, I wonder how we got from there to here.

CHAPTER VII

Starting BAR

MY CHIEF CONCERN—ACTUALLY, FEAR—at returning to the States was how I would be received at the law firm. I had visions of their saying something like this: "Chuck Trainum (or whoever) has been using your office and he is in the middle of a big, important case. Would you mind sitting in the library in the meantime?"

Of course that did not happen, and I was warmly welcomed back. I easily fell into my old ways and into my old legal practice. And I looked forward to returning regularly to Israel for short visits. But as I imagined these visits, I bumped into a hard reality: What would I do there? Yes, we did have some friends there now. But they would be working during the day. So I could have dinner with them. But I would soon run out of dinner dates. And what would I do during the day? When we lived there, I had become part of the scene. I liked that feeling. I didn't like the idea of being an outsider looking for something to do. I needed a business, a purpose for visiting Israel.

Then it occurred to me: I would write a column on biblical archaeology. So far as I knew, no one was doing this. I contacted my friend Charlie Fenyvesi, who edited *B'nai B'rith Magazine*, and proposed the idea to him. "I've already got too many columns," he said over lunch. "Why don't you start your own magazine?"

"How do you do that?" I asked.

It sounded easy: You just write up a proposal and send it to a variety of people—scholars, academic leaders, businessmen, philanthropists, community leaders, writers, etc. And then you'll have all the elements.

So that's what I did.

I received only one reply, however—from Rabbi Samuel Sandmel who taught at Hebrew Union College in Cincinnati and had served as president of the major American organization of Bible scholars, the Society of Biblical Literature. He wrote that I had an interesting idea. I've always wondered whether he might have replied because he had dated my mother-in-law when he was serving as a student rabbi in Montgomery, Alabama, before she married my father-in-law.

I then sent all the people who had received my proposal a second communication. I thanked them for their warm response and reported that we now had enough interest and money to go ahead.

My initial idea was to make the publication a simple newsletter. Greece was a land of gold. So was Egypt. Israel, however, was a land of stone. My newsletter would be a publication of ideas, not beautiful pictures. It would come out four times a year.

I would call it *Biblical Archaeology Newsletter*. In Israel, we had become friendly with two American archaeologists from Duke University, Eric and Carol Meyers, with whom we spent a week in the Sinai and who, like us, had two little daughters. On a family visit to Durham, North Carolina, we discussed the project in the Meyers' living room. Carol observed that the initials of the publication would be BAN, not a very attractive name for a biblical archaeology newsletter. She thought *Biblical Archaeology Review* would be much better. I agreed. Besides, the resulting acronym would be BAR, quite appropriate for a lawyer. And suddenly the publication became a magazine instead of a newsletter. But, still, it would feature ideas rather than pictures.

One of my plans for the magazine was to have an American editor and a Jerusalem editor. I asked Eric Meyers to be the American editor. He tentatively agreed, but when he advised the leaders of the American Schools of Oriental Research (ASOR) of his intention, he was told that if he wanted to advance within the ranks of ASOR, the major American organization of Near Eastern archaeologists, he had better decline my offer. And he did. This was a harbinger of things to come. Eric later became president of ASOR and editor of its magazine, *Biblical Archaeologist*. I decided to drop the idea of an American editor.

The wife of one of my lawyer friends was a graphic designer, and I enlisted her to "make me a magazine." My idea, which she executed, was a

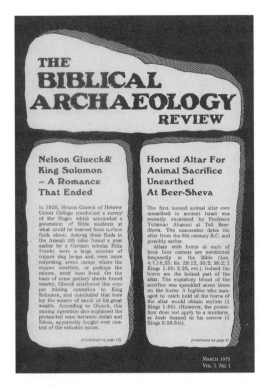

HUMBLE BEGINNINGS. The cover of the first issue of "The" BAR, published in March 1975.

cover consisting of two rough vertical blocks (like the two Tablets of the Law) within each of which an article would begin. These two tablets would, in turn, support a horizontal block more or less in the shape of the stone on which the famous Siloam Inscription is written. The inscription was discovered in 1880 carved into the wall of Hezekiah's Tunnel; it was subsequently chipped out of the wall and sent to Constantinople, the Ottoman capital. It is now on display in the Istanbul Archaeology Museum.

Frankly, the little 7-by-10-inch cover on the first BAR is pretty ugly. It somehow reminds me of the comic strip character Alley Oop, a prehistoric cave man. The issue, dated March 1975, was printed on cream-colored paper with brown ink. It consists of 16 pages and a single black-and-white picture—or rather a brown-and-cream picture. Its pages feature ideas, not pictures. How wrong I was to think that this was to be the nature of the magazine.

That first issue cost $600 to print. Since I was a lawyer, the printer agreed to trust me so that I did not have to come up with any cash in advance. A couple of small ads for subscriptions subsequently produced enough to pay him.

I wrote all the stories in the issue. In addition to six stories and an item headed "Introducing the BAR," the first issue announced the death of Harvard's G. Ernest Wright (one of the founder's of American biblical archaeology), the publication of two new journals (*Tel Aviv* and the *Journal of Field Archaeology*, both still publishing), the availability of a free 260-page book on the archaeology of Israel from the Embassy of Israel, and opportunities to volunteer on an archaeological excavation in Israel.

I also announced a policy of paying authors, which scholarly journals do not. "We have to pay the man who prints the magazine, the secretary who types the manuscript, the mailing outfit that labels and mails the magazine and that gets it to you. Why should we then fail to pay for the most important and indispensable contribution to the magazine—the authors of our articles?" In the early years we paid ten dollars for short articles and fifteen dollars for longer articles. A year's subscription was five dollars.

The masthead listed no staff because we had none. The address was my law office.

The masthead did, however, list a distinguished editorial advisory board. The first name on the board was my mother-in-law's old boyfriend, Sam Sandmel.

In "Introducing the BAR," I stated the magazine's aim "to make available in understandable language the current insights of professional archaeology as they relate to the Bible. No other publication is presently devoted to this task ... " "We will focus," I wrote, "on the new, the unusual and the controversial."

I still like this description. People want to know what's new. What's new is doubly interesting because in order to describe what's new, you often have to explain what's old and why the new is new. The same goes for the unusual. To explain why something is unusual you have to explain what the usual is.

Perhaps there's a little subterfuge involved: We're really teaching. For this purpose, the background that we give in our stories is as important, perhaps more important, than the new and unusual.

Another way to learn is to take a course in biblical archaeology. But that's not our way. That's another way. Our way is more fun. And more stimulating. Besides, you're in the vanguard of the profession when you read the articles in BAR.

Then, there's the third item I mentioned in "Introducing the BAR": "controversial." We're often charged with creating controversy. I reject the charge. But I do admit to believing that examining controversies is a good way to learn. I guess this betrays my legal background. I have an almost religious belief that examining reasoned controversy is the best way to arrive at the truth. That's the way lawsuits are conducted: Each side makes its best case, and out of this contest or controversy is our best chance at arriving at the correct answer. In the law, the judge or the jury decides who has the better case. In the academic world, it is the reader, be he a professional scholar or a layperson. And BAR strives to serve both kinds of readers.

In short, examining controversies is an excellent way to teach. Until recently, that was almost the sole way of teaching in law school. In its capacity to teach, "controversy" is like the "new" and the "unusual," the other two items that I said would characterize BAR.

But BAR does not create controversy. At most, it identifies it and exposes it. I like to say that we do not create controversy, but we do not shrink from it either.

Is archaeology more controversial than other fields? Is controversy especially intense in *biblical* archaeology?

I suspect the answer may be "yes." There is more room for controversy in archaeology because the answers are so much less certain. In a criminal case, the prosecution must prove its case beyond a reasonable doubt. This can rarely be done in archaeology. Most of the time, the archaeologist is making an educated guess—an *educated* guess, mind you, but still a guess. That is why "may be," "possibly," "probably," "likely" and the like appear so frequently in connection with archaeological conclusions. And the more general the conclusion, the more often these words appear.

The archaeologist can say with reasonable certainty that this wall was built before that one, but with less certainty when it was built and what it was part of, and, with still less certainty, who lived or worked in the building. When it comes to the big historical questions, involving thousands of observations from a myriad of fields, the problems are compounded. It is hardly surprising, therefore, that the field is beset with controversy. And it is the answer to the broadest historical questions, which are the most controversial, that people are most interested in.

That our field involves the Bible makes it that much more controversial, because we are dealing with core beliefs and strong convictions. This is not just otiose history. This matters to us. We are exploring who we are and where we came from.

In one respect, however, I think we are guilty of creating controversy. There *are* some issues, some questions that the profession laggardly does not face, does not deal with. This is true in all aspects of society. Exposing these issues and questions is part of the office of the media generally. Archaeologists are not accustomed to this kind of spotlight on what is happening in their field. They often resent it—although some few do appreciate it. An outsider can sometimes say things that insiders cannot say as easily. That is true of society generally and also of archaeology.

This aspect of controversy became a focus of BAR early on. We would ask questions that others would not ask—at least not publicly. In our third issue, I wrote an article entitled "Kathleen Kenyon's Anti-Zionist Politics—Does It Affect Her Work?"

BAR is an archaeological publication, not a political organ. I have made it a policy to stay out of politics as such, especially Middle Eastern politics. Archaeology is divisive enough, although I am sure my Zionist and Israeli sympathies come through clearly. We do, however, concern ourselves with politics as they affect archaeology. The article about Kathleen Kenyon illustrates the distinction. Kathleen Kenyon's politics *per se* are of no concern. They are of concern, however, if they affect her archaeology. And that was the question I was raising in my article. No one else would raise it publicly.

Kathleen Kenyon was one of the world's most distinguished archaeologists. She had led excavations at two of the most alluring, even romantic, sites in biblical history—Jericho and Jerusalem. Her father and Oxford don, Sir Frederic Kenyon, was author of *Our Bible and the Ancient Manuscripts*, much of which was devoted to showing how archaeology corroborated the Bible. But, like many people who work in Arab countries, she developed a natural affinity for the Arab viewpoint of the modern conflict, just as archaeologists working in Israel naturally see Israel in a more favorable light. For me, the question was whether Kenyon's sympathy for the Arab viewpoint in the Middle East struggle was affecting her archaeological conclusions.

Kenyon's antipathy for Zionism was well known and much discussed by archaeologists. In my article, I reported it and documented possible indications that her views regarding Arabs and Zionists were affecting her work. And I recounted her numerous professional differences with Israeli scholars, often as a group. Rereading the article after 35 years, I find it careful, qualified and balanced. I did not conclude that the answer to the question raised by the perhaps incendiary title was an unqualified yes, but that it was a question worth raising.

As soon as the issue came out, I sent a copy to Dr. Kenyon, with a letter to her stating that "Our pages are open, and we shall be glad to publish any response you, or someone else on your behalf, may wish to make."[7] She initially sent me a reply marked "Not for publication." We of course respected her wishes, but I then suggested to her that there were some specific items to which she might respond. This elicited a reply that we were allowed to print (and to which I replied). In this letter, she referred to my "so-called reportage" as being "such an insult to my professional integrity ... that I completely refuse to discuss your 0 ... I told you in my last letter that all real archaeologists would consider it quite unprofessional to enter into an argument with a critic, except on details of fact." She then discussed at some length her professional differences with Israeli archaeologists.

Whether I went too far is still being discussed by archaeologists (more often, by historians of archaeology). On the merits, I believe the answer is clear. She was openly anti-Zionist. In a letter to *The Times* (London) less than a fortnight after the Six-Day War, she wrote, "Israelis must not be able to keep the fruits of their invasion. Israel should be made to return to her pre-existing frontiers." She referred to Israel's creation as an "injustice" to the Arabs. Her politics were a major subject of discussion among Israeli archaeologists. Whether this anti-Zionism is reflected in her work is a moot question. There is certainly some indication that it is. On the other hand, I can be accused of implying a too clearly affirmative answer by the title I gave to the initial article (although my reply to her letter in the March 1976 BAR still reads pretty convincingly).

One thing is absolutely clear, however. Anyone reading my article, the letters to the editor that followed, Kenyon's letter in response to my article and my reply to her letter will come away with a very considerable amount of archaeological knowledge, especially about the archaeology of Jerusalem and the methods archaeologists employ in arriving at their conclusions. I think readers will also come away from this exchange with a well-balanced view of the evidence. What they conclude is up to them. In my mind, we had fulfilled our obligation to instruct.

By the end of our first year we had 3,000 subscribers. My ultimate goal at that time was 10,000. Today, we have 150,000 and more than a quarter of a million readers.

At an early point, I also enlisted several prominent biblical scholars and archaeologists for the editorial advisory board, in addition to Sam Sandmel. They included Père Pierre Benoit of the École biblique et archéologique Française in Jerusalem, a highly admired biblical scholar and shrewd commentator on archaeologically based conclusions, who later headed the Dead Sea Scrolls publication team. Père Benoit remained on the board until his death in 1987. Another early member of BAR's editorial advisory board was and is David Ussishkin, excavator of Lachish and Jezreel and now codirector of the excavations at Megiddo. He is the only academic who has been on the board since Volume 1, Number 1. (Sandmel has died.) Norma Kershaw, an independent scholar, is the other person who has been on the board since the beginning. For years, Norma would report to me all the critical things that were being said about BAR and chastise me for them. Another member of the initial board, Yigal Shiloh, who headed the major excavation of the City of David in Jerusalem, served until 1987, when he passed away from cancer at age 50.

With perhaps unjustified assurance, I advised readers in the first issue to save their copies of BAR. Perhaps they would become valuable in the future and make a fine gift to some school, church or synagogue, in turn producing a handy tax deduction.

We also established a letters-to-the-editor section that we call "Queries & Comments." Naturally we published some glowing letters from our readers, including from Tel Aviv University archaeologist Yohanan Aharoni; the head of the Hebraic Section of the Library of Congress, Lawrence Marwick; and a professor emeritus of history at Rensselaer Polytechnic Institute, Samuel Reznick, as well as from ordinary readers.

In subsequent years we stopped printing letters telling us how good we were. Instead, we began publishing letters from people who, for one reason or another, were canceling or threatening to cancel their subscriptions. As early as our second year, we published a letter from a professor at Kenyon College, who advised us that "I am renewing my subscription, though with considerable hesitancy, for I had hoped for better." He criticized our treatment of Kathleen Kenyon and found a spoof on the Dead Sea Scrolls by Woody Allen (entitled "The Red Sea Scrolls") "cheap and vulgar." Indeed, we have by now become famous for letters criticizing us, especially on religious grounds. And "Q&C," as we call it, remains one of the most popular sections of the magazine. Even academics often tell us that it is the first section they read. In 1995 we published a book of letters to the editor covering a wide range of topics. We called it *Cancel My Subscription*.

By the end of BAR's first year, I realized how wrong I had been to think that BAR would be only a magazine of ideas without beautiful pictures. By then, I knew that it had to be both. In the first issue of Volume 2, we introduced a four-page section with stunning color pictures on thick, glossy paper.

In the third year of publication, we added staff. I shouldn't say "added." Until then, there was no staff. Both new staff members were called Sue—which I have always thought appropriate for a lawyer. Both remain devoted friends and colleagues to this day.

The first was Susan Laden. I clearly recall the weekend afternoon when she and a friend came to my house. Two mothers with young children, they had heard I needed part-time help to handle subscriptions and checks. After I told them what the job was, they talked among themselves to determine who would take the job. The other woman said she didn't want the job, so Sue took it—reluctantly. BAR's first business office was in Sue's basement. Today, Susan Laden is BAR's publisher, president of the Biblical Archaeology Society and is responsible for our survival in a difficult market. Without her acumen and business ability, the organization would not have survived. People see our beautiful magazine, full of gorgeous color pictures (and ads) and think we are prosperous. On the contrary, we are always on the financial edge. It takes careful and sometimes imaginative financial balancing to keep us afloat. Sue Laden does that, as well as directing the staff.

The other "Sue" is Suzanne Singer. Like Sue Laden, she had young kids at home when she came to work for BAR more than 30 years ago. She is married to Max Singer, a Harvard Law School classmate of mine, and they had lived in Israel for four years in the 1970s. Initially, I enlisted Sue as my "Jerusalem Editor." When Sue and Max returned to the States, she became the assistant editor. BAR's first editorial office was in Sue's basement. It was not long before she became managing editor and my indispensable right arm.

One by one, the Singers' four sons, as they grew to manhood, moved to Israel permanently. One, Alex, an officer in the elite Givati Brigade, was killed in a clash with terrorists just inside Lebanon in 1987, on his 25th birthday. After Max's mother also moved to Israel, Max and Sue acquired an apartment in Jerusalem and now spend most of their time there. Sue remains a contributing editor, however, and serves as my eyes and ears in Israel.

For years, the two Sues would periodically come to my law office in downtown Washington, and we would have lunch. That was how we managed BAR as it continued to grow and flourish. We look back on those happy, happy days with a fondness that knows those times cannot be recaptured.

For me, BAR continued to be an extra-curricular activity while I supported my family by practicing law. I enjoyed both.

In the last issue of our third year, I wrote an article that was to be a harbinger of things to come. Professor Nahman Avigad of Hebrew University was heading a major excavation in the Old City of Jerusalem where he discovered the city's ancient Cardo, the main north-south street. Jerusalem and its colonnaded Cardo are prominently pictured in the famous sixth-century C.E. mosaic map preserved in a church in Madaba, Jordan. The press reported the Cardo's discovery by Professor Avigad. We subsequently learned that the part of the Cardo that Avigad had excavated was, in his view, Byzantine, rather than Roman as was at first supposed. In our report on recent discoveries in Jerusalem, we noted that in Avigad's opinion this portion of the Cardo was Byzantine, not Roman. I reported at length on a debate about the date of the Cardo that, as I understood, had followed a lecture Avigad had given at a conference. At the lecture, Avigad had shown magnificent pictures of the recently discovered street. Naturally, we wanted some of the pictures of Avigad's Cardo for our story. And Avigad, not unexpectedly, refused. So we published the story with a big black square where Avigad's Cardo picture would have gone had he made it available to us. In the caption to the black square, we said:

This space is reserved for pictures of the Cardo ... after their release by Professor Avigad. This will occur after he has first published them in his own scientific report ... Although Professor Avigad announces these finds in the press, he refuses to release pictures. Professor Avigad is by no means alone in this practice. Probably the majority of archaeologists do likewise, but Professor Avigad's restrictive release of photographs is more visible—and more objectionable—because of the spectacular nature of the finds ... We urge the abandonment of this restrictive release of photographs, particularly with respect to finds that legitimately arouse such widespread public interest.

Avigad was deeply hurt and angered. He was a soft-spoken man not given to yelling, but he felt the attack personally and deeply. "Dear Editor," he wrote in a reply which I of course published, "I know that you are happy with this kind of reporting archaeological news, you think it is

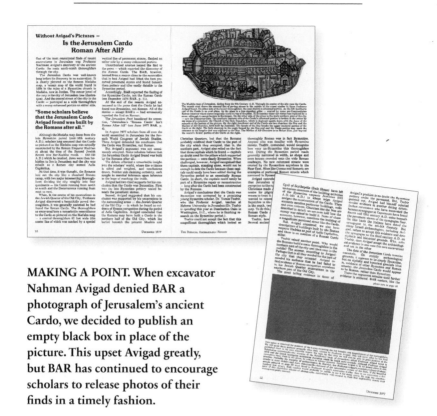

MAKING A POINT. When excavator Nahman Avigad denied BAR a photograph of Jerusalem's ancient Cardo, we decided to publish an empty black box in place of the picture. This upset Avigad greatly, but BAR has continued to encourage scholars to release photos of their finds in a timely fashion.

good for BAR. But, please, let me alone! Your journal is not to my taste." He was one of Israel's most highly respected archaeologists, an elder statesman and a meticulous excavator. For some time after this, he would have nothing to do with me. We would often hold parties for archaeologists and biblical scholars whenever I came to Jerusalem, and of course Avigad was always invited. On one occasion he came. I still remember the smile that crossed his lips when he saw me. I put my arm around his shoulder for the photographer. Jonas Greenfield, another senior scholar, said how happy he was to see this. After that, Avigad and I became friends (although I could never bring myself to call him "Nahman").

We never mentioned the photo episode, however. When Avigad wrote a popular (as opposed to scholarly) book about his excavations in the Old City, he asked me if I would be his agent for the book's publication. Of course I was honored to do so. Only then did I feel forgiven. I arranged for the book to be published by Thomas Nelson Publishers under the title *Discovering Jerusalem*. Harvard's Frank Cross called the book "a masterpiece." William Dever, whom I have already mentioned, said it was "the most important and exciting book on the archaeology of ancient Jerusalem." Seymour Gitin, director of the Albright Institute, judged it "a history that makes history ... describing the strategy of excavation and the exciting moments of discovery."

I said that Avigad forgave me, but I don't think he ever agreed with my view regarding the Cardo pictures. Withholding pictures of finds is not a habit that has died easily in the profession. Frankly, it is hard to explain. It is, so far as I can tell, a desire on the archaeologists' part to have finds first exposed in a scholarly way and in a context that they control.

More than a decade later, another senior Israeli archaeologist, Avraham Biran of Hebrew Union College in Jerusalem, made another spectacular discovery, at the site of Dan in northern Israel, where 3,000 years ago Jeroboam had set up a golden bull after the country split apart following King Solomon's death (1 Kings 12:28–29). In the 1990s controversy was already rife between the so-called "biblical minimalists," who doubted the very existence of King David and King Solomon, and those who held to the more traditional view. One thing in the minimalists' favor (William Dever calls them "biblical nihilists") was that the name "David" had never been found in any ancient inscription outside the Bible. Based on the archaeological record alone, there was no David.

Then in 1993 Gila Cook, the staff surveyor of Biran's excavation at Tel Dan, noticed some writing on a stone in an ancient wall as the afternoon sunlight glanced off it. When the stone was removed from the wall, it was found to contain an Aramaic inscription dating to the ninth century B.C.E., only a little more than a century after David was supposed to have lived. The stone had been reused as part of the wall. The inscription was part of a black basalt stela that had been put up by an Aramean king (probably Hazael, king of Damascus) proclaiming his victory over the Israelites. The broken-off inscription mentions a "king of Israel" whose name has not survived and, most startlingly, the "House of David" (*Bet David* or "Dynasty of David.") The book of 2 Kings is replete with references to Hazael and of his wars with Israel (see especially 2 Kings 10:32–33).

Based on this inscription, David had not only lived, he had established a dynasty that had lasted for at least 150 years. And the kingdom ruled by David's dynasty was important enough for Hazael to proclaim a military victory over it in an impressively inscribed stela.

I heard about the discovery at Tel Dan in a telephone call from a friend in Israel. I immediately called Biran in Jerusalem. He agreed to allow me to alert the *New York Times* to the discovery, and they ran the story on the front page. But Biran would not give the *Times* a picture of the inscription! So they asked someone to draw the letters of "House of David" supposedly in the form of these letters of the period. It looked obviously artificial and ugly, but Biran was thereby able to save the first publication of a photograph of the inscription for his own report. This, incidentally, was most unlike Biran—a jolly, opened-handed man who was warm and welcoming. If even Avraham Biran would withhold a picture from the *New York Times*, *al achat kama v'kama* (how much moreso) would other scholars do likewise.

In 2008 we published an article about the Hebrew term *opalim*, which is uniformly translated "hemorrhoids" in English Bibles. The word occurs in the story of the Israelite's battle with the Philistines at Ebenezer in which the Philistines captured the Ark of the Covenant (1 Samuel 5–6). This did the Philistines no good, however. The Lord afflicted the Philistines with *opalim*, among other things. Wisely, the Philistines decided to send the Ark back to the Israelites with an offering that included five golden *opalim*. It's hard to imagine what a golden hemorrhoid looked like. Moreover, when this passage is read in the synagogue, *opalim* is not pronounced as written, as if it were a vulgarity. Another word entirely is substituted.

Aren Maeir of Bar-Ilan University has been digging at the Philistine city of Gath, where in 2004 he came upon a couple of objects that got him to wondering whether *opalim* should really be translated as "hemorrhoids"—what Maeir found were two clay phalluses. Maeir concluded that *opalim* really had something to do with penises. Perhaps the capture of the Israelite Ark afflicted the Philistines with E.D. (This would not be the first time the Bible records this happening. When Pharaoh took Abraham's beautiful wife Sarah into his harem, thinking she was

Abraham's sister, the Lord afflicted Pharaoh with something that saved her from being violated—Genesis 12:17.)

Maeir wrote an article for BAR recounting his find and his theory regarding *opalim*. As we were preparing the article for publication in 2007, he discovered more phalluses on his dig that year, an account of which he added to his article. But when I asked him for a picture of these new finds, he initially refused. "This is not the way we operate," I wrote him. After a little more persuasion, he relented. We printed the pictures of the just-found phalluses in the article. In the caption we noted that "these two pictures of very recent finds are receiving their first publication here. BAR is grateful to Professor Maeir for making them available to our readers."

So the academic tradition of refusing to release pictures until the scholarly publication appears is not dead, just dying.

CHAPTER VIII

Maturing BAR

IN OUR SECOND YEAR, WE ADDED A few pages of color.

In our fourth year, we changed format—from a 7-by-10-inch magazine with cream paper and brown ink to a standard 8 ½-by-11-inch "book" (as they call magazines in the trade) with white paper and black ink. We also introduced our new color cover with a few more color pages sprinkled throughout the magazine.

The year after that we changed from a quarterly to a bimonthly. We still operated out of the basements of the two Sues with minimal staff and managed the organization at lunches when the two Sues would come downtown.

In 1982—Volume 8—we added color throughout the book. In 1983 we got a real office—on Connecticut Avenue—to house our now-growing staff. It was across from the entrance to the zoo, and we joked that people came to the BAR office looking for the animals in there.

One thing that didn't change, however, was the animosity of the prestigious professional organization of Near Eastern archaeologists, the American Schools of Oriental Research, known as ASOR. Note that it is plural—*schools*, not school. ASOR has schools in Jerusalem, Amman and Cyprus and committees for Baghdad and Damascus. The mother organization is in America. The schools are independent, however. They raise their own money and determine their own program. Years ago, the mother organization would help the daughter schools with financing and assistance. Today it is the other way around; the schools provide assistance to the mother organization. The chief activities of the mother organization are the holding of a scholarly conference each November with several hundred lectures and the publication of several scholarly journals and books.

I have already mentioned that ASOR leaders had advised Eric Meyers not to sign on as my American editor if he had any aspirations to ascend the leadership ranks of the organization. A variety of considerations account for this persistent ASOR attitude toward BAR. First was our name—*Biblical Archaeology Review.* In the view of some ASOR leaders, it was too close to their magazine, *Biblical Archaeologist.* Even before our first issue, ASOR considered suing me to prevent what they regarded as an illegally infringing name. In the end, however, they dropped the idea. But the thought persisted: I was encroaching on *their* territory.

ASOR's *Biblical Archaeologist* had started out as a popular magazine. It was intended to be a venue for outreach to a broader public. Over the years, however, it had become more and more rarefied, and most of its articles had little appeal for a popular, nonscholarly audience.

While the people in ASOR whose major interest was the Bible were uncomfortable with us because of this overlapping interest, the scholars whose interest lay in areas and time-periods that had little relevance for the Bible scoffed at us for the opposite reason—*because* of our biblical interest. Secular scholars sometimes look on colleagues who work with the Bible as having a slight odor. Such biblical scholars are suspected of being "too evangelical," not scholarly or worse. As a leading biblical minimalist, Niels Peter Lemche, has remarked, "to ordinary archaeologists biblical archaeologists are lowlife."

On the other hand, there is a very legitimate reason for secular scholars not wishing to be oriented toward the Bible: Their purview is broader. They don't want to be confined by always having to look at things from a biblical viewpoint. In truth, there is no reason why someone working in Jordan or Cyprus should have a special interest in the Bible. Before the peace treaty between Israel and Jordan in 1994, Jordanian archaeological publications hesitated to cite biblical materials or Israeli publications. So in a sense ASOR is riven between those who are pursuing archaeology because of their interest in the Bible and those whose archaeological interest lies elsewhere in the Middle East.

Just how sensitive the situation was is reflected in an incident involving one Tom Crotser of Winfield, Kansas, who served as director of the so-called Institute for Restoring History International. Without an excavation permit from Jordanian authorities, Crotser went looking for the Ark of the Covenant on Mt. Pisgah, from which Moses had been allowed to see (but not enter) the Promised Land (Deuteronomy 3:27) and where he had died (Deuteronomy 34:1–5). The mountain lies in Jordan opposite Mt. Nebo. And, lo and behold, Crotser found the Ark of the Covenant! Or at least so he claimed. The UPI picked up the story and the incident received wide publicity. A major American excavation of impeccable credentials was set to begin not far from Pisgah the next summer, but its excavation permit was abruptly canceled following publication of the UPI story. No reason was given for the cancellation. And the permit was canceled not by the antiquities authority, but at the highest level of the Jordanian government—by the prime minister's office.[8]

If that story reflects the Jordanian government's sensitivity about the alleged biblical connections to Jordan, the following reflects the sensitivity of Americans working in Jordan. When BAR published the story about Tom Crotser's ridiculous claim to have found the Ark of the Covenant, we were in the midst of a biblical archaeology essay contest. More than 80 entrants had been submitted. The winner was to receive a $1,500 travel fellowship to Jerusalem. Three prominent American scholars had been chosen to serve as judges. One of them was R. Thomas Schaub, professor of Philosophy and Religious Studies at Indiana University of Pennsylvania in Indiana, Pennsylvania. Schaub excavated in Jordan. When Schaub read BAR's story about Tom Crotser's foolish adventure, he resigned as a judge in the essay contest. That article, he wrote, "certainly favors the cause of those who argue for the elimination of the term Biblical Archaeology ... It is not surprising that many serious students of the Bible or of archaeology cringe when they hear or read the term Biblical Archaeology." While Schaub did not question my assertion that the Jordanian authorities had revoked the American excavation permit because of the Crotser incident, he described as "nonsense" that Jordanian authorities would "prevent or obscure serious archaeological results that may legitimately shed light on ancient history" (not exactly what I had said). I doubt that today Tom would resign over such an article. Times have changed—somewhat—especially since the

Jordan-Israel Peace Treaty of 1994. And Tom Schaub and I have had many pleasant conversations since then. I recently attended a Jordanian embassy reception to celebrate the 62nd anniversary of Jordan's independence (in 1946) and one of the placards at the reception to foster tourism featured what was prominently labeled "Biblical Jordan." It seems that much of the Jordanian sensitivity about "biblical" archaeology has evaporated.

This divide within ASOR between those who were especially inter-ested in the Bible and its background, on the one hand, and those whose focus lay elsewhere in Near Eastern archaeology became an issue in the early 1980s when the leadership proposed changing the name of its "popular" magazine from *Biblical Archaeologist* to *The ASOR Archaeologist*. "Biblical" would no longer be in the name. A unanimous ad hoc com-mittee recommended the change. The recommendation then went to the Executive Committee of the Board of Trustees. Only one member voted against the change. The recommendation then went to the full Board of Trustees. I attended the trustees meeting where the recommen-dation came up. It was about to pass until Harvard's Frank Cross, one of the world's most prominent biblical scholars and a former president of ASOR, spoke up against it: It was as if they were kicking the Bible out of the organization. The mood completely changed and the recom-mendation failed. But James Sauer, the president of the organization and former director of the ASOR school in Amman (ACOR—American Center of Oriental Research), maintained his position to the end and voted for the new name.

At one point, Leon Levy, a New York billionaire who was a major financial supporter of ASOR, invited me and Jim Sauer as well as a few ASOR leaders with whom I was friendly to a dinner. Sauer led ASOR's anti-BAR forces; he could hardly bring himself to speak to me. We met in Leon's extraordinary apartment on Sutton Place in Manhattan, which is filled with museum-quality antiquities. The dinner was an effort to make peace, a *sulha* in Arabic, between me and Jim Sauer. The evening was polite and pleasant and the talk was fascinating. But Jim held his ground. There was no room for BAR in his thinking. He did not mince words. For me, the evening demonstrated for all to see Jim's intransigence. I was not angry, however. Indeed, I very rarely get angry at adversaries, and I was never angry with Jim Sauer.

Jim taught at the University of Pennsylvania in Philadelphia and to the surprise of almost everyone, he was denied tenure. It was said this was because he had failed to publish, and he had failed to publish because he had devoted himself so wholly to his ASOR presidency. He subsequently developed a fatal nerve disorder (Huntington's disease) and died at age 55 in 1999. But before he became incapacitated he softened toward me and toward BAR. He even agreed to write an article for the magazine. In the November/December 1996 issue he was the author of an article entitled, "The River Runs Dry: Creation Story Preserves Historical Memory" which argued that even the Bible's earliest stories may contain a kernel of history.

Several years later the matter of the name of the ASOR magazine came up again. This time the suggested new name was *Near Eastern Archaeology*. It was strongly supported by the then-editor of the magazine, David Hopkins. He decided to take a poll of the members on the question. Over 80 percent voted *against* the name change. So the name was changed to *Near Eastern Archaeology*, a name that it still bears! This surely says something about the way things can work in a professional scholarly organization. And it clearly reveals the yawning gap between the leadership of ASOR and the bulk of its membership.

By the time BAR arrived on the scene, the *Biblical Archaeologist* was already more a scholarly magazine than a popular magazine. It never had more than 7,500 subscribers, and the number has steadily gone down. By our third year, BAR's circulation had surpassed *BA*'s, as it was known. And this too would hardly endear us to ASOR. Today the circulation of *Near Eastern Archaeology* is barely more than 2,000 and, as I write, it is behind about a year in publication. As a result, the June 2007 issue did not come out until May 2008. Some of its obituaries therefore list a date of death after the date of the issue of the magazine.

Other reasons might also explain ASOR's attitude toward BAR. For example, I do not have a Ph.D. I don't qualify as a member of the fraternity. In short, I am not really an archaeologist or even a scholar. I am the essential outsider.

To make matters worse, my job as a responsible archaeological journalist is to sit in judgment on the decisions and activities of my betters. As early as the September/October 1983 issue, I wrote an article entitled "Whither ASOR?" in which I described its "identity crisis." "ASOR will be a house divided if it disparages or excludes those whose chief interest is the Bible," I wrote. Incidentally, this article gave me an opportunity to describe the history of American archaeology in Israel and ASOR's enormous contributions to that history. Always lying behind our coverage of controversy is a desire to teach.

For years, I would write a review of ASOR's annual meeting. Often, I would have something critical to say, along with praise. Scholarly meetings are not accustomed to this kind of review, especially by someone who is not an academic.

I have many friends who are active in ASOR, and most ASOR scholars are pleased to write for BAR. But there is still a residue of bad feeling among some of those who are especially active in the Amman and Cyprus schools. In 2008 this surfaced in a strange way. We have given what we call dig scholarships to help students go to Israel and elsewhere in the Near East to participate in excavations during the summer. Each of our scholarships is for $1,000. In 2007 ASOR offered similar scholarships, but for $1,500 each. Some few applicants, we later learned, had double-dipped: They got scholarships from both of us. I talked to ASOR's very friendly executive secretary, Andy Vaughn, about this. I suggested comparing applicant lists to prevent double-dipping. He said he would check and get back to me; there were some in ASOR who may not want to cooperate with our organization even in this minor way, he said, which reflects the depth of the animosity. In the end, they hesitated to give us their list (they had not yet selected their winners), so we sent them our list of winners; they reported that there were no "doubles," and we went ahead and awarded the scholarships on our list.

* * * *

It is amazing—at least to me—how many of our later campaigns had their beginnings in these early years. In the July/August issue of 1983, I wrote an article entitled "The Sad Case of Tel Gezer." It had a double purpose. One was to describe this enormously important and dramatic archaeological, as well as biblical, site, and, second, to ensure that the site would be preserved, both for scholars and the public.

Gezer was also part of my personal history. I should have mentioned it in my account of our year in Israel. But I guess it was too embarrassing. Besides, the story might ruin an otherwise euphoric year in the Holy Land. We had arrived in Israel in September 1972, and by the following summer I had published *The City of David* and knew many archaeologists, some of them very well. I decided to enlist as a volunteer on an archaeological excavation—to get some practical experience with archaeology. There was little doubt what dig it would be. William Dever had been the guiding light of the Gezer expedition. It was the leading American excavation, and was also highly regarded for its educational field school. I volunteered for two weeks. Even though I knew Dever would not be there that season, I secretly anticipated that other excavation leaders would guide my understanding of some of the larger questions and decisions about the dig.

The experience turned out to be quite different. I was assigned to an excavation square supervised by a young college student. I was too embarrassed to complain, but I was "worked" like a common laborer, digging all day and exposing a wall but little else. Truth to tell, I was 43 years old and the other volunteers were kids. At the end of the day, I could do little more than flop on my cot in the tent. Besides, I had no contact with anyone higher in command. I was learning nothing, and there were no activities that week that explained anything about the site in general.

By the time Friday came, I was wondering whether I should come back for the second week. My wife Judith had arranged for our family to spend the weekend with Terry and Ann Smith and their little girl, also an Elizabeth, with whom our girls had played in the States. Terry was scheduled to pick me up Friday afternoon and drive me to Kayit v'Shayit, a modest seaside resort with a group of huts on the beach, where the rest of our families would be waiting. Terry was the *New York Times* correspondent for Israel, so when he arrived at the site, he created quite a flutter. That I drove away with him was my recognition of the week. Not long after driving away, however, I asked him to stop by the side of the road. I got out and promptly threw up. That was it. I decided I would not return for another week of this. Instead I would spend the time doing research for my book on ancient synagogues, a project which I had already begun.

That week at Gezer has been my total archaeological experience—hardly a harbinger of a career in archaeology. Many years later at a reception for Gezer alumni, I was the butt of some good-natured kidding. I am apparently the only person who flunked out of the Gezer field school.

But despite it all, I have a special devotion to the site, which was expressed in my 1983 BAR article. The article did more than simply describe the site; it called for its preservation. Gezer could well be a major tourist attraction. As far as archaeological sites go, it has everything, beginning with its convenient location halfway between Jerusalem and Tel Aviv, not far off the main highway. It is also important in the Bible. When the Egyptian pharaoh gave his daughter in marriage to King Solomon, Gezer was part of the dowry (1 Kings 9:15–17). Even before that, however, Pharaoh Merneptah boasts of conquering Gezer, supposedly taking it from the Canaanites, in the late 13th century B.C.E. Gezer dominates the famous Via Maris, the main coastal highway running between Egypt and Syria. And the mound itself offers a magnificent view in every direction.

Archaeologically, it is one of the richest sites in Israel. Its Canaanite high place, dating from about 1600 B.C.E., boasts a unique line of ten huge monoliths that stand as markers of an uncertain ceremony, perhaps to commemorate a treaty among different tribes. The Gezer stones are reminiscent of the 12 standing stones (*matzebot*; singular *matzebah*) that Moses set up at the foot of Mt. Sinai to mark the covenant between God and the tribes of Israel. The Israelites sacrificed bulls to the Lord and dashed part of the blood against the stones; another part they placed in basins (Exodus 24:4–7). There is even a large basin at the base of one of the standing stones at Gezer.

Elsewhere on the site is the largest tower foundation in all of Palestine, a tower that was once part of the city's Middle Bronze Age fortifications (c. 1650 B.C.E.). A beautiful six-chambered gate, first noticed by Yigael Yadin, was long thought to have been built by King Solomon.

SIGNS OF AN ANCIENT COVENANT. Erected by the biblical
Canaanites more than 3,500 years ago, these massive standing stones still
dominate the mound of ancient Gezer. BAR has repeatedly promoted the
restoration of this important archaeological site, but thus far no one has
come forward to fund and lead the project.

Today, that claim is hotly disputed by some archaeologists, but the excavators of Gezer (and others) maintain that the gate's Solomonic date and attribution are sound.

By 1983 Gezer had gone to seed, however, and it was difficult even to get to the site. The ancient walls were disintegrating. Graffiti were painted on the monoliths of the Canaanite high place. Overgrowth made it difficult to see what the archaeologists had left. No fence protected it from stone looters. To illustrate the degree of neglect, I printed some "before" and "after" pictures of the site in my article.

To encourage action, I wrote that BAR had deposited $5,000 in a special Gezer Preservation Fund and challenged others to step up to the plate. "The money would remain in the account for three years," I wrote, and would be available to the group or institution that would undertake the restoration of Gezer. I mentioned several possibilities—from the Israel Department of Antiquities and Museums and its National Parks Authority to Hebrew Union College, the Harvard Semitic Museum, the National Endowment for the Arts and Humanities and the United States Government. "Those who love the Bible ... have a special interest in and responsibility for Tell Gezer," I said.

"The Gezer project," I continued, "was initiated by two archaeological giants—George Ernest Wright of Harvard University and Nelson Glueck of Hebrew Union College. Both men, unfortunately, are now dead. But they left thousands of friends, students and devotees who cherish their memory. They would not have left this work unfinished. In honor of their memory, we cannot either."

Alas, there were no takers, not a single expression of interest. The money languished in its special account until we transferred it to our regular account three years later.

I failed but I was persistent. A decade later I returned to the subject. Writing in the form of a public memo to the director of Israel's National Parks Authority, "You are really missing a good bet!" I began. "Gezer has enough magnificent remains to attract even the most jaded tourist," I continued, but it "is rarely visited even by aficionados because it is so difficult to get to—unmarked and neglected ... Gezer must be restored."[9]

It was like dropping a pebble into a lake that made no ripples. In the early years of the new century, I tried a different attack. One feature at Gezer that I have not talked about is its magnificent water system. It has not been explored, however, for a century—since the excavations led by the Irish archaeologist R.A.S. Macalister. The date of this magnificent water system is still uncertain. What we know is that the ancients, in order to reach the water table inside the city walls, dug a stepped shaft down nearly 25 feet that led to a long tunnel that sloped downward into the heart of the hill and ended in a cave where the water could be drawn. All this has now been filled with rubble. It has been impossible to explore this water system for a hundred years.

I thought of arousing some interest in the water system—and therefore the site. When Ronny Reich, a friend and archaeologist, said he thought he knew where the source of the water was outside the city walls, we decided to test his speculation. I raised money to do a GPR (Ground Penetrating Radar) study to see if there was an underground anomaly at the point where Ronny thought the tunnel led. The result was positive. A bright red spot appeared on the GPR chart just where Ronny said the outlet to the tunnel should be. So we did a trial excavation. Unfortunately, there was nothing there.

In 2007, a new excavation of the site was undertaken by Steven Ortiz, then associate professor of archaeology at the New Orleans Baptist Seminary. I have been trying to convince Steve to open the water tunnel. But clearing the tunnel of its accumulated debris is a major project. Steve is receptive, however, and I predict that we will eventually do it. This, plus Steve's excavation, may well lead to the preservation and consolidation of the archaeological remains of Tell Gezer. I have not given up.

The campaign to restore Gezer didn't raise any hackles. No individual or body was being accused of not doing its job. If I wanted to encourage the restoration of sites, fine. That was the attitude of the profession. Actually, in our own small way, we did manage to encourage and foster site preservation. I even created the BAR position of "Preservation Liaison," a position that appeared on BAR's masthead until 2008. We contributed to the impressive restoration of David Ussishkin's important excavation of biblical Lachish, about 25 miles southwest of Jerusalem. We also contributed to the restoration of the so-called "Winter Palaces" at Herodian Jericho, excavated by Hebrew University's Ehud Netzer. Painstaking effort was required to preserve the frescoes that covered the decorative-looking *opus reticulatum* walls of the Roman-period palaces.

We also undertook a project on our own: the restoration and consolidation of a site of enormous biblical importance that had been completely ignored. It may have been ignored because the name of the archaeological site is little known and hard to remember. Who or what was Izbet Sartah? Actually, Izbet Sartah is very probably the site of biblical Ebenezer, where the Israelites mustered before their disastrous battle with the Philistines in which the Ark was captured.

The site is located in the low hill country, an area that was inhabited by the early Israelites. Their enemies, the Philistines, lived on the adjacent coastal plain. I'm no military expert, but I think it's clear why the Israelites got pasted. They went down into the Philistine plain where they were no match for the Philistine chariots with their metal wheels. As the Bible itself reports: "There was no smith to be found in all the land of Israel, for the Philistines had said to themselves, 'The Hebrews might make swords or spears.' So all Israel would go down to the Philistines to repair any of their plowshares, mattocks, axes or sickles" (1 Samuel 13:19–20). Joshua too referred to the fact that the Israelites could not drive out the dwellers in the plains (this time the Canaanites) "because of their iron chariots" (Joshua 17:18; see also Joshua 17:16). In the plain, the Israelites were fighting *mano-a-mano*, while the Philistines were fighting from their chariots. No wonder it was disastrous. The Israelites should have waited for the Philistines to come up to the hill country where the Philistine chariots would have been relatively useless.

I have to add that the Ark the Philistines captured did them no good. As I reported in the last chapter, according to the prominent Israeli archaeologist Aren Maeir, the captured Israelite paladin gave the Philistines E.D., which is part of the reason they decided to return the Ark to the Israelites, together with five golden phalluses similar to the ones made of clay Maeir found in his excavation of Philistine Gath.[10] In any event, the Israelite defeat at Ebenezer and the encroaching Philistine threat demonstrated the need for a government that was stronger than early Israel's group of tribes. Thus was born the Israelite monarchy.

The views from Ebenezer are spectacular. The ancient battle comes alive as you look down on the lush green plain toward Aphek where the Philistines mustered. Ebenezer was excavated many years ago by Moshe Kochavi of Tel Aviv University and his student Israel Finkelstein. They discovered the walls of a typical, though beautifully preserved, Israelite house, known as a four-room house. A four-room house consists of three long rooms (the middle one usually open to the sky) and an adjoining broad room along the back wall of the house. Dozens of four-room houses have been excavated, but the one at Ebenezer is perhaps the best preserved of them all. In addition to other less-well preserved buildings, Ebenezer has

LOST BUT NOT FORGOTTEN. In 1979, BAR restored the little known archaeological site of Izbet Sartah, probably biblical Ebenezer, where the Israelites mustered for battle with the Philistines. It includes this well-preserved example of an early Israelite "four-room house" (bottom). But local authorities have not followed up on plans to turn the site into a park. Today the house is barely visible, overgrown and covered with weeds (top).

more than 20 silos for storage and a cistern for water collection. It is a good place to see how early Israelites lived.

The excavators at the site also discovered an inscription that may be the earliest Hebrew writing ever found. The inscription appears on a small 6-inch-wide pottery sherd. The letters are clearly ancient Semitic. Hebrew is only one of several Semitic languages, however, a language family that also includes Canaanite. The basis for identifying the letters as Hebrew is the fact that the site where it was found was inhabited by Israelites. The letters make no sense as words, however. The sherd was apparently a scribe's tablet used for practicing the Semitic alphabet. But this nevertheless says something important about a society that had people learning how to write and become scribes 3,000 years ago. Replicas of the inscribed pottery fragment could easily be made available to tourists visiting the reconstructed site.

Ebenezer has all the ingredients that call for site restoration and preservation. By 1978, when we first published our articles about Ebenezer and its inscribed pottery sherd, I had appointed Georg Majewski as our Preservation Liaison. Georg was a well-informed, can-do retired engineer who was active in amateur archaeological activities in Israel. (Alas, he has recently passed away at age 88.) In 1979, we announced that BAR would preserve and restore Ebenezer and that the work would be coordinated by BAR's Preservation Liaison and directed by Professor Kochavi. We were as good as our word. We even put up attractive signs explaining the site and its significance. The work was paid for by contributions from BAR readers. One of these readers visited the site after the work had been completed and wrote that it was "an inspired choice." Professor Kochavi wrote me a letter of appreciation in which he described a meeting of the various public and private groups that had a stake in the development of the site. The meeting included representatives from Tel Aviv University, the Department of Antiquities, the National Parks Authority, the municipality of Rosh Ha'Ayin where the site is located, and a charity group known as The National Fund for Israel. All agreed, in Professor Kochavi's words, "that every effort should be made to proclaim the site as a national park." These institutions also agreed "to take care of the site and protect it from man and nature."

For several years this was done. But the site was never declared a national park. And then "man and nature" took over. The signs were used for target practice. They were full of bullet holes when I visited the site years later. When they no longer served that purpose, they were simply knocked down. In the meantime, the site had become completely over-grown. It was difficult to identify any of the archaeological features. And the site was now adjacent to a garbage dump.

I haven't given up on Ebenezer, however. As I write, I have been in touch with the new mayor of Rosh Ha'Ayin ... We're making progress.

Other projects and campaigns also engaged us as BAR matured. Unlike our efforts at site preservation, which were applauded on all sides, some other efforts created discomfort, to say the least. One was what I called "archaeology's dirty secret." Archaeologists love to dig. But they don't always like to write reports. A failure to write a report on an excavation is tantamount to looting. An archaeological excavation is, by any other name, destruction. This destruction is justified only because what is learned during this destruction is made available to others, both scholars and the public. There is no other justification for this destruction. A particular area of a site, once dug, cannot be re-dug. In archaeology; testing a hypothesis cannot involve repeated experiments.

In many cases, however, no final excavation report is ever written. There are many reasons for this. The major one is that it's just very, very hard to write one. And, for this too, there are many reasons. Writing a major excavation report is not something you can do in a week or a month. It takes years of concentration and devotion and analysis, often to the exclusion of things that would be much more fun. And excavation direc-tors are, alas, quite human. In addition, there are people, including good archaeologists, who just can't write very well.

There are also other psychological impediments, including the fear of criticism or even failure. What if the report is harshly judged by one's colleagues?

Then there are the technical issues. The scientific tests and analyses that can be performed on the mountains of materials that are retrieved from a modern excavation are almost endless. Where to stop? What is enough? And should the scholar make some more general judgments—insights on a larger social or historical canvass—to make the report more significant? Or would such large conclusions be too "iffy"?

Finally, excavators often fail to provide adequate funds in their budgets for post-excavation expenses related to research and publication. In short, the cry goes up as justification, "I have no money."

My initial thought was to hold a conference that would address all the issues involved in the problem. In the mid-1980s, I started to raise money to support an international conference to address archaeology's "dirty secret." I often came close, but ultimately failed. In the 1990s, I decided to try some venues where the expenses of such a conference would be minimal. A major biblical archaeology conference was being held at Lehigh University in Lehigh, Pennsylvania, in the spring of 1994. A bevy of leading archaeologists would be assembling, and they were traveling there at someone else's expense! I decided to hold an additional private session at the Lehigh conference in which I invited scholars who were already presenting to give papers on the field's publication problem. This turned out to be quite feasible and produced a series of insightful papers in the subject. We published them as a small volume under the title *Archaeology's Publication Problem*.

Before BAR raised the issue, it was generally recognized as a serious problem *sotto voce*, but rarely publicly discussed even in scholarly venues. All of the participants in our Lehigh symposium recognized the seriousness of the publication problem. Hebrew University's Amihai Mazar called it "a professional disease." His colleague Ephraim Stern acknowledged that the problem had been "almost completely ignored by the profession." However, as Phil King said in his opening address, "We don't want to embarrass anyone," so it was agreed that no specific names would be mentioned. One archaeologist was quoted as saying, "We all carry around with us, like millstones around our necks, this terrible burden of unfinished or unwritten excavation reports."

Moreover, the problem was getting worse. In the period from the end of the Second World War to 1959, only (only!) half of the excavations in Israel failed to produce a report. By the 1970s, it was 75 percent. By the 1980s, it was 87 percent. Even in the best years, the results were terrible!

I followed up the Lehigh conference with a session at the 1996 annual meeting of the Society of Biblical Literature. These papers were subsequently published as Volume 2 of *Archaeology's Publication Problem*.

One proposal that I put on the table to alleviate the problem somewhat was the creation of a new profession—an archaeological editor/ writer who would be trained to assist dig directors in writing their final reports. I tried to interest several people in Israel in creating such a course. I even had money to pay them. But, in the end, they weren't interested. Someday, I think this suggestion will be picked up again. When, however, remains a question.

Of course, as I have stated, from the outset I wanted to hold a major conference to address all aspects of the publication problem. Out of this failed effort grew something even better. One of the people I spoke to in the early 1990s was the New York philanthropist Leon Levy. At one point I thought I had a letter from him agreeing to subsidize a "publications conference" with a grant of $250,000 (including the publication of papers). Leon suggested we include two scholars in the planning: Harvard's Lawrence Stager, who headed the Leon Levy Expedition to Ashkelon, the most important American excavation in Israel; and Philip King, whom we have already met in these pages and who originally involved Leon in the Ashkelon dig. I was delighted to have the involvement of these two friends who were also major figures in the archaeological world.

Leon graciously invited the three of us to lunch in his New York office (with food prepared by his private chef) for a planning session. The morning of the lunch, I flew to New York and arrived on time, only to learn that a sudden snowstorm in Boston resulted in the cancellation of all flights out of Logan Airport. So Leon and I had a fine lunch in his office accompanied by good conversation, but carefully avoiding discussion of the publication conference the four of us had been scheduled to discuss.

My expectation that we would reschedule the meeting, however, never materialized. Instead, on his own initiative, Leon decided on something far grander. As I had said in my talk at the Lehigh conference: "Money matters ... Money won't solve the problem by itself ... but money would help." Leon decided to provide it. With his wife Shelby White, he created

The Shelby White–Leon Levy Program for Archaeological Publications, which provides grants for the writing and publication of old excavations that have gone unpublished. From its inception in 1997, the program has awarded nearly $10 million in grants to more than 150 scholars. Phil King directs the program out of an office at the Harvard Semitic Museum.

But problems still remain. I still think my suggestion regarding the creation of the profession of an archaeological editor/writer is a good one. The archaeological editor would be an expert in organizing the research needed for an excavation report and knowing how to get it written. Obviously, when it comes to a specialized skill like writing an excavation report, a professional who has spent many years practicing the skill is going to be better at it than someone who is attempting to write a report for the first time.

The archaeological editor would also help the dig director decide what *should* be in the report and how it should be published. These are major, largely unaddressed issues that archaeologists often overlook. Is print publication of the entire excavation report outmoded? What should an excavation report include? An archaeological editor would help the professional address these concerns.

Leon Levy passed away in 2003. He had been fast friends with Phil King for decades. They indeed made an odd couple—a Catholic priest from Boston and a Jewish professional investor and philanthropist from New York. But they got along famously. Leon called Phil his "rabbi." Phil was also a dear friend of Shelby's, and that relationship survived Leon's death. Shelby and Phil work closely together on the administration of the grants program and on the support of the Leon Levy Foundation for Larry Stager's dig at Ashkelon.

Leon also gave me a small grant to support the publication of the Biblical Archaeology Society's two volumes on *Archaeology's Publication Problem*, and I remained friendly with Leon and Shelby. Contrary to common belief, however, Leon never made a major contribution to the Biblical Archaeology Society.

As the years went by after Leon's death, Phil's health declined, so I decided to make a suggestion. I called Shelby and told her, "Don't wait until Phil dies to do something for him." We discussed several options. The one she chose was a chair in Phil's name at Harvard. On November 9, 2006, the Philip J. King Professorship was announced at a gala dinner at Harvard. Shelby looked smashing in her designer clothes. And for the first time ever, I saw Phil wearing a priest's collar. Shelby made a little speech in which she graciously told the select audience that I had suggested the chair in Phil's honor. I was grateful.

* * * *

In the meantime, the early years at BAR had been spent not only putting out a first-class magazine, but also implementing ideas for increasing BAR's reach and making it more attractive. One of these was the "Backwards Subscription," which is still good for a laugh at our marketing meetings. Since our circulation was rapidly increasing, especially in those early years, we decided to offer our newer subscribers packages of back issues. These sold unusually well. So we announced something unique in magazine history as far as I know: The Backwards Subscription. Instead of a packet of back issues bundled to create a themed package, why not sell people all of the back issues, the issues they missed before they became subscribers? BAR comes out every other month. Why not provide them with another issue—one that they missed—on the off month? Instead of starting with the first issue, we would start with the latest one that they had missed—the issue just before they had started their subscription—then work backwards from there. It was a brilliant idea that proved quite popular! But it was a fulfillment nightmare! People who started subscribing at different times were supposed to get a different back issue every two months. Just keeping track of who got what was almost impossible. But this was only the first major problem. Finding the issue each "Backwards Subscriber" was supposed to get and then mailing it out was even more challenging, not to mention time consuming. We soon discontinued the offer.

We also tried a newsletter, in addition to the magazine, but that too soon petered out.

In the magazine, we added a section called "BAR Jr." that was intended for children. Unfortunately, we were never able to develop material attractive enough for kids, so we soon dropped that idea.

After two years of publication, we developed something that proved to be more successful—a travel/study program. We started with archaeological tours (led by Lorna Zimmerman, who thereby got into the tour business and subsequently started her own travel agency, which continues to this day and makes the travel arrangements for many of our tours). We soon added three-day and six-day BAR seminars, taught by prominent scholars at various places in intimate settings. In addition to those held in the United States, we added a two-week-long seminar at the University of Oxford and a "Seminar at Sea" (held on a Caribbean cruise) every February. Our latest addition to this program has been what we call the "Bible and Archaeology Fest," held each November in conjunction with the annual meetings of ASOR (American Schools of Oriental Research) and SBL (Society of Biblical Literature). These meetings are held in a different city each year. Hundreds of leading scholars gather to give often technical papers to their scholarly colleagues. We take advantage of their all being together in the same city at one time by asking them to lecture to our group of interested laypeople. Those laypeople who sign up for the three-day-long Fest, as it is known, can attend their choice of morning and afternoon lectures. In addition, a prominent senior scholar gives a plenary lecture on Friday evening, and the Society hosts a banquet on Saturday that is attended by scholars as well as lay participants who enjoy the close interaction that this setting provides. Several hundred people now attend the Fests.

For years we had a special after-dinner talk at the Fest banquet. One year, however, the speaker was late. So, to kill time until he arrived, I asked two scholars to sit with me on the podium and take questions from the audience. This proved to be so popular that we adopted it as a continuing format. Each year I ask two scholars to sit with me on the podium and we answer questions.

In those early years (but in later years as well), we also had to worry about ways to increase revenue. The magazine simply could not sustain itself on circulation revenue alone. Other publications—newspapers as well as magazines—used to live on advertising. But we didn't have any products that would have special appeal to readers of a biblical archaeology magazine. What were we going to sell—picks and trowels?

In our third year, we created for our readers (and their children) special Biblical Archaeology Society T-shirts that featured an ancient pot inscribed "Dig It." The T-shirts were available in both English and Hebrew. We didn't make much money, but it was fun. So we expanded the operation. Sue Laden and I traveled all over the world looking for appropriate merchandise—cartouche pendants from Egypt; a replica of an ancient Egyptian necklace; dolls from a kibbutz; an olive-wood crèche set and a ram's-horn shofar from Israel; glass goblets from Hebron; a brass umbrella stand from Turkey; shawls from Morocco; watches with Hebrew letters; and a kit to make papyrus. Gradually the merchandise program grew and grew, but we never seemed to make any money from it. Finally, after the program grew so that it produced revenue of three-quarters of a million dollars and only cost us approximately $750,000, we decided to drop it. We still sell things, but mostly books and DVDs.

In 1984, buoyed by BAR's success, I decided to create another magazine called *Bible Review*. It would publish straight biblical articles—without an archaeological component. The first issue came out in February 1985. It was a marvelous little magazine, full of engaging stories and festooned with full-color pictures of the finest biblical art. By this time, I was easily able to assemble a host of prominent biblical scholars for the editorial advisory board and, equally important, to enlist many leading scholars to write for the magazine.

As I look at the early issues to illustrate what the magazine was all about, I feel renewed excitement. I want to tell you about all the enticing stories it featured. Don't you want to read an article by David Noel Freedman from our first issue entitled "What the Ox and the Ass Know—But the Scholars Don't"? That issue also included articles about different ways of looking at the birth of Jesus, problems of translating words that occur only once in the Bible, and how to understand the love poetry of the Song of Songs. The second issue included an article by Harvard's Frank Cross on how the Dead Sea Scrolls reveal the text behind the final text of the Bible. Another article discusses images of God in Western art. I could go on and on.

In my enthusiasm, I felt that *Bible Review* had an even greater potential than BAR. After all, I reasoned, many more people are interested in the Bible than are interested in archaeology. But *BR*, as we called it, never approached BAR's circulation. In the end, it could not sustain itself financially. *BR* lasted for more than 20 years, until we folded it into BAR in 2006.

In 1987, I acquired a Jewish magazine called *Moment*. By then I was personally grappling with Jewish issues and ideas—not religious but secular. I wanted a Jewish voice. I knew it would be too difficult and expensive to start from scratch. I looked for an existing magazine I could acquire. There is a saying that if you are Jewish, you never have an empty mailbox. Most Jewish magazines and newsletters are free or come with membership in a Jewish organization. Membership in some of these organizations runs into the hundreds of thousands. *B'nai B'rith Magazine* comes with membership in that society's fraternal organization. *Hadassah Magazine* comes with membership in the women's Zionist organization. There are many others. Little independent magazines, like *Commentary* on the right and *Tikkun* on the left, have always struggled and need to be supported. Besides, they are gray, essentially pictureless magazines and that was not what I had in mind. The closest to what I envisioned was a magazine called *Present Tense*. But it had recently folded. The only other one was *Moment*.

Moment had been started 17 years earlier by Elie Wiesel and Leonard (Leibel) Fein. Not long after, Elie dropped it and left it to Leibel. "I like beginnings," as Elie later told me. He likes to get in with new ideas and then get out. After 17 years, Leibel was a little tired of the struggle—any Jewish magazine is a struggle. We made a deal and I acquired *Moment* for a little over $100,000.

By this time, I thought I knew a little about publishing small magazines. I had successfully launched two of them. I would need a little help the first year, but after that it would be able to sail on its own. From ten friends and philanthropists who gave me $25,000 each, I raised $250,000 for acquisition and operational costs that would see me through the first year. I published my first issue as editor in September 1987.

As would so often be the case, editorially all went well. But at the end of the first year, I knew I would need a subsidy for another year. So I went back to the well. By the end of the second year, however, I realized that I had been wrong in thinking that I could produce *Moment* without a continuing annual subvention. I could either drop the magazine or be resigned to having to raise at least $100,000 a year—forever! I chose the latter. It proved to be a continual and burdensome struggle. The people and the issues I grappled with editorially, however, made it all worthwhile.

Early on, I called Wiesel, whom I had never met, and we agreed to have lunch in New York. He was, as I expected, gracious and willing to help. Indeed, he offered to become a member of my editorial advisory board. I rejected his offer: "I want you, not your name," I said. Elie and I have had a wonderful relationship over the years, but as things have turned out, his contributions to *Bible Review* and BAR have been more significant than his help with *Moment*. He wrote a series of ten articles on major and minor biblical characters for *Bible Review*, which I was naturally very proud to publish.

On one occasion, Elie said he would like to meet Phyllis Trible, with whom I had worked on several articles. Phyllis is probably the country's leading feminist biblical scholar. I of course said I would be glad to arrange a meeting, and the three of us subsequently had lunch together. I decided in advance that I would say little, leaving these two giants to get to know one another. And that's what I did. But the lunch, though cordial, was a failure. The conversation was prosaic. "What are you working on ...?" kind of talk. Maybe the auspices weren't right. Maybe they needed a specific topic to pursue. Maybe each was too reticent to be forward. To me, it also showed that even great scholars were just like the rest of us.

Another meeting proved more successful: I separately asked Elie and Frank Cross, perhaps the country's leading Bible scholar, if they would agree to a joint interview to be published in *Biblical Archaeology Review*. Both said yes. Elie lives in New York but was teaching at Boston University, so he was in Boston two days a week, and Frank was nearby at Harvard. So we arranged a date at the Harvard Semitic Museum for the interview. One of the few pictures I have hanging on my office wall is of the three of us joking together after the interview. Needless to say, it was a moving experience to listen to these two larger-than-life figures talk about the Bible from their slightly different but complementary perspectives. Naturally I enjoyed probing the differences. For each, the Bible was central to his life. Wiesel entered the biblical world almost from infancy. He has spent his life exploring its layers of meaning. He recalled how at age four he came home from synagogue and shouted to his grandmother that the hitherto childless Sarah had finally become pregnant. Cross also relates to the Bible in an emotional way, but he has spent his scholarly life exploring the history of its formation and the ancient world in which these events occurred. For me, it was a gripping experience exploring these different perspectives with the two of them.

Editing a magazine has always been a learning experience. I didn't start with an interest in selling my ideas to others but saw magazines as an opportunity to explore new worlds. *Moment* surely provided new opportunities of this kind. Jewish culture is exceptionally rich—and it was all available to me through the pages of *Moment*. For example, in the same issue in which I published an interview with then-Israel Defense Minister Yitzchak Rabin, I published an article by left-leaning Israeli novelist Amos Oz.

The interview with Rabin was especially memorable for me. It took place in his office in Tel Aviv. He had recently complained that the press was misquoting him, so he had his own burly man in the room with his own tape recorder to make sure I did not misquote. Less than thirty seconds before the end of the interview, I looked down at my tape recorder and realized I had depressed the "play" button instead of the "record" button. There would be nothing from the interview on my tape. I gulped but graciously thanked Rabin and walked out with the burly man who had also taped the interview. In desperation, I explained to him what had happened. I asked if he would make a copy of his tape and send it to me in Washington. Instead, he removed his tape and simply gave it to me. I threw my arms around his broad shoulders and embraced him like a long-lost brother. The interview promptly appeared in *Moment*.

Moment also gave me an opportunity for some exciting travel. Sue Singer, then my executive editor, and I traveled to what was then known

A FULL LOAD. By 1998, I was editing three magazines in addition to BAR. *Bible Review* dealt with topics that were more directly focused on the Bible. *Moment* was a magazine of Jewish culture and society. *Archaeology Odyssey* dealt with the archaeology of the Mediterranean and Near Eastern worlds. We ultimately closed *Bible Review* and *Archaeology Odyssey* and sold *Moment* to a foundation controlled by the then managing editor.

as the FSU, the Former Soviet Union, to explore the condition of the previously suppressed Jewish communities, not only in Russia but also in such far-flung places as Uzbekistan and Azerbaijan. We went to Berlin before the wall came down and crossed over to East Berlin. We explored communist Czechoslovakia and visited the Nazi death camps. These were all exciting adventures.

From the lofty to the pedestrian, my acquisition of *Moment* affected another change in my life: With three magazines, I decided it was no longer feasible to edit and manage them as a sideline. It was time to give up the law. In fact, it was only a small step. My magazine time was encroaching so heavily on my time in the law office that I was hardly practicing law anymore. In one sense, it was a small step. In another sense, it was major. I kind of lost my identity. When people would ask me at a party what I did, I could no longer say, "I am a lawyer." After 20 years as an editor, this is no longer a problem—"I am the editor of an obscure little magazine," I say now. But at first it was, I admit, a loss of stature. Being a Harvard lawyer gave me some of the confidence I had needed. But being a lawyer was more than my identity. I loved the law—and still do. After all these years away from the law, I still revere it. I still read legal publications, like the *American Bar Association Journal*, that continue to come to me. In the newspaper, I read articles about court cases with special interest. And most of my friends in Washington are still lawyers. Outside of Washington, my friends are mostly academics. So in a sense, I'm still leading a double life. And I continue to have some brushes with the courtroom, as my struggle with the Dead Sea Scrolls will illustrate.

Once I left the practice, however, I pursued my full-time editorial duties with zest. Indeed, I had enough energy to launch one more magazine. In early 1998, we published the premiere issue of *Archaeology Odyssey*. *Biblical Archaeology Review* combined archaeology and the Bible; *Bible Review* emphasized the first part of that title, biblical. What about another magazine, I reasoned, that emphasized the second part of that title, archaeological. It would cover the world around the Bible—the ancient civilizations of Mesopotamia, the worlds of Greece and Rome and everything in between. The articles wouldn't need to have any direct relationship to the Bible, but anyone interested in the Bible should be interested in what was going on around biblical civilization, both before and after the time of the Bible. That is what *Archaeology Odyssey* would cover. The cover of the premiere issue featured the famous golden mask found at Troy and asked, "How Historic Is Homer?"

With the inauguration of *Archaeology Odyssey*, I was publishing and editing four bi-monthly magazines—24 issues a year. We were spitting out an issue every two weeks!

Within the industry, we are what is known as a niche publisher—a publisher whose content appeals to a small group of especially committed readers. Most publishers start by looking for a niche that isn't occupied—or at least isn't crowded. My view was different. I didn't look for the idea that I thought would interest the reader. Rather I proceeded from what interested me! Then my job was to make the public interested in what I was interested in. My excitement and enthusiasm no doubt helped me along. And in those early years, we were solvent—an achievement in itself for these kinds of magazines. That would change, however—although not for a while.

We published *Archaeology Odyssey* for eight years—until the first issue of 2006—but finally had to close the magazine down at the same time we discontinued *Bible Review*. It was small comfort that all magazines (and newspapers), even the big ones, were going through difficult times. At about the same time, we (technically, the non-profit organization that owned it) sold *Moment* magazine to my managing editor (technically, to the non-profit organization that she controlled) for a pittance. While it was a sad day, it was also a great day for me. I could spend all my time on the magazine that was my first love and that I loved most. I have never been happier.

CHAPTER IX

Freeing the Scrolls

I WAS ASHAMED. I WAS EMBARRASSED FOR the man. He was a caricature of a fawning Jew debasing himself before nobility. Ben Zion Wacholder was an Old World professor teaching rabbinic literature and law at Hebrew Union College in Cincinnati, Ohio. He was small and stooped and old and white-haired. He spoke with an accent. And he was almost blind; he could tell time only by holding his watch to within an inch of his eye. Since he could not easily read, he hired students to read to him. Of course he had a prodigious memory. And he had just published a book on the Dead Sea Scrolls. He had a problem with the book, however. Most of the Dead Sea Scrolls were unavailable to him. It was like trying to clear a forest with one hand tied behind your back.

"Wonderful! Wonderful!" repeated Ben Zion Wacholder in his accented English. He was responding to John Strugnell, Oxonian and professor of Christian origins at Harvard University, who had just finished delivering his paper at a 1985 conference of Dead Sea Scroll scholars at New York University. Strugnell was the star of the conference. The exclamations of other scholars clearly agreed with Wacholder's assessment of Strugnell's paper. Except for a young scholar who had studied with him, Strugnell was the only one at the conference who gave a paper on a new—that is unpublished—scroll. The rest of the scholars were left to re-chew the old lettuce.

It was there at the conference table around which we all sat that I first felt emotional about the issue—the failure to publish the Dead Sea Scrolls.

The issue was not new to me, however. Strugnell had played the same trick before—teasing his colleagues with an unpublished Dead Sea Scroll to which he alone had access. In April 1984, a three-day conference of scholars had been held in Jerusalem. Although Strugnell did not attend, a paper of which he was the senior author was read at the Jerusalem conference by the junior author, Elisha Qimron, who would later sue me for publishing the text that was the subject of their paper. The text, known as MMT (from the phrase *Miqsat Ma'aseh Ha-Torah,* "Some precepts of the Law" that appears in it) was recognized at the conference as extraordinarily important. Although Strugnell and Qimron's paper was about the text, the text itself was not disclosed. The two authors of the paper told the assembled scholars that MMT had survived in six copies, reflecting the text's importance, although none of the copies was complete. Strugnell and Qimron believed that MMT was a letter from the leader of the Dead Sea Scroll sect, the Teacher of Righteousness. It was probably addressed to the high priest of the Temple in Jerusalem. If their dating was correct, it was the most ancient of the Qumran literary documents. In their own words, this letter is "undoubtedly ... one of the most important documents from Qumran." Only five or six of MMT's 130 lines, however, were revealed to the assembled scholars.

Like those at the New York University conference, most of the scholars at the Jerusalem conference were nevertheless grateful and respectful. On the other hand, there was also a clear rumbling of discontent. As I reported in BAR:

"While a flush of excitement surged through the scholars listening to the paper, there was also a deep concern—concern that the remainder of the letter is still unavailable to scholars more than 30 years after its discovery."

David Noel Freedman, an internationally known biblical scholar, called the situation with regard to the unpublished scrolls "very distressing." He was not the first. As early as 1976, Professor Theodor Herzl Gaster of Columbia University complained:

"Many of us who stand outside the charmed circle of the 'Scrolls team' in Jerusalem deplore the fact that, after nearly twenty years, so relatively little has been made generally available to us ... [T]he prevailing policy will, by the hazards of mortality, prevent a whole generation of older scholars from making their contribution."

AFTER THEIR DISCOVERY in 1947, the bulk of the Dead Sea Scrolls remained unpublished for nearly a half century. In 1991, the Biblical Archaeology Society published two volumes of previously unpublished scrolls, one for texts reconstructed with a computer and the other of photographs of the unpublished scrolls. With our help, the scrolls were freed and the scroll monopoly was broken. This scroll, known as MMT, was to figure in a lawsuit against me. I lost!

Morton Smith, also of Columbia and a member of my editorial board, bitterly commented that some scholars "have now withheld Qumran material from the public for over 25 years."

Perhaps the most famous complaint was that of Oxford's Geza Vermes in 1977:

"The world is entitled to ask the authorities responsible ... what they intend to do about this lamentable state of affairs. For unless drastic measures are taken at once, the greatest and most valuable of all Hebrew and Aramaic manuscript discoveries is likely to become the academic scandal *par excellence* of the twentieth century."

At first, I simply collected and reported these views. This, however, triggered comment in the wider press. For example, *Newsweek* picked up on my report in BAR on the Jerusalem conference. It also collected other scholarly comment. For example, James Charlesworth of Princeton Theological Seminary called the situation "the scandal of our time."

And of course as time went on, the drumbeat of my own complaints became more persistent. Thus, in my report on the New York University conference in 1985, I wrote:

DR. JECKYL AND MR. HYDE. An original member of the scrolls publication team, John Strugnell of Harvard University became chief scroll editor in 1984. Strugnell was a strong-willed and brilliant scholar, but he was dismissive and even hostile to critics, who complained of his secretive and possessive treatment of the unpublished scrolls. When one of his anti-Semitic tirades was published both in a Hebrew newspaper and in BAR, Strugnell was removed as chief editor in 1990.

"The leitmotif throughout the three-day New York conference, however, was the fact that after nearly 40 years, a substantial mass of Dead Sea Scroll materials has not been published and remains inaccessible to scholars generally."

At this point, I tried to emphasize Strugnell's brilliance, competence and conscientious effort to get the material out, while also being critical of him. I referred to him as a "superb scholar ... Whatever he produces is universally acknowledged to be first-rate. It would surely be unfair to single him out for criticism ... He serves as an example here simply because he was there." I gave him credit for assigning some of his texts to his graduate students.

One of the other papers at the New York University conference—by Michael Knibb of King's College London—discussed an important Hebrew text known as the Damascus Document found in Egypt at the end of the 19th century. Additional fragments were later found among the Dead Sea Scrolls but were unavailable to Knibb. Also relevant to Knibb's analysis was the polemic nature of MMT, the Dead Sea Scroll discussed by Strugnell and Qimron in their Jerusalem conference paper in 1984. The only way that Knibb knew that MMT was polemical, however, was that Strugnell and Qimron had earlier said so in their Jerusalem conference paper: Knibb referred to MMT's "'distinct polemic nature'—as the editors have described it."[11] Knibb could not confirm this from his own knowledge of the text. He only knew what the editors had told him. (By the time Strugnell and Qimron got around to publishing the text with their commentary in 1994, they had changed their minds. They decided that "the tone of the polemic in MMT is [only] moderate ... [T]he addressee is treated with respect.")

What led to this deplorable situation?

* * * *

The dramatic saga of the discovery and recovery of the scrolls is well known. Some Bedouin shepherds near the northwestern shore of the Dead Sea were looking for a lost goat or sheep, so the story goes, when one of them threw a stone into a cave to scare the animal out. Instead of the sound of a bleating sheep, however, they heard the sound of breaking pottery. When one of them went in to explore, he discovered some clay jars, one of which had broken. Inside the jars were rolled-up ancient documents wrapped in linen.

While the details are obscure and uncertain, seven scrolls eventually were divided between two Bethlehem middlemen into two lots, one of four and the other of three. The smaller lot was offered for sale through still more middlemen to Professor E.L. Sukenik, father of Yigael Yadin. At that time, Yadin was chief of operations of Israel's underground army, the Haganah. This was in 1947, during the final days of the British Mandate over Palestine. Arab and Jewish Jerusalem were already divided by a barbed wire fence. The initial negotiations for the three scrolls were conducted between Sukenik and his Arab interlocutor through the barbed wire. In the end, Sukenik had to take a bus to Arab Bethlehem to finalize the deal and pick up the scrolls. It was a dangerous trip. Both his son and his wife thought it too dangerous and urged him not to go. Tensions were especially high because half a world away at Lake Success, New York, the United Nations was nearing a vote on a resolution to partition Palestine into a Jewish state and an Arab state.

Sukenik disregarded his family's advice and took an Arab bus to Bethlehem to pick up the scrolls. He recalled that his hand trembled when he first held one of the scrolls, the book of the prophet Isaiah. He returned to Jerusalem with the scrolls. Within hours of his return, on

November 29, 1947, the United Nations passed a resolution by the necessary two-thirds, effectively creating a Jewish state for the first time since the Romans destroyed Jerusalem and the Temple nearly two thousand years before. Joyous celebrations broke out as Jews took to the streets. For Sukenik, the conjunction of events was almost messianic—the recovery of a 2,000-year-old scroll of Isaiah and the re-creation of a Jewish state in Zion. As anticipated, the next day seven Arab armies declared war on the new Jewish nation, which would officially declare itself a state nearly six months later, on May 15, 1948.

The other four scrolls were purchased by the Metropolitan of the Syrian Orthodox Church, Mar Athanasius Yeshue Samuel. When he was unable to sell the scrolls from Jerusalem, he brought them to the United States where he placed his famous ad in the classified section of the *Wall Street Journal*: "Four Dead Sea Scrolls for Sale. Biblical manuscripts dating back to at least 200 BC ... Ideal gift to an educational or religious institution ... Box F 206."

On June 1, 1954, when this ad appeared, as luck would have it, Yigael Yadin was in the United States on a lecture tour. He was now a famous archaeologist. Someone called his attention to the classified ad and Yadin made secret arrangements to purchase the scrolls—which he ultimately did for $250,000, a paltry price even then.

All seven of the intact scrolls were now in Israel's hands. A special building, called the Shrine of the Book, was built for them on the grounds of the Israel Museum and within a reasonable time they were published by Israeli and American scholars—all except one of the scrolls, which could not be unrolled at that time.

Almost from the moment the scrolls came into scholarly hands, the question naturally arose as to where they had been discovered. The answer came in 1949 when an officer in the Arab Legion noticed freshly turned dirt in front of a cave near the Dead Sea. Inside were scroll fragments that had been part of some of the scrolls the Bedouin had recovered. This was it—Cave 1!

In 1951, G. Lankester Harding, the British director of the Jordanian Department of Antiquities, and Father Roland de Vaux of the École biblique in Jerusalem, began to excavate the major archaeological site in the area, about a half mile from Cave 1. The site was known as Qumran and also as Khirbet Yahud—"the ruin of the Jews." They hoped their excavation would uncover more scrolls or at least fragments of scrolls and other context for their creation and deposit in the cave. The discovery of scrolls hidden in the cave was considered a one-time event. As Harvard's Frank Cross put it, "It was generally assumed that by a stroke of fortune an isolated cache had been found. Apparently it occurred to few scholars that Cave 1 was other than a chance hiding place, or storage place, chosen by some odd but happy quirk of an ancient mind."

The Bedouin made no such assumption. They continued looking for other scroll caves. In early 1952 they found Cave 2, not far from Cave 1. It contained only a few fragments, but this was enough to alert the scholarly community to the possibility of other manuscripts in other caves.

The race was on: the scholars versus the Bedouin. Members of the Ta'amireh tribe to which the original Bedouin discoverers belonged also hired themselves out as workers on Harding and de Vaux's excavation at Qumran. They were learning how to be archaeologists—or at least how to dig.

Qumran sits on a marl terrace of crumbly sandstone overlooking the Dead Sea. Behind it for miles on the Dead Sea littoral are steep, high, rocky limestone cliffs. It was in these cliffs that the Bedouin found both Cave 1 and Cave 2. When the scholars organized a team to search for more caves, they sensibly centered their search in the limestone cliffs. And indeed they did hit pay dirt—once. Among the 270 caves they explored, they found Cave 3, containing the famous Copper Scroll, perhaps the most mysterious of the Dead Sea Scrolls, with descriptions of 64 locations where vast treasure had been buried.[12] So far none of the treasure has been found.

The Bedouin were not so clever. They wasted their time searching and digging in the caves in the marl terrace as well as in the limestone cliffs. Among them were the Bedouin workers who were doing the digging at Qumran. When they were not excavating at the site, they were digging elsewhere in whatever cave they could find.

Among these caves was what has become known as Cave 4, located right under the noses of the archaeologists supervising the excavation of Qumran. For all practical purposes, Cave 4 is a part of the site. There the Bedouin removed fragments of nearly 600 Dead Sea Scrolls (not even one, however, was intact)! Finally, the archaeologists got wind of the Bedouin excavation, but by that time, 80 percent of the scrolls had been removed, and the anonymous Bedouin were represented by Kando, the infamous and wily antiquities dealer who played such a major role in the Dead Sea Scroll drama. In Cave 4 itself, the professionals were simply left with a mop-up operation.

The small percent of Cave 4 scrolls professionally excavated nevertheless provided valuable confirmation that the other 80 percent had in fact come from Cave 4. But for this, the scholars would have to rely on Kando's word. There was still another danger—that Kando would sell the fragments as he got them from the Bedouin to buyers all over the world (it is estimated there were 15,000 fragments). If that happened, the fragments would never be able to be pieced together. Some kind of deal had to be made with Kando to prevent this from happening.

Ultimately Harding and de Vaux made an arrangement with Kando that they would pay one Jordanian dinar (pegged to the British pound, about $2.80 at the time) for each square centimeter of script. This arrangement saved the Cave 4 fragments for the scholarly community. The Jordanian government set aside 15,000 dinars ($42,000) for the purchase of the Cave 4 material, but these and other funds were soon exhausted. Kando continued to bring more and more fragments in a steadily flowing stream to the Palestine Archaeological Museum in east Jerusalem. At this point, institutions from the United States, England, Germany, Canada and the Vatican made financial contributions, with the understanding that after the fragments were published, contributors would receive a proportionate share of the fragments. (The Jordanian government later expunged this understanding without, however, returning the contributors' money.)

It was not until 1958 that Kando brought in the last of the fragments. They were all there together in the Palestine Archaeological Museum—a major and critical achievement.

Long before this, however, it was clear that arrangements also had to be made for the study and publication of the thousands of fragments that had come in to the museum. Word went out from de Vaux to international scholars and from them to others that appropriate younger scholars who were needed in Jerusalem to work on the fragments. In this way, a team of eight scholars was assembled, headed by de Vaux himself.

The idea of a team may imply a formal organization, but that was not the case. The team was a fluid group of individuals who sometimes worked together on a project. It included two Americans (Frank Cross, who was later to distinguish himself at Harvard as the most prominent and influential Dead Sea Scroll scholar in the United States; and Father Patrick Skehan of Catholic University in Washington), a Frenchman (Abbé Jean Starcky), a Polish priest from Paris (Father J.T. Milik, who was generally regarded as the most talented of the group in fitting the fragments together and reading the faint script), a German (Claus-Hunno Hunzinger, who soon resigned and was replaced by a French priest, Father Maurice Baillet, whose membership was also short-lived) and two Englishmen (John Marco Allegro, the atheist of the group; and John Strugnell, fresh out of Oxford). Roland de Vaux, the head of the team, served mainly in an administrative capacity (in addition to leading the excavation of Qumran).

Working in Jerusalem, the team's initial task was to prepare the fragments physically so they could be studied. Cross has described the fragments as they came in:

> Many fragments are so brittle or friable that they can scarcely be touched with a camel's-hair brush. Most are warped, crinkled or shrunken, crusted with soil chemicals, blackened by moisture and age ... Often a fragment will exhibit an area of acute decay and shrinkage ... The bad spot may draw the entire fragment into a crinkled or scalloped ball, so that the fragment is almost impossible to flatten.[13]

After the cleaning process, the fragments were placed under glass on long tables in a room that became known as the scrollery. Then the process began of trying to assemble fragments of the same document. This was based on the identification of joins, the identity of handwriting, the sense of the text and even the condition and coloration of the parchment.

The next step was to assign the various manuscripts thus assembled (mostly with 90 percent of the document missing) to individual scholars on the team for publication. This was done informally. The various members of the team tended to have different specialties, which quite naturally became the basis for assignments. Starcky was an Aramaicist, so the Aramaic documents went largely to him. To Cross and Skehan went the biblical texts (fragments of more than 200 different biblical manuscripts were found in Cave 4). It was all a very friendly affair.

In those early years, there were some remarkable achievements. Working in Jerusalem, the team transcribed thousands and thousands of scroll fragments. With a transcription, a scholar can easily read the letters (if letters are uncertain, this is noted) without breaking his eyeballs looking through a magnifying glass at an ancient parchment that is about to crumble.

A separate project later proved to be key to the release of the scrolls. Three other scholars (Father Joseph Fitzmyer of Catholic University, Father Raymond Brown of Union Theological Seminary in New York and Willard Oxtoby of the University of Toronto) prepared a concordance of the Cave 4 fragments. (A separate concordance of the non-Cave 4 fragments was prepared by Javier Teixidor.) A concordance lists each word in a document together with a few words before and after the concorded word. The concorded words are then arranged in alphabetical order. With a concordance, the team of scholars could quickly identify any particular word in the Cave 4 fragments and compare it with its use in every other document from Cave 4. This was immensely helpful to individual scholars studying individual documents. It was the tool by which they could tease out the meaning of words, comparing their use in a variety of contexts.

Initially, all this work on the Cave 4 fragments proceeded with remarkable efficiency and speed—until 1960. On May 11, 1960, John D. Rockefeller, Jr., died. And with his death, the financial support of the project also died. No longer supported in Jerusalem, the team dispersed, coming together sporadically in the summer or at scholarly conferences.

Individual team members continued to work on their assignments at home, using photographs and occasional visits to Jerusalem.

Other infirmities in the system also became evident. The team had no formal organization, no structure, no plan, no rules, no way to assign duties, no way to choose members or expel them, and no way to choose a chief editor should a new one become necessary. When Père de Vaux died in 1971, the team chose as chief editor Père Pierre Benoit who, like de Vaux, was affiliated with the École biblique. Benoit was a beautiful man; I don't mean his looks, although he was indeed handsome, especially in his cassock. He was kind and pure and mild. But he was not a strong editor. In later years, we were friends, and I spoke to him about the delays in the publication of the Cave 4 materials. "What can I do?" he told me, "I urge them to publish."

The root of the publication problem lay in another scholarly tradition. When a scholar is assigned responsibility for the publication of an archaeological artifact, including an inscription, he or she has complete control of it.

There is nowhere you can go to find a formal statement of this rule. Perhaps worse, there is nowhere you can go to find out the limits of this tradition. The principle was expanded beyond reason in the case of assignments to publish Dead Sea Scrolls.

For example, the rule usually pertains to an archaeological artifact that has been uncovered in a professional excavation. The right of publication belongs to the excavator. In the case of the Dead Sea Scrolls, however, the team members were not the excavators. They were chosen arbitrarily from among bright young people with little more experience or standing than that. The claims they thereafter made equivalent to ownership were astounding.

Publication of artifacts in the scholarly world is a term of art that can mean many things, from just publishing a photograph of the artifact, to including a drawing, to including a short discussion with some technical notes (a so-called "diplomatic" edition), to engaging in a full study with extensive commentary. In this regard, the team members individually decided that they would publish their hoard only in the context of a full and detailed scholarly analysis with commentary. One especially egregious example involves Milik's fragments of the pseudepigraphic book of Enoch. Thirty years after the original assignment, Milik finally published a 439-page text-cum-commentary. In the meantime, Enoch scholars all over the world had to wait, often postponing their own publications because they could not do their work without taking into account the Cave 4 Enoch fragments that Milik was hoarding.

To make matters worse, it gradually became clear that some of the assignments to individual scholars were so massive that the assigned scholars could not possibly publish all their texts-cum-commentary in their lifetimes.

Instead of making reassignments to senior scholars, however, the team members adopted another stratagem: assigning a text to one of their graduate students. The enmity this produced in excluded scholars was palpable. This device meant that a graduate student could work on an unpublished Dead Sea Scroll at Harvard, for example, but not at Yale. It gave team members a lock on some of the brightest students.

That was not the end of it. When, by the vagaries of mortality, a member of the team died, he reserved the right to bequeath his scroll assignment to a colleague, who then assumed the same privileges as his testator. That is, there was no time limit on publication; the assignee could and did keep the text itself secret until the full *monte* of his scholarly commentary was completed.

And all the time, no non-team scholar was permitted to see a text even if it might be critical to his or her own research.

In June 1967, during the Six-Day War, the Palestine Archaeological Museum, where the Cave 4 texts were stored in east Jerusalem, fell to Israeli forces. The Dead Sea Scrolls were now controlled by Israel, rather than Jordan. It seemed to me that the continued responsibility for the delay and the unavailability of the texts to other scholars lay with Israel. As I wrote in BAR, "If Israel has control, it also has responsibility. It should exercise both."

I would have expected that at the very least Israel would have demanded that some Jewish scholars be added to the *Judenrein* scroll team that had been appointed under Jordanian auspices. After all, these were

Jewish documents. But it did not. Instead, Israel confirmed the team of scholars that had been established when Jordan controlled the scrolls.

Essentially, Israel did not act because it did not want to appear boorish, unrefined and grabby (Jewish?). Years later, I talked to the two major Israeli players, Yigael Yadin and Avraham Biran who was head of the Israel Department of Antiquities in 1967. When an emissary of the queen of Holland came to Biran asking permission to continue working on some inscriptions, Biran replied to the emissary, "What do you think we are? Are we here just to grab things?" Biran went on to tell me, "And that was the attitude we had toward the Dead Sea Scrolls ... We did not want to appear as barbarians who prevent other scholars from doing their work."

In later years, Biran realized he had made a mistake. "It's only, as I say, years later, and partly because you started the whole battle for the publication ... Look, you're right," he told me. "I didn't anticipate ... "

Yadin too had concurred in the decision to leave the original team in control, although he maintained that one condition of this permission was that publication "proceed quickly."[14]

Nearly 20 years after Israel captured the Palestine Archaeological Museum (now renamed the Rockefeller Museum), little more had been published. In 1985 I editorialized about Israel's responsibility:

> The rules of the game must be changed. And the appropriate Israeli authorities must change them ... It is clear what should be done: Photographs, including infrared photographs of all unpublished Dead Sea Scroll materials, should be published immediately ... At the very least, Israel, through a committee of its own, could negotiate with the scholars who have unpublished scroll materials to work out an agreeable time schedule for publication and to negotiate reassignments of materials that cannot be published within, say, the next two or three years.[15]

If I would have expected support from some Israeli scholars, I would have been disappointed. We printed a letter of support from a Presbyterian minister, but none from Israeli scholars—because we received none.

In the early 1980s, Père Benoit was diagnosed with what was to be terminal cancer (he died in 1987). In 1984 he resigned as chief editor. During Benoit's 13-year tenure only two volumes were published in the official series of scroll publications, *Discoveries in the Judaean Desert.*[16] Benoit was replaced by John Strugnell. How Strugnell was chosen is by no means clear, but the Israel Department of Antiquities concurred in the appointment.[17]

A weak and indecisive director of the Department of Antiquities, Avi Eitan, did ask Strugnell for a timetable as to when the various categories of scrolls would be published. He never got it.

Soon after Strugnell replaced Benoit as chief editor, a similar change occurred in the Department of Antiquities. Eitan was replaced with Amir Drori, a former general. Drori too pressed Stugnell for a timetable. The Israelis also created a secret three-person oversight committee that informed Strugnell he no longer had the sole right to reassign publication rights. In an interview on National Public Radio, Strugnell was asked, "Does the Israeli oversight committee have the power to take control of the documents?"

Strugnell replied, "I meet with them and they make suggestions and we discuss them and the ones that are reasonable I accept, and the ones that are not reasonable, I don't."

Interviewer: "So you control the documents, not the Israeli government?"

Strugnell: "We try not to put it so bluntly."

Finally, Strugnell did submit what he regarded as a timetable (which of course was kept secret). And he did begin reassigning publication rights. And some of the people to whom he gave assignments were Jewish. Progress was being made. But Strugnell and Drori were both strong-willed. Relations between the two of them soon grew hostile.

When I finally obtained a copy of a timetable, which I promptly published in BAR, it was a one-page "Suggested Timetable" issued in the name of the Israel Antiquities Department and unsigned. There was no indication that Strugnell had agreed to it. And nobody had any expectation that it would be met. When I wrote the Antiquities Department asking who "suggested" the timetable, whether anyone agreed to it and what would happen if the deadlines were not met, I was thanked for my "sincere concern" and told that the Suggested Timetable was "what we wish to bring to the attention of the public."

Even if the timetable had been agreed upon, there was no assurance that the scholars would meet the deadlines. When I asked Drori what would happen if someone failed to meet the deadline in the Suggested Timetable, he replied, "I don't know . . . I don't have the right to take it away." According to Strugnell, the government of Israel had no right to reassign the scrolls for publication. "I am the chief editor," said Strugnell.

In the July/August 1989 BAR, we published the now-famous (or infamous) cover of a beautiful picture of the inner courtyard and pool of the Rockefeller Museum boldly labeled in a bright red strip: "The Dead Sea Scroll Prison."

"Israel's Department of Antiquities and the Committee of Israeli scholars appointed to oversee Dead Sea Scroll publication has now joined the conspiracy of silence and obstruction," I charged.

This coverage generated more stories in the mainstream press. The *New York Times*, the *Washington Post*, the Associated Press and hundreds of other newspapers and magazines carried articles based on BAR's reporting. The *New York Times* story was featured in the short index on the front page. The cause was getting legs. The theme was the same in all the articles: A small group of scholars who control the scrolls, with the sanction of the Israeli government, decides who gets to see what and who gets to study what. The public and other scholars are excluded.

The Israeli press had ignored BAR's coverage, but with the international press writing about it, even the *Jerusalem Post* observed that "BAR has waged a four-year campaign to make the scrolls accessible to anyone who wants to study them."

Why, after four years of our campaign to free the scrolls, was the story finally grabbing international attention? Several readers raised this question. The reason, I suggested, was that I had raised the "decibel level." For four years, I wrote, "We had been gently prodding. We appreciated the difficulties facing the scholars assigned publication rights; we respected them as great scholars; we liked them as human beings. We hoped gentle prodding would be enough ... Unfortunately, you sometimes have to yell to get attention."[18] I later applied this lesson on how to get public attention by "yelling"—and got into trouble.

Magen Broshi, the curator of the Shrine of the Book, where the original intact scrolls were housed, told me that BAR has "done a wonderful job, performed a great service and is really responsible for all the movement toward publication." But, he added. "Don't be a bully."

I didn't listen. I kept pounding away. "*At Least* Publish the Dead Sea Scrolls Deadline!" I screamed in a headline.[19]

By this time, two of the original team of eight scholars had died (Starcky and Skehan) with major incomplete assignments. Their unpublished texts were simply reassigned on the basis of what I called the "buddy-boy" system. The assignee would now decide who, if anyone, was permitted to see the text. "Release the Dead Sea Scrolls to Other Scholars" read a headline for an article in BAR in which I urged the new team members to allow other scholars to see the unpublished texts even while team members continued to work on their publication.

Not surprisingly, rumors were swirling around that the unpublished scrolls contained material that would somehow upset Jewish or Christian beliefs. Other rumors laid the blame for the delay at the door of a Vatican fearful that the scrolls would undermine Catholic doctrine. The scroll team, after all, was dominated by Catholic priests. (Strugnell, too, had converted to Catholicism.) Our view of these rumors was unequivocal:

> We firmly believe that there is no—repeat, no—doctrinal reason for the delay in the publication of the Dead Sea Scrolls. We are close enough to the scholars—of all faiths—involved to give you our assurance that they would have absolutely no part in any suppression for doctrinal reasons or even any delay in publication for such reasons. They may be slow, but they are people of great rectitude and scientific objectivity.[20]

The *New York Times* ran an editorial suggesting that the real reasons for the delay included "greed for glory, pride, or just plain old sloth" and characterized the team members as "dawdling scholars." The editorial concluded, "Archaeology is particularly vulnerable to scholars who gain control of materials and then refuse to publish them."

Robert Eisenman, a scholar from California State University at Long Beach, who would later become a major player in the ultimate release of the scrolls (and who has not received the credit he deserves) is a maverick, outside the mainstream of scholarship. He can be irritating, and he is not always easy to get along with. When he applied to Strugnell and the Israel Department of Antiquities to see certain scrolls (sending copies of his request to other scholars), that raised the issue of accessibility very specifically. Of course, he was not given access. When the Associated Press asked Strugnell about this, he replied, "My problem is to get the scrolls published, not satisfy the vanities of particular scholars."

Strugnell also replied directly to Eisenman. I quote Strugnell's reply because it reflects better than anything I know Strugnell's dismissive hauteur and condescension:

> I don't propose spending time to correcting the factual errors and understandings you make about the history of the Qumran Editorial Project; I have rarely seen more per page—they do not improve your reputation for competence in these matters ... I am puzzled why you felt constrained to broadcast your 'letter' with its deadline (the only one, *ni fallor* [Latin, for "lest I'm mistaken"], that you have ever sent me) to half the "Who's Who" of Israel. I do not propose to follow your example. As a rule I do not write answers to public letters—I make just this one exception in your case, hoping it will inspire you in any further letters to politer and more acceptable norms; or is *adab* [Arabic for "good manners"] so much different among the lotus-eaters?

The situation was reaching high pitch. Even *Time* magazine was covering it. One "scholar in the field," who declined to give his name to the *Los Angeles Times* for fear of retribution, told the paper, "I find it hard to believe that a few scholars can stonewall the Dead Sea Scrolls and keep them from scholarly access for much longer. The situation has become an embarrassment in the field."

"Let's find a dark place where we can open it."

"WHO CONTROLS THE SCROLLS?" In the March/April 1991 BAR, we lampooned the two scroll committees' lack of direction with this cartoon that pictured a cart being pulled in six different directions by two three-headed horses. The scrolls are in a safe, as chief scroll editor John Strugnell falls off the back of the cart. BAR, as a little dog, barks at the cart while the drivers head off looking far a dark place where they can open the safe and look at the scrolls.

At the same time, it was becoming obvious that Strugnell was having other problems. He regularly appeared disheveled. His hair was uncombed. A short, stumpy man, he now walked with a limp. He constantly had a three-day beard. And he was clearly an alcoholic. I recall visiting him one day in his cell at the École biblique. His files were kept on shelves in old beer cartons. Beneath his bed was a case of beer. An American scholar who would become a chief editor for the biblical scrolls and a young female graduate student who would later become a leading Dead Sea Scroll scholar were also in the room. They would look at each other furtively as Strugnell reached for another beer every 15 minutes, while he and I talked.

The Israelis clearly wanted to control Strugnell, but without creating a crisis. They urged Strugnell to speed things up, to make a more definite time schedule, to add new members to the team. In addition to the Israeli oversight committee, in 1990 a highly respected text-critical Bible scholar from Hebrew University, Emanuel Tov, was appointed co-editor in chief, or something like that. He was secretly appointed to work with Strugnell. Tov's appointment was made without Strugnell's approval. Strugnell was simply "informed" of this appointment. But nothing was made public. The first time I talked to Tov about his appointment, he denied any knowledge of it. The public—and BAR—were left to wonder what was happening. In addition, a second co-chief editor was appointed for the biblical scrolls; he was Eugene Ulrich, a former Strugnell student teaching at Notre Dame. "Who Controls the Scrolls?" we asked in a headline. "In the Land of Kafka, Where the Marx Brothers Rule" was the BAR headline we printed over a cartoon in which the scrolls in an iron safe were on a cart pulled by two three-headed horses going in six different directions. One of the horses was labeled "Israel Oversight Committee" and the other "Chief Scroll Editor(s)." The drivers holding the reins included two members of the original team and the director of the Antiquities Authority.

In an interview with the *Jerusalem Post*, Ulrich, the new co-chief editor, declared that the editing process had not gone too slowly, but too quickly: "The editing of the scrolls has in fact suffered not from foot-dragging but from undue haste." In Ulrich's view, quick publication would "shackle" the public with poor scholarship.

As we pushed on with our campaign to release the scrolls, one of the members of the Israel Oversight Committee, Jonas Greenfield, a major scholar and a long-time friend, publicly declared me "an enemy of Israel."

In an ABC television newscast, an unrepentant Strugnell described our campaign for the release of the scrolls. "It seems," Strugnell said on national television, "we've acquired a bunch of fleas who are in the business of annoying us." This led to BAR's most famous cover. In the March/April 1990 issue, I put on the cover a picture of a scowling Strugnell in a television frame. Below this picture was the flea quotation. Otherwise, the cover, including Strugnell, was covered with large fleas. I placed identifications on some of the fleas—the scholars who had objected to the fiasco of the scroll publication team. (Scholars from many countries were represented, but none from Israel.) I identified the biggest flea as BAR.

Inside I commissioned a political cartoon, quoting defenders of the status quo. Magen Broshi, the curator of the Shrine of the Book, was quoted from an interview on *Good Morning America*: "There's no urgency; it's not like we're dealing with cancer." From John Strugnell: "We're not running a railroad. Even trains are sometimes late."

Under pressure, the team was expanded and new scholars were added. This focused attention on something that had largely been ignored since the late 1950s—the concordance of the Cave 4 fragments that had been compiled by Joseph Fitzmyer, Raymond Brown and Willard Oxtoby. Each word in the fragments was listed on a three-by-five index card, listing each reference to the word, noting in which texts the word could be found and quoting the adjacent words in that text. In those early years, when the members of the team were working in Jerusalem the file cards were readily accessible to them. When, 30 years later, new scholars were added to the team and they were working in their home bases far from Jerusalem, the concordance was in effect unavailable. Then, all of a sudden, someone remembered it. Strugnell decided to make a few copies of the concordance available for members of the team—a fatal mistake.

Strugnell had someone (Hans-Peter Richter) take the three-by-five cards and line them up one above the other, seven cards to the page. He then had each page photocopied and the photocopies gathered together as a book. The title page advised that this was "A Preliminary Concordance ... Including Especially the Unpublished Material from Cave IV." Thirty copies were "Privately Printed in Gottingen, 1988 ... on behalf of Professor John Strugnell, Harvard University." In the center of the page, in all caps and underlined, were the Latin words "<u>EDITORUM IN USUM</u>," or "for the use of the editors." For all others, the very existence of the concordance remained a secret.

I had long before heard rumors about a concordance that had been assembled in the late 1950s. I tried to confirm its existence in an early interview with the then-director of the Department of Antiquities, Avi Eitan. Its

CLASSIC COVER. In a 1990 ABC News interview, John Strugnell described BAR and other critics as "fleas who are in the business of annoying us." On the cover of the March/April issue, we featured this quote along with a scowling Strugnell on a TV screen surrounded by fleas. Each flea is labeled as a prominent critic of the scroll publication team. The largest flea is labeled "BAR."

existence was important because it proved that by the late 1950s the team of editors had transcribed all of the unpublished scrolls. The texts of the Dead Sea Scrolls could have been released then. They were not because the team scholars did not want anyone else to see them until they had completed their book-length commentaries on the texts. Eitan was extremely cagey with me about the existence of the concordance:

> HS: I understand that shortly after these Dead Sea Scroll materials were brought to the museum in the 1950s ... a concordance [was made] of 25,000 cards with every word that appeared in these Dead Sea Scroll materials. Is that right?

Eitan: I must say this is again at a time before I held this position and I'm not too familiar with these details ...

HS: I understand that concordance now sits in this very building. Is that true?

Eitan: Maybe so.

HS: Well, the first thing I want to know is whether you can confirm that it exists, and you say you can't.

Eitan: No, what I'm saying is you are driving at a certain point. I'd like to know what point you are driving at.

HS: I must say it seems unusual to me and strange that you really don't want to say whether such a concordance exists. Let me ask you this: If such a concordance exists, wouldn't it be a very valuable aid to scholars working on Dead Sea Scroll problems?

Eitan: Yes.

HS: So if it exists, shouldn't scholars generally be told that it exists?

Eitan: That the fragments of the scrolls themselves exist and that they are here is much more important than the fact that a concordance like this exists.

This concordance later proved to be the key to the release of the Dead Sea Scrolls.

* * * *

As Strugnell's health was deteriorating, in the fall of 1990 he gave an interview to Avi Katzman, a journalist with the Israeli newspaper *Ha'aretz*. I soon learned about it and arranged with Katzman to publish a modified English version, including additional details, in BAR. The interview clearly exposed Strugnell not simply as anti-Zionist, but as a rabid anti-Semite—as had been widely rumored.

Katzman noted that, although Strugnell drank beer throughout the interview, he did not appear to be drunk. He was lucid and spoke in a firm voice.

When Katzman asked him if he was "anti-Israel," Strugnell replied:

"That's a sneaky way of coming at the anti-Semitic question, isn't it?"

When Katzman asked him directly if he was an anti-Semite, Strugnell denied it: "I've spent my life studying Semites from Ethiopia to Baghdad. I don't know anyone in the world who's an anti-Semite."

He described himself as an anti-Judaist:

[Judaism] is a folk religion; it's not a higher religion. An anti-Judaist, that's what I am. I plead guilty. I plead guilty in the way the Church has pleaded guilty all along, because we're not guilty; we're right. Christianity presents itself as a religion which replaces the Jewish religion. The correct answer of Jews to Christianity is to become Christian. I agree there have been monstrosities in the past—the Inquisition, things like that. We should certainly behave ourselves like Christian gentlemen. But the basic judgment on the Jewish religion is, for me, a negative one.

Katzman asked him what annoyed him about Judaism. Strugnell replied:

The fact that it has survived when it should have disappeared ... For me the answer [to the Jewish problem] is mass conversion ... It's a horrible religion. It's a Christian heresy, and we deal with our heresies in different ways. You are a phenomenon that we haven't managed to convert—and we should have managed.

As for Israel:

I dislike Israel as an occupier of part of Jordan ... The occupation of Jerusalem—and maybe of the whole State—is founded on a lie, or at least on a premise that cannot be sustained.

He compared Israel to the Crusaders:

One of the great building periods was the Crusades; but, basically, they were unsustainable. That's me on Israel ... Am I opposed to Zionism?

I think we've had enough of it but you can't say it's not out there. It would've been nice if it hadn't existed, but it has, so it's covered by a sort of grandfather clause.

In a separate sidebar to the interview in BAR, I expressed compassion for the man, but contempt for his views. I wrote:

Initial reaction to the interview ... can only be shock and disbelief. A distinguished theologian at Harvard Divinity School, a professor of Christian Origins, a man who has spent his life studying the Dead Sea Scrolls, harboring thoughts like this? Impossible! Unfortunately, it is possible. The stories, the rumors, the gossip we had heard, but refused to print, have turned out to be true.

I then called for his dismissal as chief editor: "It is clear that Strugnell cannot be permitted to function any longer as chief editor of the Dead Sea Scrolls." I quoted Professor Morton Smith of Columbia University regarding the reluctance of the Israeli authorities to do anything: The Israelis, said Smith, should "stop shaking in their shoes over what people might think of them at Harvard."

I urged the Israelis to throw open the doors and release the scrolls.

The immediate scholarly reaction to our publication of the Strugnell interview was different. I called the dean of Harvard Divinity School, Mark Edwards, to see what he thought of it. When I telephoned his office, I was told he was out with a cold. When I called later, he was in a meeting. Then he was in an all-day meeting. After repeated calls, his secretary told me he would not speak with me. Only when *Time* called did he take the call and condemn Strugnell's remarks as "personally repugnant."

From 85 of Strugnell's academic friends and colleagues, I received a letter for publication in BAR. Despite the interview, they "remain deeply grateful to a man who has contributed so much to the study of ancient Judaism."

Of course, I printed the letter. The roster of signatories included some of world's greatest scholars. The letter attributed Strugnell's untoward remarks to his mental imbalance at the time:

"While we find these remarks [in his interview] abhorrent, it is our understanding that they were made at a time when he was seriously ill. We cannot know how much his illness influenced what he said."

There was no question that Strugnell was inebriated and suffering from manic-depression. He soon entered a psychiatric hospital for treatment. Whether this can serve as an explanation for his anti-Semitic rant is another question, however. Drunks and mentally impaired often go off the deep end, but the content is not simply undetermined. Why did he not rant at Catholics or his colleagues or his wife or the Antiquities Authority, rather than Jews? The alcohol and mental problems simply unlocked what was already there, at least in embryo.

As a matter of fact, it was not simply the alcohol or mental illness that unlocked Strugnell's anti-Semitism. It had been widely acknowledged previously in the halls of academia. One scholar (who was Jewish and signed the letter to BAR!) told a reporter that when in the past Strugnell would make derogatory remarks about Jews, she would call Strugnell on it and he would laugh and back down. Another signer of the letter acknowledged that Strugnell was known for anti-Semitic "slurs."

As I put it in the magazine:

Certainly but for his illness, Strugnell would not have expressed himself in these crude terms publicly. But beneath this name-calling lies a far more sophisticated, intellectual, carefully developed form of anti-Jewish polemic. It is the repudiated doctrine of a past age. It is the view that Judaism is a not a valid religion, the view that Christianity is the true Israel and the Jews the false Israel, the view that the Jews are 'stubborn' because they have not accepted Christ, the view that the New Testament has invalidated the covenant reflected in the Old Testament, the view that Christianity has 'superseded' Judaism and that Judaism should disappear.

Eugene Fisher, the director of the secretariat for Catholic-Jewish Relations of the National Conference of Catholic Bishops, wrote a strong piece in BAR declaring that "supersessionism," as it is known, had been definitively rejected by the Catholic Church. While it had been a common belief in ages past, Fisher noted that it had never been the official doctrine of the church. "The statements by Professor John Strugnell (now, I understand, hospitalized)," Fisher wrote in BAR, "are classically anti-Semitic. They deserve to be condemned publicly for what they are: not only sick, but sinful."[21]

At the end of 1990, Strugnell was silently removed from his position as chief editor (or co-chief editor). As I described it in an op-ed piece in the *New York Times*, he was "fired." But his scroll assignments remained his to publish, to give to his students, or to bequeath to a colleague.

* * * *

As I mentioned earlier, the limited publication of the concordance in 1988 for the use of the editors was itself kept secret. Joseph Fitzmyer, who was one of the principal compilers of the concordance in the 1950s, learned of its publication when he received a communication asking if he was interested in buying a copy for $300. With that, the secret was out. It was soon common knowledge.

When Ben Zion Wacholder, with whom I began this chapter and who would play a key role later in breaking the scroll monopoly, found himself in a taxi with Strugnell at a scholarly conference in Israel, he asked Strugnell if he could get a copy of the concordance for the library of Hebrew Union College. Strugnell suggested Wacholder send him a letter "and we'll take it up." So Wacholder did. And a copy of the concordance was sent to the Hebrew Union College library. Whether the copy was sent because of Wacholder's request or because the college was one of three institutions—two in the United States and one in England— where security copies of the photographs of the unpublished texts had been deposited is unclear.

In any event, Wacholder was able to use his college's copy of the concordance. With his purblind eyes he perused the concordance cards. Then he shared the treasure with his graduate student, Martin Abegg, who was accustomed to reading to the old man. Abegg was writing his doctoral dissertation on the War Scroll, one of the seven intact Dead Sea Scrolls that had been published, but there were several other fragmentary copies of this scroll among the hoard from Cave 4. Abegg hungered to see them. Here in his hands was the opportunity to view the secret copies. He was soon able to reconstruct from the concordance some of the texts that he needed for his dissertation. When he took the results to his mentor, Wacholder was startled. Abegg recalls Wacholder's first reaction: "We must publish this material."

Abegg also vividly recalls his own reaction to this: "I will never be able to get a job," he thought. "No one will ever hire someone who plagiarizes these texts." To publish this material would contravene a basic scholarly tradition. Abegg consulted his friends. Their advice: "Don't do it! You'll never work." He asked his pastor. He said, "Do it!" He consulted his father: "It looks to me like the ethical shoe is on the other foot. I think you should do it."

The deciding factor, however, was a feeling for his mentor. As Abegg has expressed it:

> Here was a man who was one of a very special generation who had been uprooted from Eastern Europe during World War II, who had spent their whole lives studying Jewish literature and law and knew it by heart, and yet had been kept away from this material all these years. For Ben Zion and others like him, I finally made the decision. Yes, I would agree [to publish it].[22]

With the help of his computer, Abegg found the task infinitely easier, and work proceeded apace. It was at this point that Wacholder telephoned me to talk about our publishing the material. I knew immediately that I wanted to publish it. There were two problems: (1) The process of reconstructing the text had just begun; and (2) We didn't have the money to publish it. I suggested to Wacholder that we publish the material in fascicles. This would solve both my problems. As to the first, we would be able to publish the first fascicle quickly because we would include only 25 of the texts in a book of a mere hundred pages. Then, with the sale of the first fascicle, we would get enough money to publish subsequent fascicles, and so on.

Wacholder agreed and on September 4, 1991, the Biblical Archaeology Society published Fascicle One of *A Preliminary Edition of the Unpublished Dead Sea Scrolls*. I began my foreword with these words:

"This is a historic book. A hundred years from now this book will still be cited—not only on account of its scholarship, but because it broke the monopoly on the still-unpublished Dead Sea Scrolls."

In their own introduction, Wacholder and Abegg wrote:

If we are not totally mistaken, the works published in this fascicle alone will shed new light on the history, social structure and literature of the group of men and women who founded this community, ultimately known to us as the Essenes. Some current hypotheses as to the nature of these people and their literature will be confirmed; others will necessarily require revision or abandonment.

Abegg, incidentally, has had a stellar academic career. He is now a leading Dead Sea Scroll scholar—with a job.

Abegg recalls his first encounter after the publication of Fascicle One with Emanuel Tov, now the chief editor of the Dead Sea Scrolls. It was in November 1991 at the annual meeting of the Society of Biblical Literature. Abegg had a special reverence for Tov; it was Tov who had introduced him to the Dead Sea Scrolls when Abegg was studying at Hebrew University in Jerusalem. When Fascicle One came out, however, Tov was still fiercely resisting the release of the unpublished texts. Abegg was immediately apprehensive when he spied Tov at the book exhibit. Tov greeted him in Hebrew: "*Banim gidalti v'romumti*." Abegg immediately recognized the quotation—from Isaiah 1:2: "I have reared children and brought them up." It was only that night that Abegg recalled the end of the line: "*v'ham pashu vy*"—"And they have rebelled against me."

The rupture was not permanent, however. Abegg and Tov subsequently became good friends again and continue to work together on scroll materials to this day. This is a tribute to Tov's character, who was also very antagonistic to me personally, but with whom I now have excellent relations.

Strugnell characterized the publication of Fascicle One as "stealing." "What else would you call it but stealing?" he declared. I answered in an op-ed piece in the *New York Times*, saying that under international law the scholars who have been hoarding the scrolls are fiduciaries, trustees for all mankind. They do not own the scrolls. We the public are the beneficiaries of their trust. By keeping them secret and as if they owned them, they are in breach of trust. "We are taking only what is rightfully ours," I said. "It is they who are the lawbreakers. It is they who are stealing from all of us."

The publication of Fascicle One received widespread publicity and recognition. Abegg's computer caught the popular imagination—the latest technology applied to uncover the text of the ancient scrolls—and it was quickly dubbed "Rabbi Computer." Editorials (following frontpage news articles) in the *Washington Post* and *New York Times* were typical.

Said the *Times*:

> The first volume of the reconstructed text has just been published by the Biblical Archaeology Society of Washington, D.C. More will be forthcoming as the researchers press on with their work ... Amazingly, two scholars at Hebrew Union College in Cincinnati have now broken the scroll cartel ... Mr. Wacholder and Mr. Abegg are to be applauded for their work ... The committee, with its obsessive secrecy and cloak and dagger scholarship, long ago exhausted its credibility with scholars and laymen alike.

Likewise, the *Post* said:

> Mr. Shanks and others on his side of the issue believe the scrolls will be best understood if they are treated like any other such source material— that is, made as freely available as soon as possible to all ... Judging their effort by the material that is known, they believe they've been remarkably successful, and they intend to do more. Some of the authorized scholars are irked; they doubt the accuracy of the effort and question its propriety.

Some even talk of lawsuits. They'd do much better to accept the fact that things are inevitably going to move a lot faster now.

We ultimately published four fascicles of texts reconstructed by Wacholder and Abegg. These fascicles did more than simply release the texts. As the title page announces, these texts were "reconstructed and *edited*." Wacholder and Abegg were able to improve a number of the readings. When the scroll photographs were finally released, they could make further improvements by comparing the concorded texts with the texts as they appeared in the photographs.

Some scholars harshly criticized the quality of the reconstructed texts in Fascicle One. Eugene Ulrich told the *Times* that no scholar could "base solid work" on these computer-reconstructed texts. But in time this criticism turned to praise. One of the early doubters was James Sanders, director of the Ancient Biblical Manuscript Center. As he later told me, "I've revised my opinion. They're g-o-o-d. They're amazing!" Hartmut Stegemann, who taught at Göttingen University and who had arranged for the private printing of the concordance at the university, wrote me not long after Fascicle One came out: "I checked the reliability of this preliminary edition ... Congratulations to this almost perfect way of publication!... [It] is a trustworthy representation of about 98 percent of the textual evidence." As late as 1994, Professor Lawrence Schiffman of New York University wrote in the *Religious Studies News*, "Virtually everyone in the field regularly uses these volumes."

With the publication of Fascicle One, the scroll monopoly was broken.

* * * *

At the same time we were working with Wacholder and Abegg on Fascicle One, we were working on an entirely different Dead Sea Scroll project. Wacholder and Abegg gave the scholarly world the Hebrew (or Aramaic) text of the scroll fragments in modern Hebrew letters, as transcribed in the 1950s. It in effect reproduced the text of the fragments as transcribed by the original publication team. But at this point, scholars could not check the transcription in Fascicle One against the scroll fragments themselves—or against photographs of the scroll fragments. This still remained unavailable to the scholarly community at large.

Just as the original team of scholars had engaged another team of young scholars to construct the concordance, they had also engaged a superb Arab photographer named Najib Albina to take pictures of the fragments, both with ordinary film and with infrared film. These photographs are extraordinarily valuable, for in many cases they are more legible than the scrolls themselves. Over the years, the text of the scrolls would often deteriorate and become unreadable. The photographs often provide better evidence of what the scrolls originally said than the fragments themselves.

Very near the time we began work on what became Fascicle One, I received a telephone call from a California lawyer named William Cox, who was calling on behalf of an unnamed client. When he wouldn't tell me who his client was, I almost hung up on him. I told him that I was not interested in talking to him. Fortunately, he convinced me to stay on the line. In fact he was calling on behalf of Robert Eisenman, who had copies of Najib Albina's photographs of the scrolls, taken more than 30 years earlier—nearly 2,000 of them. He wanted us to publish them. I did not hesitate. Of course, we would.

I must say at the outset that I don't know where Eisenman got them. To this day, he has refused to tell me—even to give me a hint. Eisenman had contacts with some prominent political figures in Israel, who may have been the source. He was also close to a far-right philanthropist named Irving Moskowitz, who ended up financing our publication of the photographs (I was not aware of his political views at the time Eisenman enlisted him). Eisenman may well have gotten the photographs through Moskowitz, who had superb connections in Israel. Another less likely possibility is that Eisenman somehow got access to a security copy that had been deposited with the Ancient Biblical Manuscript Center in Claremont, California, or even from another copy held by the Huntington Library in San Marino, California.

I later learned that Eisenman had originally sought to publish the photographs with a leading international academic publisher in the

Netherlands, J.J. Brill of Leiden. Brill anticipated charging $800 for its microfiche edition and netting $200,000 from the deal. When it became clear to Brill at a Dead Sea Scroll conference in Madrid that the Israelis would vehemently object to the publication of the photographs (thus endangering Brill's prospects of publishing books by them), Brill withdrew its commitment to Eisenman.

Doubtless aware that he lacked the scholarly prestige that would adequately distinguish the publication, Eisenman sought the association of an eminent West Coast scholar, James M. Robinson of the Claremont Graduate School in Claremont, California. Robinson was both a major scholar as well as somewhat of a renegade himself. He was the hero of the Nag Hammadi codices, a dozen tattered books containing 52 tractates of early Christian literature. They were found by peasants near Nag Hammadi in Egypt two years before the Bedouin discovered the first Dead Sea Scrolls. The Nag Hammadi codices too languished unpublished by a team assembled to publish them. The scholars on the French team, like the Dead Sea Scroll team, had intended to publish the texts only when their commentaries were completed. Finally, in 1970, with help from UNESCO, the Nag Hammadi codices were given to Robinson and his colleagues, who promptly decided to publish translations without commentaries. The first translations appeared two years later. By 1977 all were published. The Nag Hammadi codices thus became available to everyone, for which Robinson has received worldwide plaudits. Robinson's involvement with Eisenman in the publication of the photographs of the Dead Sea Scrolls gave it a scholarly heft it would not otherwise have.

When the two cartons of photographs arrived by mail from Eisenman, my assistant and I spent the day, from early morning to night, designating the photographs for each page of the two volumes.

The names of Eisenman and Robinson, in that order, appear on the title page. They appear not as editors, but as having "prepared [the edition] with an introduction and index." Their three-page introduction (dated June 5, 1991) is followed with an index of 1,787 photographs keyed to the number assigned to them in the Palestine Archaeological Museum.

I wrote an 11-page "Publisher's Foreword," with 22 plates of supporting documents labeled "Figures 1–22."

The two-volume folio-sized set (priced at $200) came out on November 29, 1991. By that time, however, we had been upstaged.

This part of the story goes back to an imperious West Coast philanthropist named Elizabeth Hay Bechtel, whose money helped support early Dead Sea Scroll research. She also provided the money to found the Ancient Biblical Manuscript Center (ABMC), whose mission was to collect high-quality photographs of important biblical manuscripts for scholarly study. The ABMC was directed by the distinguished biblical scholar James Sanders, whom I have already mentioned. Mrs. Bechtel was also associated philanthropically with the Huntington Library, a major research institution near Pasadena, so she sent its photographer, Robert Schlosser, to Jerusalem to make copies of Najib Albina's negatives for the ABMC. While Schlosser was in Jerusalem, Mrs. Bechtel and Sanders had a falling out and a bitter struggle ensued for control of the ABMC. (Mrs. Bechtel eventually lost.) When Schlosser returned with the photographs (negatives), Mrs. Bechtel met the plane. A set of the photographs was eventually deposited with the ABMC, which signed an agreement with the Israeli authorities to keep the photographs secret. But Mrs. Bechtel also obtained a separate copy for herself. These she deposited in a special safe constructed for this purpose in the Huntington Library. The Huntington's research interests are worlds away from concerns with the Dead Sea Scrolls, so there the microfilm lay forgotten and untouched for a decade. Mrs. Bechtel died in 1987.

In 1990 William A. Moffett was appointed librarian (director) of the Huntington Library. When he read about BAR's efforts to free the scrolls, he realized he had a copy of them. But paradoxically, the trigger was provided by the scroll cartel itself. When Strugnell was removed as chief editor, a triumvirate was created to advise the publication team; the triumvirate consisted of Emanuel Tov, Eugene Ulrich and Father Emile Puech of the École biblique. Part of the committee's assignment was to protect the secrecy of the scrolls. The committee had of course followed BAR's campaign closely, and this led them eventually to focus on the copy of the photographs in the Huntington. This set was Mrs. Bechtel's personal copy. It was, in effect, a loose cannon. Neither the Huntington nor Mrs. Bechtel had signed a secrecy agreement. The scroll committee decided that they had better take action to protect against a leak at the Huntington.

On July 23, 1991, Eugene Ulrich wrote Moffett a letter oh-so-warmly expressing the committee's "gratitude" for the care the Huntington Library provided in preserving this copy of the photographs: "Your contribution in this regard to the field of Dead Sea Scrolls scholarship has been much appreciated by ourselves and our predecessors." The time has come, however, the letter went on, for the Huntington's copy to be transferred. "It is important to us that no copies of them be retained hereafter in your care." The letter closed by thanking the Huntington "for the care until now you have given the treasures in your trust."

The letter of course had just the opposite effect on Moffett. Shortly after we published Fascicle One of Wacholder and Abegg's reconstructed texts in September 1991, Moffett announced that he would open his microfilm of photographs to everyone. On Sunday, September 22, 1991, the *New York Times* featured the story above the fold on its front page.

This was two months before we came out with our two-volume edition of the photographs.

If anyone thought the Huntington's announcement would end the matter, they were wrong. The Israeli contingent had just begun to fight. The Israel Antiquities Authority (as it was now called) and the new chief editor, Emanuel Tov, immediately faxed the Huntington a peremptory letter as if dressing down a schoolboy: "Your legal and moral obligation ... clearly forbids [your release of the photographs] ... We expect you to honor the terms of the agreement and save us the trouble of taking legal steps. We expect your immediate reply."

The Huntington was sure of its ground, however. It had signed no agreement to maintain the secrecy of the photographs. Only the ABMC had signed such an agreement (as had the two other depositaries of security copies of the photographs, Hebrew Union College and Oxford University.) The Huntington was in receipt of Mrs. Bechtel's personal copy—and she had signed nothing.

Moffett replied politely, but firmly: "You, I am confident, respect and understand the principle of intellectual freedom we are committed to uphold."

"When you free the scrolls, you free the scholars," Moffett told the press.

The Israel Antiquities Authority (IAA) called an emergency meeting for December in Jerusalem that was to include Moffett of the Huntington, as well as representatives of the three institutions that held security copies and who had signed secrecy agreements. There, according to the IAA, they would decide on procedures for granting access to the photographs, while also protecting assigned scholarly rights to publication. In its own words, the IAA wanted "to facilitate access." The Israeli authorities wanted any outside scholar allowed to see the scroll photographs to sign a statement saying that the scholar would not publish an edition of the scrolls. Moffett declined to attend the meeting. It was never held.

The IAA took to the press. Drori, describing the Huntington's release as "not ethical," characterized Huntington's announcement as "a mere publicity stunt." According to the *New York Times*, some of the scroll editors with assigned texts described the photographs held by the Huntington as "stolen property." The Jewish Telegraphic Agency reported that the Huntington's move "was bitterly attacked by the Israel Antiquities Authority as tantamount to trafficking in stolen property and as a flagrant violation of a longstanding agreement."

The press's editorial comment, however, was withering. *New York Times* columnist William Safire described the scroll monopolists as "a little band of academics representing no interest but their own arrogant selfishness." He called the IAA officials "insular jerks ... Prime Minister Shamir should shut them up."

IAA director Drori went so far as to charge that the source of the pressure to release the scrolls was anti-Semitic: "It seems," he mused, "to have something to do with the fact that Israel and Jews are in control."

Shortly thereafter, however, the IAA gave up. It simply dropped its opposition. On the contrary, it promptly began work on its own microfiche copy of the scrolls that would be available to everyone—which were published several years later by Brill.

As for the Huntington, it is doubtful that more than two scholars have ever looked at its copy of the photographs. The photographs were much more accessible in BAR's two-volume set and subsequently in the IAA's set.

I guess it can be argued that the Huntington stole our thunder. Simply by making the announcement of free access, they captured the front page of the Sunday *Times*. But I have always been grateful to the Huntington and for Bill Moffett's firm stand. (Unfortunately, he died of bladder cancer in 1995 at age 62.) The Huntington is big and powerful. They are not easily pushed around. I naturally wonder, with considerable trepidation, about what would have happened if BAR had stood alone in the publication of the Eisenman and Robinson photographs. I believe I would have been sued over the publication of the photographs and the texts reconstructed from the concordance. The IAA had already forbidden its archaeologists to write for BAR (something it would do again during the forgery crisis described in a later chapter).

By 1996, director Drori's fury had subsided and we talked about the old days (he died in 2005). Indeed, he had considered suing me, he said: "We think [note the present tense!] your publication [of the scroll photographs] is illegal ... We think, even now, that we are one hundred percent right, [but] I decided not to go to court about it." He also considered suing the Huntington: "I think what the Huntington did was an awful thing—to break the law. It was a one-sided decision of the Huntington. They didn't ask us. The pictures were stolen material ... We were one hundred percent right. No doubt about it. But I decided not to go to court."

Because of the Huntington's release of its photographs, I didn't get sued by the Israel Antiquities Authority. But I did get sued. And I lost. But that's for the next chapter.

CHAPTER X

Losing in Court

THE LAWSUIT AGAINST ME AND BAR GREW out of the pugnacious "Publisher's Foreword" I wrote in the two-volume set of scroll photographs. Both Eisenmen and Robinson had strongly urged me not to publish it, as they thought it would be inappropriate to a scholarly production. But I had other reasons for taking a belligerent stand: I feared the IAA would sue me, and I wanted them to know that if they did, they would have a fight on their hands. One commentator called me "leather-lunged."[23]

In retrospect, my fear of being sued was entirely justified, as detailed in the preceding chapter. For the IAA, what I was doing was stealing. Perhaps my belligerence lent a note of caution to the IAA's thinking and ultimate decision not to pursue their supposed legal claims.

The poster child for my "Publisher's Foreword" was the scroll text known as MMT. It provided an excellent example of the scholarly abuses in the handling of the scrolls more generally. As mentioned at the outset of the previous chapter, MMT was first brought to the attention of the wider scholarly community at an archaeology conference in Jerusalem in 1984 in a paper by John Strugnell and his junior colleague Elisha Qimron. Their presentation electrified the otherwise staid scholarly conference. Here was a document that the two scholars—who were preparing it for publication—readily acknowledged was "highly important." But while they *described* the text in their paper, they released only six of its 130 lines—and 40 years after the assignment.

MMT, they said, was the only letter identified among the more than 900 Dead Sea Scroll manuscripts.[24] That fragments from six copies survived reflects its importance. The letter seemed to come from the head of the community at Qumran, the Teacher of Righteousness, and was probably addressed to the high priest of the Temple in Jerusalem. The heart of the document is approximately 20 legal rules, mostly dealing with purity laws, in which the stricter laws of the Dead Sea Scroll community are contrasted with the more lenient laws of the priestly hierarchy in the Jerusalem Temple. In short, this document was crucial to understanding what divided the Qumran community from mainstream Judaism of the time—and perhaps what led to their separation. The text of MMT also revealed that the Dead Sea Scroll community followed a different calendar, a solar calendar with a 364-day year (in contrast to the lunar calendar of mainstream Judaism).

MMT was important for understanding the roots of Christianity as well as the history of ancient Judaism. As mentioned in the previous chapter, MMT stands for *Miqsat Ma'aseh Ha-Torah*, which officially translates as "Some precepts of the Torah." Martin Abegg—who, with "Rabbi Computer," had recreated the transcripts from the secret concordance— cogently pointed out that this translation of the name MMT "unfortunately obscures MMT's relationship to Paul's letters."[25] In fact, MMT is the same phrase in Hebrew that Paul uses in Greek, meaning the familiar "Works of the Law" (see Romans 3:20,28 and Galatians 2:16, 3:2,5,10). A better translation of the Hebrew would be, as is sometimes used, "Some Works of the Law." In short, if you want to understand what Paul meant by "Works of the Law," then study MMT.

For the history of Judaism, MMT is, if anything, even more important. The earliest extant rabbinic code is the Mishnah, dating from about 200 C.E. It presents a fully developed legal (*halakhic*) system governing all aspects of life. This system must have had a substantial development over a long period of time. How did this complex, subtle legal structure evolve? On what sources did the laws of the Mishnah draw?

The Mishnah was followed by the Talmud several hundred years later. For Rabbinic Judaism (the form of Judaism to which modern Judaism is heir), the Mishnah and Talmud are known as the Oral Law. According to tradition, it was handed down from God to Moses at Mount Sinai. But where did this legal structure come from? What are its roots in the period before the Roman destruction of the Temple in 70 C.E.? MMT offers important apercu in answering these questions.

MMT© When we published the reconstructed Hebrew text of the ancient MMT manuscript (see p. 127) in our 1991 Facsimile Edition of the Dead Sea Scrolls, scroll scholar and MMT co-editor Elisha Qimron sued for copyright infringement in an Israeli court. Though Qimron's scholarly reconstructions of the text were later shown to be minimal, he won the case. Legal experts continue to debate the court's reasoning and application of copyright law.

In my "Publisher's Foreword," I recounted how university courses were being taught on MMT, but only at schools where the professor had been given a copy by the official editors. Then stray copies went almost everywhere; Strugnell referred to them as "daughters of the Xerox machine." To have an underground photocopy of MMT was a kind of status symbol among scholars.

One of these underground copies found its way to a Polish bibliographer and librarian named Zdzislaw J. Kapera. In 1989 Kapera had organized an international scholarly conference on the Dead Sea Scrolls in Mogilany, a small village south of Krakow. He invited almost all Dead Sea Scroll scholars (and some like me who were not) and enough attended (perhaps out of curiosity to see post-Communist, post-Holocaust Poland) to have a very successful conference. The papers were printed in two volumes by Kapera's own press, which he calls The Enigma Press. In addition, the participants passed the "Mogilany Resolution," which protested the delay in publication of the Dead Sea Scrolls and demanded access to the unpublished texts.

After the conference, Kapera established a journal, *The Qumran Chronicle*, for scholarly articles on the Dead Sea Scrolls. When one of the samizdat copies of MMT fell into Kapera's hands, he promptly published it in *The Qumran Chronicle*. This was the first publication of MMT, a historic accomplishment.

His victory was short-lived, however. The Israel Antiquities Authority and the scholars who controlled the scrolls were furious.

Another Dead Sea Scroll conference was held in Madrid in March 1991, sponsored by the Universidad Complutense. My own invitation to the conference was apologetically cancelled a week before the conference; the organizers succumbed to pressure from the Israel Antiquities Authority, who had their own plans for the conference and they didn't want me interfering. Kapera, the editor of *The Qumran Chronicle*, would be attending and he was their target.

At the conference, the Israeli authorities confronted Kapera in what scroll scholar Philip Davies called a 20th-century version of the Spanish Inquisition. They accused Kapera of stealing, of unethical conduct, and of trampling scholarly norms. They heaped scholarly opprobrium on him. They threatened him with a lawsuit. IAA director Amir Drori sent a letter to Kapera, a letter that he pointedly copied to the head of the Polish Academy of Sciences. The letter accused Kapera of "a violation of all legal, moral and ethical conventions and an infringement on the rights and efforts of your colleagues."

Kapera caved. He agreed to stop distributing copies of *The Qumran Chronicle* containing MMT and to destroy all his office copies. And he apologized in writing for his transgressions.

I recounted all this in my "Publisher's Foreword" to Eisenman and Robinson's collection of scroll photographs. In my best smart-alecky, finger-in-the-eye style, I wrote that "outsiders must still await publication of the commentary [of MMT] if they want to see the text"; then I added in parentheses "(unless they look at Figure 8)" which was included in my "Publisher's Foreword." Figure 8 was a copy of the text of MMT taken from *The Qumran Chronicle*.

Earlier in the "Publisher's Foreword," I had referred to Figure 8 as "Strugnell's transcription of MMT." And I referred to Strugnell's work on the commentary together "with a colleague," whom I did not name. The colleague was in fact Elisha Qimron. For this omission, the heavens fell.

I of course knew that the yet-unpublished commentary was the work of Strugnell *and* Qimron, the young Ben-Gurion University scholar whom Strugnell enlisted to help him understand the intricacies of Jewish law and philology. When I had written about MMT in BAR, I had always identified both men by name. Why, then, did I omit Qimron's name from my "Publisher's Foreword"? Simply because I was being harshly critical and I did not want to bring this criticism down on the head of an innocent, young, untenured professor. I readily admit that no one—or practically no one—believes this, but it is true. I had no reason to omit Qimron's name as "the colleague," except that I did not want to bring obloquy on a young scholar who was not really guilty of any wrongdoing. But Qimron interpreted my omission of his name as depriving him of what he hoped would be his "fame" for his work on MMT.

Qimron filed suit against me and BAR in an Israeli court. It has been called "one of the most dramatic cases ever tried in the history of copyright law,"[26] and elsewhere "a copyright case of biblical proportions."[27]

Elisha Qimron is a small, shy, timid-looking man with an almost expressionless face. In conversation, he looks down, almost apologetically. In a BAR article,[28] I once compared him to Peter Lorre in *The Maltese Falcon*—inscrutable and diffident, glancing here and there. The comparison is apt. For, like Peter Lorre's Joel Cairo, inside his quiet exterior, Qimron is fierce, tenacious, aggressive and tough as nails. And of course, in addition, Qimron is a superb scholar.

His lawyer, Yitzchak Molcho, was one of the most prominent members of the Israeli bar. A close friend of Prime Minister Benjamin Netanyahu and his personal attorney, Molcho was also active politically, eventually serving for a time as head of Israel's negotiating team with Yasser Arafat and the Palestinian Authority. (The question naturally arises as to how Qimron got to know Molcho. Rumor has it that Qimron's sister is married to a well-known Jerusalem physician who knows Molcho.)

As Qimron is a superb scholar, Molcho is a superb lawyer. He knew the Israeli judicial system well and used it to his client's advantage. He virtually wiped up the floor with us.

For example, he did not precede the lawsuit with claims and negotiations for a public apology. He simply filed a formal complaint with the court, initiating the lawsuit. He simultaneously went into court seeking a Temporary Restraining Order. He asked the court to order us to immediately stop selling or distributing the two-volume set of photographs anywhere in the world—in advance of any trial and without notice to us. *And the court granted his motion!* It was all done, in legal jargon, *ex parte*, without the other side participating. Molcho could easily have advised us that he was going to court, in which case we would have had our own law-yer in court to oppose his motion. He had my fax number, demonstrated by the fact that he promptly faxed me the court's order *after* it was entered. This would never have happened in an American court. An American judge would have, at the very least, inquired as to the applicant's efforts to notify the defendant so he could defend himself. The Israeli judge appar-ently felt there was no time even to fax me a notice of the motion, nor time to notify me of the court hearing at which the motion would be decided.

My own efforts at finding the right Israeli lawyer were less successful than Qimron's, despite my legal background. A good friend and excellent lawyer was working with a large Tel Aviv law firm, and I simply retained the lawyer in that firm whom my friend recommended. My lawyer filed a motion to dismiss the case on the grounds that the Israeli court did not have jurisdiction since I was in America and the "Publisher's Foreword" was published in America. The court denied the motion, ruling that the Israeli court had jurisdiction because three copies of the set of photographs had been mailed to Israel by American purchasers and also because the books of photographs were advertised in BAR, which was distributed to a handful of Israeli subscribers.

My lawyer wanted to appeal the ruling. He had good grounds for appeal. But I said no because the jurisdictional defect could easily be cured whenever I came to Israel. If the complaint were served on me in Israel (which would be very easy to do and in fact was done just before I gave a public lecture at Hebrew Union College in Jerusalem), there is no question that the Israeli court would have jurisdiction. I decided to get a new lawyer.

All this proved critical because, according to Israeli procedure, the time had passed for me to demand to see Qimron's drafts of the MMT com-mentary he and Strugnell were writing. I needed this in order to determine what Qimron (as opposed to Strugnell, who had not joined the suit) had supplied to the final draft of the reconstructed text. Once this time period had elapsed, it was up to the court's discretion whether I could "discover" (the technical legal term) Qimron's working papers that would reveal just what his contribution to the reconstructed text of MMT had been.

We filed a motion to obtain this material. Since the time period in which we had a right to obtain the material had passed, it was a matter of the court's discretion. Our motion was denied.

This was a critical loss. It meant that we were never able to determine whether Qimron's claims as to his contribution to the reconstruction were correct. (As it turned out, they were not, but that is getting ahead of the story.) The only thing we could examine was the text of MMT as printed in the attachment to my "Publisher's Foreword." According to scholarly convention, anything added by the scholars to the original text found in the cave was contained in brackets, indicating a reconstruction. But the copy we had printed was such a bad copy that, try as we might, we could not determine the reconstructions. Here and there, we could see—with a magnifying glass—a bracket indicating the beginning of a reconstruction, but we could not find the end. Or, in other cases, we could find an opening bracket, but not a closing one.

At the time, we did not realize that the denial of our motion for discovery would be a critical loss, because even if we could identify the reconstructions, we could not analyze this difficult Hebrew text. I was not a scholar, and there was no scholar in Israel with expertise in this area who had any sympathy for our position.

The core issue in the case was whether Qimron had a copyright in the reconstructions to MMT. If he did, we violated his copyright by "copying" his copyrighted creation without his permission.

At this point, I have to describe what must appear to a non-lawyer to be a subtle distinction in copyright law—the distinction between expression (which is copyrightable) and facts (which are not). Let's say someone says that something looked blue. Anyone can report that it was blue; that fact is not copyrightable. But let's say that someone writes that it gave off a hue that reminded him of the feeling he had when he first studied the early paintings of Picasso's blue period. That way of expressing blueness is copyrightable.

Obviously the line is often difficult to draw. That is what makes lawsuits. How about the reconstructions in MMT? It's especially difficult because the scholars doing the reconstructing are really trying to find the words of the ancient author of the text. And that ancient text is not copyrightable.

We could not even identify the reconstructions that Qimron had made to the text. We were entirely dependent on Qimron's testimony in this regard. In court, Qimron referred only to two "examples" of his reconstructions. In one case, a letter was missing from a word. If the missing word was completed with one Hebrew letter (an *ayin*), it would mean "animal hides"; if completed with another Hebrew letter (an *aleph*), it would means "lights." With Qimron's understanding of Jewish law, he was able to say that the missing letter was an *ayin* and the word meant "hides." As another example, Qimron testified that, with his knowledge of the Jewish context of the discussion in MMT, he was able to place a fragment of MMT horizontally that Strugnell had previously placed vertically.

In her opinion, Judge Dahlia Dorner, who presided at the two-day trial, cited these two and only these two examples as evidence of Qimron's contribution to the reconstruction.

The court was clearly under the impression that these were only two of many examples. But even if there were other examples, was the resulting text of MMT, which had been written by an ancient theologian, copyrightable under 20th-century copyright law? Were the reconstructions themselves copyrightable? Was there enough new "writing" to constitute a "writing" under copyright law?

Judge Dorner decided the answers were "yes."

Regarding my failure to mention Qimron by name, Qimron testified that when he saw himself identified simply as "a colleague," he was "shocked." "I can't describe the feeling," Qimron had told the court. "It's as if someone came and took away the thing I had made by force, telling me: 'Go away! This belongs to me' ... During the years I worked on [MMT], I did almost no other work ... [My] whole family lived very frugally ... When my wife complained, I would tell her, 'Look, this is our life; we will achieve fame.'"

The judge adopted this testimony: When Qimron saw that his name was omitted, wrote the judge, "His dream to achieve fame had vanished ... [He] felt that he had been robbed of his life's work ... He decided that he had to file suit ... to save his honor."

We appealed Judge Dorner's decision to Israel's Supreme Court, which, in a lengthy opinion, affirmed the judgment of the lower court. The court recited that Qimron had worked on the reconstructed text for 11 years. "From the 67 fragments that he received from Strugnell," according to the court, "[Qimron] was able to construct a 121 line text ..., 40 percent of which are completions that are not found in the writing on the fragments."

The court cited the same two examples about which Qimron had testified and which the trial court had cited—the reconstruction of *orot* with an *ayin* rather than an *aleph*, and the placement of a fragment of MMT horizontally rather than vertically. It later turned out that, according to a major Dead Sea Scroll scholar who examined the photographs that we published, these two examples are apparently the only reconstructions that Qimron made. The rest were made by Strugnell in the late 1950s and early 1960s. Moreover, it turned out that Hebrew University professor Menachem Kister had originally suggested the horizontal placement of the MMT fragment. Qimron simply adopted Kister's suggestion.[29]

The court noted that "the primary purpose [of my publication of MMT in my "Publisher's Foreword"] was to publish the Deciphered Text in defiance of the research 'monopoly' given to the international team of scholars." This was of course true, but it was stated as a justification of Judge Dorner's award. "Shanks is not an innocent infringer," said the Supreme Court.

In justification of the amount it awarded for damages, the court noted that Qimron "was prevented from being the first to publish [MMT], and because of this the level of the sales of the book in which he published the Deciphered Text, together with Strugnell, at a later date, was damaged. This violation also injured [Qimron's] reputation and lowered his expected income from lectures."

The court awarded Qimron 100,000 shekels in damages (more than $40,000 at the time). Under Israeli law, the loser in a lawsuit must pay the winner's attorney's fee. With proceedings in two courts, with lawyers' fees for both sides and an award of 100,000 shekels to Qimron, the case cost us over $100,000, a very hefty sum in the mid-1990s.

The case has been widely discussed in the law journals, which have harshly criticized the courts' reasoning and application of the law.[30] One law review article, after referring to this case as "a publisher's nightmare," described the outcome this way: "The final end of such a nightmare, of course, would be an award of damages on a scale unprecedented in the foreign country. This nightmare came true for Hershel Shanks."[31] The leading multi-volume treatise on copyright law in the United States is known as *Nimmer on Copyright*. It is written by David Nimmer, son of the famous legal theorist Melville Nimmer. David Nimmer wrote a 221-page erudite legal article (with over a thousand footnotes) severely critical of the Israel Supreme Court's opinion.[32] "Sound copyright doctrine should always doom the claim of any scholar to copyright over the reconstruction of an antecedent manuscript," he said. "Qimron's suit constitutes an attempt to use copyright law not to promote the progress of science, but as an engine of suppression ... For the wealth of reasons posited above, Qimron lacks copyright over his reconstruction."

In 1994, MMT as reconstructed was published with commentary by Oxford University Press as Volume X in the official Dead Sea Scrolls publication series *Discoveries in the Judaean Desert*. The authors were listed as Elisha Qimron and John Strugnell, not John Strugnell and Elisha Qimron. Many in the Dead Sea Scroll scholarly community have never forgiven Qimron for this grab for notoriety. In the academic community Strugnell would clearly be regarded as the senior author (just as he was in the paper read by Qimron at the scholarly conference in Jerusalem in 1984). Not only had MMT been assigned to Strugnell, but everything in the published volume—from the table of contents to the text itself—makes clear that Strugnell was heavily involved in its writing and scholarship. Moreover, in every other published scroll volume, when a second scholar was brought in to assist the original editor or to take over after an editor's death, the scholar with the original assignment was always listed first. This small detail revealed much about Elisha Qimron's character.

But that was not all. Volume X of *DJD* (as the series is known) also has a unique copyright notice. In every other volume in the series (which has now reached almost 40 volumes), the copyright owner of the text is listed as "Oxford University Press." In Volume X, the copyright owner is "Elisha Qimron." But this notice is followed by a long qualifying sentence beginning: "Without derogating in any rights vesting in the Israel Antiquities Authority with regard to the Scrolls' fragments, photographs and any other material ..." This obviously reflects a hard-fought negotiation between Qimron's attorney and the IAA, which was fearful that Qimron's unusual claims would infringe on its own rights to MMT.

Indeed, Qimron's rights as defined by the court decision were so broad that even after the publication of Volume X a scholar could still be prevented from "copying" MMT as reconstructed by Qimron and Strugnell. Qimron had already written Wacholder and Abegg threatening them with a lawsuit if they made "any use" of the reconstructed text of MMT in reconstructing their own text of MMT from the concordance prepared in the 1950s. If Qimron could assert these rights *before* the publication of Volume X, he would continue to do so *after* the publication of Volume X.

Although today it is generally acknowledged that Qimron will not sue a scholar who quotes (that is, "copies") his reconstruction of MMT, under the court's decision, he would have a good case. Indeed, when Oxford don Geza Vermes published the fourth edition of his translation of the scrolls, he refrained from including a translation of MMT, even though the translation would be his own. Vermes noted that the Israeli court had "ordered [Shanks] to pay $43,000 to Professor Qimron ... In the circumstances, I have decided to postpone the full translation of MMT until the legal storm has blown over." Subsequent editions of Vermes's book do include a translation by Vermes of MMT. While technically (and legally), Vermes and other scholars could be sued for doing this, it is generally agreed that now there is no danger.

Although the copyright notice in Volume X is unique, the paragraph relating to permissions to reproduce the copyrighted material used the standard language: "Enquiries ... concerning reproduction [of copyrighted material] should be sent to the Rights Department, Oxford University Press." So I sent a letter to the Rights Department of Oxford University Press requesting permission to reprint the copyrighted 135-line text of MMT. The request was granted and we published MMT, both the original Hebrew and the English translation, in BAR.[33]

Through his lawyers, Qimron promptly threatened to have us held in contempt of court for publishing MMT in BAR. We of course directed his lawyers to the permission granted by Oxford University Press. Oxford had even waived any fee for the reproduction rights. And nearly 200,000 copies of BAR had now been distributed all over the world.

With some masterful lawyering, Qimron's lawyers managed to convince Oxford University Press that it had made a mistake in granting us permission to reprint MMT. We got another letter from Oxford:

We have been in correspondence with Professor Elisha Qimron's lawyers and have agreed to write to you again ... We feel obliged to protest at the nature of your approach to us for permission: Your request of 12 July 1994 was disingenuous ... because it ignored the previous (March 1993) court injunction against your publishing this text.

In the end, Qimron decided not to pursue the matter further, however. Obviously, it would be impossible to put the genie back into the bottle. Since we had Oxford's permission to do what we did, we could hardly be guilty of contempt of court.

But even that was not the end of the matter. With the publication of Volume X of *DJD*, it became possible to compare what was finally presented as the reconstructed text with the various fragments as they had been photographed and transcribed in the late 1950s and early 1960s. This comparison was made by an internationally prominent Dead Sea Scroll scholar, Florentino Garcia Martinez, when he was asked to review Volume X of *DJD* in *The Journal for the Study of Judaism*. His findings were devastating. He found:

1. The selection of fragments belonging to each manuscript, the totality of the isolated fragments, their transcription [and] translation ... were substantially completed in 1961 [before Qimron was involved with MMT]. 2. The combination of various manuscripts in a more or less unbroken text (...the composite text) was also substantially completed in 1961.

In an article Qimron had written defending and explaining his contributions to the reconstructed text of MMT, he cited only two examples, the same two examples he cited in his court testimony: (1) the reconstruction of an *ayin* rather than an *aleph*, and (2) the horizontal placement of one small fragment.[34] Apparently, these were Qimron's only contributions to the reconstruction of the text! Based on his testimony, however, the court had concluded that he was responsible for a substantial number of reconstructions. The Israel Supreme Court praised the trial judge for having "thoroughly examined the process of Qimron's work"; she had concluded, the Israel Supreme Court said, that Qimron "assembled from 60 to 70 fragments of ... a composite text of 121 lines."[35]

Badly embarrassed by Garcia Martinez's review and its conclusions regarding his contribution to the reconstruction of MMT, Qimron demanded that Garcia Martinez "apologize in print for defaming my character. Needless to say, I reserve the right to utilize all legitimate means at my disposal to redress this wrong if Garcia Martinez chooses to ignore this demand."

We printed Qimron's demand under the headline "Israeli Scholar Bares His Fangs—Again!" But in the end Qimron decided to drop the matter "to avoid further controversy and save my time and energy." Apparently, he had had enough of the courtroom.

I would not want to leave the impression that Qimron made little contribution to the *interpretation* of MMT (in contrast to the *reconstruction* of the text). By all accounts, he made an enormous contribution to the interpretation. But not to the text, only to the interpretation. This interpretation is extensively expressed in Volume X of *DJD*, but we did not copy that. Moreover, interpretation—insofar as it consists of ideas—is not copyrightable. He has a copyright in the expression of his ideas, but not in the ideas themselves. As reflected in Strugnell's foreword to Volume X, Qimron contributed mightily to Strugnell's *understanding* of the text, but not in its reconstruction: "By 1959," wrote Strugnell, "the six copies of MMT had been identified, transcribed, materially reconstructed and partly combined into a common text, but how were such odd fragments to be understood?" That is where Qimron came in.

Perhaps understandably Qimron has barely been able to speak to me when I have seen him at scholarly conferences (which mostly he does not attend). But it is he who won! At the end of the legal case I was left on the floor bloodied (but unbowed). It is I who would more understandably decline to speak to him. Or is it that, as one commentator has remarked, "Regardless of how the various courts in fact ruled, Shanks would appear to be the winner in the grand sense. His attack on the cartel has succeeded."[36]

Paradoxically, my post-lawsuit relationship with Qimron offers a striking contrast to my relationship with Strugnell.

To the end, Strugnell (who died in 2007) maintained that, all things considered, the pace of publication had not been slow. As he wrote in a 2001 publication, "Hysteria and *cris à scandale* are really uncalled for, nor do they reflect any credit upon the knowledge or judgment of such critics."[37] But Strugnell never exuded the vitriol that characterized Qimron. On the contrary, we had a pleasant relationship in his later years after he returned to Cambridge.

The contrast between Strugnell and Qimron is striking. I have had no effect on Qimron's life, except for the obloquy he brought on himself with his litigiousness. Strugnell could claim with considerable justification that I ruined his life. He was dismissed from his position as chief editor of the scroll publication team, he was disgraced by his anti-Semitic interview, and he was forced into retirement from his professorship at Harvard. Yet we could regularly agree to have a meal together whenever I was in Cambridge. I refer to him as a Christian gentleman. But he is also what I call an intellectual anti-Semite. He was not prejudiced against Jews, only against their "silly" religion. He would not burn them at the stake. He would not even deny them tenure. Indeed, he would warmly associate with them. But he could never understand their theological obtuseness.

All this did not prevent the two of us from enjoying our association, although we sometimes (respectfully) disagreed. The marks of his mental and physical deterioration were clear, however. And they soon became worse. I recall the last time I saw him. I had to help him up the stairs to his third-floor flat. I left him alone slumped in a chair in his stench-filled apartment.

FIRST DISCOVERED in 1979 by Sorbonne scholar André Lemaire in a
Jerusalem antiquities shop, this small inscribed ivory pomegranate was
long considered to be the only surviving relic from Solomon's Temple.
Now, some Israeli officials and archaeologists question the authenticity of
this and many other finds that have surfaced on the antiquities market. I
believe the pomegranate inscription is authentic, a position supported by
leading paleographers.

CHAPTER XI

Two Extraordinary Inscriptions— The Pomegranate and the Ossuary

The Ivory Pomegranate Inscription— A Relic from Solomon's Temple—Or Is It?

IN THE SUMMER OF 1979, SORBONNE PROFESSOR André Lemaire was staying in Jerusalem and, as is his wont when in the Holy City, he made the rounds of antiquities dealers, looking for ancient inscriptions. It was July as he recalls it that a dealer invited him to the back of his shop—Lemaire still won't tell me who the dealer was—and showed him a tiny ivory pomegranate that was inscribed on the shoulder of the ball (or grenade). The inscription was engraved in paleo-Hebrew letters, the kind that were used before the Babylonian destruction of Solomon's Temple in the sixth century B.C.E. About a third of the ball had broken off, so the inscription was incomplete. The part that survived, however, could be easily read:

"(Belonging) to the house (temple) of [xxx]h; holy to the priests."

It was a startling inscription. Only the last letter of the name of the God to whom the temple was dedicated survived, an *h*. The rest had

177

broken off. But the missing letters were almost surely the Hebrew letters that would spell *Yahweh*, the personal name of the Israelite God. Based on the shape and form of the letters, the inscription could be dated to the eighth century B.C.E.

In the flat bottom of the pomegranate was a hole, apparently for a rod. The pomegranate itself was the head of a wand or scepter from the Temple. Several of these pomegranate scepters had been recovered, but they had no inscriptions.

Given its date and the restored name of the God, it seemed clear that this pomegranate had once been part of the paraphernalia of the priests in Solomon's Temple! If so, it was the only surviving relic from the Temple.

Lemaire, a former priest who left the priesthood many years ago to marry, is a mild-mannered, soft-spoken, even self-effacing scholar who lives modestly in Paris. He is one of the world's two or three leading paleographers of ancient Semitic inscriptions. He lives for his scholarship and is widely admired not only for his scholarship, but also for his character. His reaction to the inscribed pomegranate was completely in character: He wrote a careful, precise but short note about it that he published (in French, of course) along with black-and-white pictures in the *Revue Biblique*, the arcane journal of Jerusalem's École biblique et archéologique Française. Although he had seen the inscribed pomegranate in the antiquities shop in 1979, the note in the *Revue Biblique* did not appear until 1981.

The publication made not a ripple. No other publication—in French or English—picked up on it.

I met Lemaire at a scholarly conference and was naturally eager to see his scholarship in the pages of BAR. We talked about an article on the Canaanite goddess Asherah, who figures importantly in the Bible. This appeared in the November/December 1984 issue. In the course of preparing this article, however, André (we were soon on a first-name basis) told me of the notice in the *Revue Biblique* about the inscribed ivory pomegranate. Of course, I immediately knew that I wanted to publish a more extensive article about the inscription on the pomegranate in BAR. We postponed the article about Asherah and began working on the pomegranate article.

I wanted to illustrate the article with a full-page color photograph of the pomegranate. Could it be obtained? This was more than four years after Lemaire had seen it in the antiquities shop. The antiquities dealer had told Lemaire that he himself did not own it. Naturally, the owner was never identified. Now Lemaire wanted to know from the dealer if a color picture of it could be obtained for publication. Could the antiquities dealer still locate the owner? Had it changed hands in over four years? Would the owner consent to having a color picture published? With bated breath I waited. The answer was ultimately yes, the antiquities dealer could get a picture of it.

Four years after the publication in the *Revue Biblique*, Lemaire's article appeared in BAR—in the January/February 1984 issue—with a stunning full-page photograph in color.

After we published our article, the next question was where was the pomegranate? Lemaire had not seen it since 1979. And he had no idea who owned it, let alone where it came from. He had carefully examined it for authenticity and was satisfied on this score (a conclusion that was buttressed in my mind by the fact that in at least five years, there had been no attempt to sell it for a huge sum or otherwise to capitalize on it).

I strongly felt that the public should have an opportunity to see the pomegranate with its inscription. In the May/June 1984 issue of BAR, we lamented that no one knows who owns it—except the owner himself and the antiquities dealer who showed it to Lemaire. "We can only plead with the owner to identify himself—or at least allow the Israel Museum to display it anonymously, so that the public can view this beautiful relic, which can now be seen only in BAR's lifelike color photographs." We also called on Israel's attorney general and the director of the antiquities authority to look into the matter.

The best sleuths in Jerusalem, however, could not find the tiny object—a little more than an inch-and-a-half high. We know it was smuggled out of Israel because in 1985 it was displayed in an exhibit in Paris's Grand Palais. Then it disappeared again.

In 1987 a tour guide named Meir Urbach (son of the eminent Talmud scholar Ephraim Urbach), who often escorted dignitaries around Israel, approached the Israel Museum: The pomegranate was available for purchase. The circumstances of the purchase are clouded. A purchase price of $550,000 was negotiated. (The initial purchase price of the pomegranate in the shop where it was first shown to Lemaire was reportedly $3,000.) But of course the museum did not have a half-million dollars lying around. Then suddenly, as if from heaven, the museum received an anonymous gift of one million Swiss francs (at that time about $675,000). This was enough to purchase the pomegranate and pay the ever-present middlemen.

The money was placed in a numbered Swiss bank account and the museum sent Israel's preeminent paleographer, Professor Nahman Avigad of Hebrew University, to Basel to make sure a fake was not substituted for the real thing when the price was paid and the precious package delivered. Avigad came home with the real thing, which was then placed in a special room of the museum with a narrow beam of crystal light focused on it. Amid great fanfare, it was reported that this was the first and only relic ever recovered from Solomon's Temple. The opening of the museum exhibit was the first item on TV news in Israel that night. The museum stayed open until midnight to accommodate the crowds.

Sixteen years later, in 2004, a scientific committee appointed by the Israel Antiquities Authority examined the inscription on the pomegranate and found it to be a forgery.

The Antiquities Market and Looted Antiquities

EVEN IF THE POMEGRANATE WITH ITS INSCRIPTION was authentic and had been used in Solomon's Temple, other questions relating to it arose. Should André Lemaire have been in an antiquities dealer's shop prowling around for such things? Should BAR have given publicity to the artifact by publishing it, thereby adding to its value on the antiquities market?

Many scholars, especially field archaeologists, detest the antiquities market and, derivatively, antiquities dealers. The artifacts they sell, in the jargon of the trade, are "unprovenanced": We don't know where they came from. The dealers usually say they come from old collections that have just been put on the market, but that's an obvious ruse.

If we don't know where they were found, they have no archaeological context that would tell us much more about the object in its setting. Some archaeologists say that an unprovenanced object, without context, is worthless. But this is going too far. I usually reply, "It may be *worth less*, but it is not *worthless*."

But that's not the worst of it. Most of the artifacts you see in the antiquities shops have been looted. These objects represent nothing less than the destruction of our cultural heritage (although some may simply have surfaced after a rain or turned up when a farmer was seeding his field).

I surely agree that looting is a scourge. It is worse than ever today. Looters should be caught and jailed—in small cells. But the fact is that the only way to discourage looting is to catch the looters on the ground. It often helps to involve the locals in the vicinity of a site; when they understand the cultural treasure that is near where they live, they often develop a local culture that effectively discourages looting.

Everyone, including the severest critics of the antiquities market, admits, however, that the campaign of some archaeologists to shun the market has had no effect whatsoever on looting. Looting is worse than ever. So shunning the antiquities market is simply a statement of principle, not a means to reduce looting. Even when legal markets are closed, the market simply migrates elsewhere and the scholarly community never hears of these cultural treasures.

And shunning the antiquities market is not cost-free. It comes with a price. It deprives us of cultural treasures of extreme importance. Think of the Dead Sea Scrolls. Almost all of them were looted and purchased by scholars—of course through middlemen—from the Bedouin who looted them. The scrolls are generally recognized as the greatest archaeological find of the 20th century—and often dismissed by scholars who want to shut down antiquities shops as the exception to the rule concerning shunning the antiquities market. Of course there are many others who argue that we must look at objects that come to us via the market.

Recently, a three-foot-high stela from the market enriched our understanding of the Jewish roots of Christian messianism. In addition to being reported in BAR,[38] it was reported on the front page of the Sunday *New York Times*.

Another recently surfaced inscription provides the historic background to characters in the Hanukkah story.[39]

A royal inscription in which a Moabite king brags of his military victories and his great construction projects was found in an antiquities shop by an Israeli scholar and is now displayed in the Israel Museum.[40]

More than 90 percent of ancient coins, which teach us so much about our past, come from the antiquities market.

Recent books and articles in BAR reveal a culture of magic, illuminated by strange inscriptions in so-called Aramaic incantation bowls, virtually all of which come from the antiquities market.[41]

Are we to ignore all of this because the objects come from the antiquities market and were probably looted?

Othmar Keel, a distinguished Swiss scholar who has spent a lifetime studying the iconography on seals and other archaeological artifacts, most of which are unprovenanced, told me in an interview, "I don't think a history of the ancient Near East can be written without relying on unprovenanced material."[42] Indeed, all leading paleographers—Frank Cross, Joseph Naveh, Kyle McCarter, Dennis Pardee, Pierre Boudreuil, Felice Israel and, of course, all Dead Sea Scroll scholars—publish and rely on unprovenanced finds. As Alan Millard, a leading British scholar, told a forgery conference, "If they're not published, they are virtually destroyed."

For the scholars who shun any contact with the antiquities market, however, it is a matter of moral principle. It is not simply a difference of opinion: Any contact with the antiquities market and its unprovenanced artifacts is consummate evil.

Taking this position, the Archaeological Institute of America (AIA) and the American Schools of Oriental Research (ASOR), the two major scholarly organizations of archaeologists in the United States, will not publish unprovenanced artifacts in their scholarly journals. Nor will they permit papers on artifacts that come from the antiquities market to be read at their scholarly conferences.

Yet they are hypocritical: They interpret the prohibition to apply only to the first publication of the artifact or inscription. After it is published elsewhere, it can be discussed in their journals. Andrew Vaughn, the executive secretary of ASOR, once explained to me how he (and many others) get around the prohibition: He wrote his doctoral dissertation on ancient seals, many of which are unprovenanced and in the hands of private collectors whom he visited. In order to discuss the objects in ASOR's journal, he had to "jump through hoops," to use his language. First, he had to publish the unprovenanced materials in journals that had no objection to the publication of artifacts that come from the antiquities market. Then he would publish articles discussing them in ASOR's own scholarly journal.

Many junior, especially untenured, faculty members are fearful of any involvement with unprovenanced material, lest this damage their prospects for advancement or tenure. As I said, to those scholars who despise the antiquities market, this is not a matter of debate. It involves the difference between rectitude and evil. William (Bill) Dever, my long-time friend who figures in an earlier chapter of this autobiography, is one of America's two or three most distinguished archaeologists. He has recently retired, so he is not subject to the kind of pressure that would affect a younger untenured professor. But Dever is a field archaeologist and even he is affected by those who shun the market on principle, as illustrated by the following story:

We recently published an article on some fascinating small house shrines that were unprovenanced and came from the well-known collector of biblically related artifacts, Shlomo Moussaieff. As a result of this article, another house shrine was brought to our attention in the collection of a collector who wished to remain anonymous lest he be subject to the vitriol that some sections of the academy now heap on collectors. This newly surfaced house shrine was unusual in another respect. It was apparently consecrated to a divine couple, as indicated by the double (two-seated) throne inside. Did this deity have a wife? This is a subject of deep interest to Bill Dever. So I asked him to write an article for BAR that treated this house shrine as it related to the much-discussed question of whether Yahweh, the early Israelite God, had a consort. Bill said he would write the article, but only if the house shrine were previously published, so that he could say that he was just discussing an unprovenanced arti-fact that had been previously published. I agreed. We simply published a picture of the house shrine on the page preceding Bill's article, so he came within the exception to the rule against publishing anything from the antiquities market.[43]

I sometimes wonder whether the reason field archaeologists so roundly condemn any association with unprovenanced artifacts is that these artifacts are often much more exciting than the finds dug up in professional excavations. Not that they are more important. There is no comparison of what we learn from unprovenanced artifacts to what we learn from professional excavations. The latter involve much detail, often dull but necessary detail, and careful, often lengthy and painstaking study, but they sometimes lack the excitement and immediacy of an important relic. And field archaeologists may miss this, especially when they see the attention lavished on exciting unprovenanced finds.

Why is it that what may appear to be the most dramatic artifacts are often found by looters rather than professional archaeologists? Certainly professional archaeologists trumpet their most stunning finds—when they find them. But they do so less often than the looters. "The looters know where to look," says Shlomo Moussaieff. Often the most beautiful artifacts are found in tombs, a favorite target of looters. But this is not the whole story. The puzzle remains.

The Ossuary Inscription—"James, Son of Joseph, Brother of Jesus"

IN 2002, EIGHT YEARS AFTER WE PUBLISHED Lemaire's article on the ivory pomegranate, I was having dinner with him in a fine Jerusalem fish restaurant across from the King David Hotel when he told me about some-thing that had recently come to his attention. He had been at a gathering in Shlomo Moussaieff's elegant apartment overlooking the Mediterranean from the 14th floor (the whole floor) of a fashionable Herzliya hotel, when

Lemaire was approached by another collector, Oded Golan, who asked Lemaire if he would help him read an inscription. Lemaire later went to Golan's apartment in downtown Tel Aviv to look at the inscription. It was engraved on an ossuary, a limestone box in which the bones of the deceased were placed about a year after death, when the flesh had desiccated and fallen away. This was a Jewish custom mainly in the Jerusalem area that lasted for about a century, ending with the Roman destruction of the Holy City in 70 C.E. The inscription that Golan was having trouble reading was indeed a difficult inscription to decipher. One of Israel's leading paleographers, Ada Yardeni, had already looked at it and struggled to read it. Lemaire did too. It took him several days to decipher the heavily cursive script. The inscription indentified the woman whose bones had once lain within: Although unnamed, she was the daughter of Samuel the priest and was brought from Apamea to be buried in Jerusalem.

Before Lemaire left, Golan showed the scholar pictures of some other pieces that he kept in a warehouse, unlike the prize pieces featured in the vitrines of his apartment. One was another ossuary, this one with an inscription that was easily read:

"James, son of Joseph, brother of Jesus."

It was not a particularly elegant looking ossuary. It was slightly trapezoidal rather than rectangular, as if the manufacturer had not been very competent. The box was about 21 inches long, 10 inches wide and 12 inches high. The only decoration was a single framing line and two very faint rosettes on the long side opposite the inscription. The rosettes were so faint Golan hadn't even noticed them.

I later talked to Golan about why he hadn't appreciated the importance of this inscription. "I never realized God could have a brother," he said, hardly a surprising comment for an Israeli Jew. Moreover, all three names in the inscription were quite common in the first century. Even someone more familiar than Golan with the New Testament would have difficulty recognizing the name James on the ossuary. The reason is that the Aramaic letters on the ossuary spell "Yaakov." This is the Hebrew name of the patriarch Jacob, easily recognizable by any Israeli. It takes a special arcane bit of knowledge to realize that Aramaic Yaakov came to be translated, via

Sorbonne scholar André Lemaire, who first published the ivory pomegranate inscription and the James ossuary inscription.

the Greek then Latin of the New Testament, as James in English rather than Jacob. So it was entirely understandable that Golan hadn't recognized "Yaakov" as "James." (Incidentally, if the inscription was forged, as some would later claim, the forger would have to know that Aramaic Yaakov became James in English translations of the New Testament.)

When Lemaire told me about the ossuary at our Jerusalem dinner, I naturally suggested an article about it in BAR. Two questions immediately presented themselves of which I was well aware: (1) As with any item from the market, was the inscription a forgery?; (2) Was this Yaakov a reference to James, the brother of Jesus of Nazareth (Matthew 13:55; Mark 6:3), leader of the Jerusalem church following Jesus' crucifixion (Acts 15; Galatians 2:9)? Or was this simply another James whose father happened to be named Joseph and who happened to have a brother named Jesus?

Based on his paleographic study, Lemaire was confident that the inscription was authentic. Nevertheless, I thought it the better part of caution to have the inscription examined by a scientific expert. I contacted Amos Bein, head of the Geological Survey of Israel, who agreed to assign two members of his staff to study it, for which the magazine paid. Their examination found nothing suspicious.

I also consulted one of the world's leading Aramaicists and Dead Sea Scroll scholar, Father Joseph Fitzmyer, who lived in Washington. His examination was especially important because he found a problem. The word "brother" was spelled incorrectly in the inscription—or rather in a way that was not adopted until hundreds of years after the time of Jesus.

When Father Fitzmyer proceeded to research the matter, however, he found the same spelling in one of the Dead Sea Scrolls. Then he also found this spelling in another ossuary inscription. "I stand corrected," he told me. The implication of this was that if this inscription was a forgery, the forger had to know Aramaic better than Joe Fitzmyer!

I was satisfied that the inscription was authentic and I was comfortable publishing it. The second question was more difficult: Was this Jesus the Jesus who is called Jesus of Nazareth in the New Testament?

Lemaire thought it was. That was good enough for me to publish it, although this kind of thing can never be established with certainty. Lemaire's conclusion was based on a statistical study of the size of the population at the time, the frequency of these names (found on all inscriptions from the period) and the probability that the three names would occur in this order as James, followed by father Joseph, followed by brother Jesus. Lemaire concluded that there were probably 20 people in Jerusalem at the time who would fit this profile. That would give it a 5 percent chance that this Jesus was Jesus of Nazareth. But at this point, another factor enters the judgment. We have thousands of ossuaries. Most people 2,000 years ago were identified simply as "X son of Y." This formula appears frequently on ossuary inscriptions. Indeed, there are at least two ossuaries inscribed "Jesus son of Joseph." The names were so common that no one thought to relate these ossuary inscriptions to Jesus of Nazareth. But it is very unusual to mention a brother on an ossuary. Indeed, in all the known ossuaries, this has occurred only one other time. Lemaire suggests two possible reasons for mentioning a brother in an ossuary inscription: First, because the brother is responsible for the burial; or, second, because the brother is well known and the deceased would want to be associated with him. It is the latter that substantially increases the likelihood that the Jesus referred to in this inscription is Jesus of Nazareth. On this basis, Lemaire concluded that "it seems very probable" that this Jesus is indeed Jesus of Nazareth.

Before we published Lemaire's article, I was asked to appear on a television program in Toronto. By coincidence, I also received a call from a TV producer from Toronto named Simcha Jacobovici, who wanted to talk to me about working with him. I declined the opportunity, although

I was going to be in Toronto. When I resisted his importuning, he asked me if I would be willing to give an interview to the Toronto newspapers, including the *Toronto Globe*. I agreed to this. Of course, Simcha arranged the interview in his own offices, so naturally I had to talk with him as well.

I admit I was impressed with him. He was intelligent, informed and articulate. He had produced several award-winning programs, including one entitled "Falasha: Exile of the Black Jews." In the end, I confided to him about our forthcoming article on the James ossuary. We agreed to make a television production about it.

In November of that year, the American Schools of Oriental Research, the Society of Biblical Literature and the American Academy of Religion would be holding their annual meetings in Toronto, which would bring together more than 8,000 archaeologists and biblical scholars. I contacted the Royal Ontario Museum and arranged for the museum to exhibit the James ossuary in a special room during the meetings and for a few weeks afterward, provided of course that Golan could get permission from the Israel Antiquities Authority (IAA) to take the ossuary out of the country.

Golan applied for a temporary export permit, noting on the application that the shipment was insured for a million dollars and quoting the inscription on the ossuary. He had no difficulty in obtaining the permit from the Israel Antiquities Authority. But this would later be the source of intense enmity of the IAA's director, retired general Shuka Dorfman, toward me. I was completely unaware of it at the time. All I knew was that Golan, the owner of the ossuary, had applied for a temporary export permit and that the permit was granted. (To this day, Shuka will not speak to me. Nor will he permit his archaeologists to write for BAR. We still manage to report on all the important finds from IAA excavations, however.)*

Back in Washington, we held a press conference on October 21, 2002, featuring Lemaire's article on the ossuary. The next day the ossuary was on the front page of the *New York Times* and practically every other paper in the world. This was soon followed by intense media coverage in *Time*, *Newsweek*, etc. as well as on ABC, NBC, PBS, CNN, etc.

---

*Late bulletin: In January 2010 Shuka and I had a sulkha (an Arab peace meal) in Jerusalem. We are now friends.

THE JAMES OSSUARY sits proudly in its display case during a special 2002 exhibit at Toronto's Royal Ontario Museum (top). The inscription on the ossuary (bottom) reads "James, son of Joseph, brother of Jesus." It has been declared a forgery by a committee of the Israel Antiquities Authority. But BAR, together with every leading paleographer who has opined on the matter, has defended the authenticity of the inscription.

When the ossuary arrived in Canada, the museum carefully transported it from the airport and proceeded to unpack it. It was enclosed in a cardboard box rather than a wooden crate. Inside, it was encased only in layers of bubble wrap. When museum officials removed the bubble wrap, they found the limestone box inside had cracked into five separate pieces. The front page of the *Sun*, Canada's leading tabloid, blared in 72-point white type on a black background, "Oh, My God—2,000-year-old relic linked to Jesus cracked on way to ROM."

Until this time, the owner of the ossuary, Oded Golan, had requested anonymity in our coverage. And we respected that. But the Israeli newspaper

Queen: Butler didn't do it Pages 3, 28-29

THE SATURDAY SUN

$1.99

POWER PLAY

NHL STICKERS!
COUPON, PAGE 2 ■ DETAILS, PAGE S11

Details: Page S28

Don't Miss Tonight's Draw!

IMAGINE THE FREEDOM

Vol. 17 No. 6   TORONTO, NOVEMBER 2, 2002   128 PAGES   WEATHER MAP: Page 65

OH, MY GOD!

2,000-year-old relic linked to Jesus cracked on way to ROM
— Page 3

AFTER

BEFORE

— Sharks' Biblical Archaeology Review/AP

— Royal Ontario Museum/Reuters

A LIMESTONE box said to have contained the bones of Jesus' brother James was found to have cracks in it yesterday when the crate it was travelling in was opened by Royal Ontario Museum staff. The box, called an ossuary, arrived in Toronto after being shipped from Israel via New York. ROM said it will be repaired and ready for its international public debut Nov. 16.

WHILE EN ROUTE to its world premiere at the Royal Ontario Museum, the James ossuary broke into several pieces. As shown on the front page of the Canadian *Sun*, one of the cracks even went through the inscription. Fortunately, museum conservators easily repaired the fractures and, in the process, gained significant insight into the inscription's authenticity.

Ha'aretz soon smoked him out, and the paparazzi descended on him. He soon became a very public figure.

After the ossuary broke, I asked Oded (we were now on a first-name basis) whether he was going to make a claim against the insurance company or against the shipping company that had packed the ossuary. Despite the fact that he had engaged what he described as the leading company in Israel for such purposes (Atlas/Peltransport Ltd.), it had been packed unbelievably poorly, in a way that would almost guarantee that it would break. Yet Oded said he was not interested in making a claim. The money, he said, was unimportant. Strange. Why was this? Was it because he knew there was no monetary damage? Was there no monetary damage as a result of the breakage because it was fake—and Oded knew it? It is this kind of reasoning that began to build the case against him. (Remember this later in the book when we consider his storing the ossuary on an unused toilet on the roof of his apartment building.)

Fortunately, the Royal Ontario Museum had a superb restorer on staff who mended the ossuary prior to the exhibit. The cracks were barely visible. One of the cracks ran through the inscription and this gave the museum the opportunity to examine the inscription from the side, where any evidence of forgery would more likely be visible. All of the museum's extensive tests confirmed the authenticity of the inscription.[44] Its conclusion was the same as the Israel Geological Survey's earlier examination—the ossuary inscription was old and authentic.

The ossuary was exhibited in its own room in the museum against a wall that dramatically proclaimed, "Jacques, fils de Joseph, frère de Jesus." We arranged a special viewing for the scholars at the conferences. Even scholars closely affiliated with ASOR snuck in to see it, despite the organization's policy statement that cautioned members to refrain from exhibiting unprovenanced artifacts. While ASOR officially ignored the exhibit, the Society for Biblical Literature held a special session on the ossuary in the grand ballroom of the hotel where it was meeting. The session was attended by nearly 1,200 scholars, many times more than any of the hundreds of other sessions at the meetings. André Lemaire spoke at length, explaining why he considered it clearly authentic, based on his paleographic examination. The former president of ASOR, Eric Meyers, nevertheless questioned the authenticity of the inscription simply on the basis that it had come from the antiquities market, a position that was consistent with his intense animosity toward the antiquities market.

The public flocked to the museum exhibit—more than 100,000 in seven weeks, forming lines around the block. The museum wanted to extend the exhibit for another month. But the IAA, by this time furious at me, would not extend the permit even for a month. They wanted the ossuary back in Israel.

In the months after the exhibit, Simcha Jacobovici and I met in Tel Aviv to film a TV special about the ossuary in Oded's apartment. And New Testament scholar Ben Witherington and I wrote a book about the ossuary and the character of James that was published by a major American publisher.[45]

Later, like the tiny pomegranate inscription, the James ossuary inscription was declared to be a forgery.

But was it?

CHAPTER XII

A Royal Israelite Inscription— The Yehoash Plaque?

EXACTLY WHEN THE YEHOASH (OR JEHOASH IN English) plaque surfaced on the antiquities market is unknown. Unlike the ivory pomegranate inscription and the James ossuary inscription, the Yehoash inscription was suspected of being a forgery from the moment it was seen by senior paleographers.

It consists of 15 lines of ancient Hebrew script on an 11-by-9-inch black stone plaque and describes the collection of money for repairs to the Jerusalem Temple. It closely parallels the descriptions of the same events in 2 Kings 12:5–17 and 2 Chronicles 24:4–14. According to the Bible, Yehoash reigned more than a century after Solomon built the Temple and by that time it needed repairs. If authentic, the Yehoash inscription would be the first royal Israelite (Judahite) inscription ever discovered. If authentic, it could well have been a plaque that had actually hung in the Temple of Solomon—or an ancient copy thereof. Indeed, rumors had it that it had been discovered in the Muslim cemetery just outside the eastern wall of the Temple Mount, perhaps when someone was digging a new grave. So it could well have come from the Temple. Or it might have come from the area of recent extensive unsupervised Arab excavations on the Temple Mount.[46]

Early on the Yehoash inscription was shown under mysterious circumstances in a Jerusalem hotel to Israel's senior paleographer, Joseph

TOO GOOD TO BE TRUE? This 15-line Hebrew inscription, known as the Yehoash inscription, describes repairs to the Jerusalem Temple by King Yehoash in the ninth century B.C.E. Like the ivory pomegranate and the James ossuary, the inscription is currently at the center of controversy as to whether it is a forgery or authentic.

Naveh, who immediately thought that it was probably a forgery. It was then offered to the Israel Museum, which had it in its possession for more than a year and a half while examining it—and ultimately declined to purchase it. Too dangerous.

It was also taken to the Geological Survey of Israel which found it to be authentic.

After that, the plaque disappeared.

Rumors about the plaque swirled around the antiquities market. Then articles about the rumors were published in *Ha'aretz* and the *Jerusalem Post.* The matter thus came to the attention of then Education Minister Limor Livnat. Here was an inscription that, if authentic, would provide evidence for Israel's claim to the Temple Mount. If authentic, it would demonstrate the accuracy of the biblical accounts. It might even prove that the Temple was decorated in gold, because gold globules were found in the patina. What was the Israel Antiquities Authority (then a part of the Education Ministry) going to do to locate the inscription? Livnat demanded to know. Locating the plaque then became a top priority of the antiquities authorities. Forgery did not seem to be a question at that time.

But locating the plaque was not an easy task. At one point, the owner of the plaque was represented by one of Israel's leading law firms, Israel, Herzog, Fox and Neeman. One of these lawyers, Isaac Herzog, was a member of the Knesset, Israel's parliament. But the lawyer-client privilege prevented the police from requiring the lawyer to identify his client. The owner of the plaque and its location remained elusive.

In the days that followed, Amir Ganor, head of the IAA's theft investigation unit, intensified his search for the plaque. The mystery man who had brought the Yehoash plaque to the Geological Survey for examination had told the geologist that he had gotten the geologist's name from Oded Golan. Ganor was thus alerted to the name Oded Golan. Ganor's sixth sense also led him to suspect the Tel Aviv collector of having the Yehoash inscription: Golan had the ossuary. What about the Yehoash plaque? Ganor was already building up a head of animosity against this fellow over the ossuary. Not that Ganor (yet) thought the ossuary was a forgery, but rather it was Golan's underhanded way of dealing with it—not telling the IAA about it—that angered Ganor. Ganor had paid a routine visit to the collector's apartment not long before the world learned of the ossuary, just looking for looted items and taking the temperature of the antiquities market. Golan hadn't even mentioned the ossuary that was about to explode in Ganor's face. Ganor was "furious" at Golan for not telling him about the ossuary.[47]

When Ganor finally caught the mysterious man who had taken the Yehoash plaque to Naveh and then to the Israel Museum and the Geological Survey—a man named Tzur who often used the name Tzuriel—Tzur identified Golan as "the guy that trained me to do everything." According to one reporter who talked to Ganor, Tzur identified Golan as the owner of the plaque.[48] This was music to Ganor's ears. It confirmed his suspicions, although at this point the issue was still not forgery, but the location of an immensely valuable looted object.

According to the same source, when Golan denied any connection to the plaque, Ganor obtained a search warrant for Golan's apartment—and found nothing. Ganor grilled Golan daily for 30 days, from late February to mid-March 2003, but came away with no information about the plaque. He did learn about Golan's warehouses where he stored antiquities; Ganor searched those as well—still no plaque. Finally, with Golan in handcuffs, he took Golan to his parents' apartment during the night. Golan's parents were sleeping. The banging on the door awakened them; they let the police and their handcuffed son inside. The search of their apartment proceeded as Golan and his parents looked on. The search was completed, all but the parents' bedroom, without finding anything.

When the police began to enter the bedroom, Golan broke. He said he would deliver the Yehoash plaque if they would not press charges against him for lying that he knew nothing about it. Two days later, Golan's lawyer delivered the Yehoash plaque to the police.[49]

It's a strange story. It didn't make sense to me. Why did Golan resist for so long? Why didn't Golan tell them earlier that at one time he had the stone in his possession and that, as he now claims, it belonged to an Arab dealer from East Jerusalem? Why did Golan break only when they were going to search his parents' bedroom? After all, there was nothing in there. I talked to Amir Ganor about what he thought: "Why didn't Golan tell you sooner?" I asked. Ganor had no explanation.

I then talked to Golan himself. His story didn't make much more sense than Ganor's. Golan claims that he had given the Arab antiquities dealer (who has since died) a promise that if Golan did not return it, he would be liable for its value. Golan admits he lied when he denied having the inscription in his possession, but he did not lie when he denied owning it. He claims from the beginning he told the investigators that he could get the plaque for them, but they would not accept this offer. It all sounds fuzzy.

In any event, the IAA now had the plaque. On May 17, 2003, the IAA held its own press conference, featuring Education Minister Limor Livnat with her finger pointing to the Hebrew writing on the plaque, proving that the Jewish Temple was a historical reality, that it was not the fiction that a chorus of Arab "temple deniers" had been feeding to the media.

Until now, the IAA's (and Ganor's) focus had been looting, not forgery. Ganor felt certain that the James ossuary had been looted—and it probably was. And of course the Yehoash plaque was too. An Israeli law provides that any antiquity recovered after 1978 belongs to the state. If the ossuary had been looted after this date, it belonged to Israel, not to Oded Golan. Similarly with the Yehoash plaque. Ganor and the IAA wanted these extraordinary relics for the State of Israel.

True, questions as to authenticity had been raised. But as for the James ossuary inscription, the forgery claim had not been made by what scholars consider "serious" people. Apart from a woman whom no one in the community of paleographers had ever heard of (Rochelle Altman), there were people like Eric Meyers who despised the antiquities market and raised the issue only in general terms—anything that comes from the market is likely to be a forgery, especially if it is "too good to be true." As for the Yehoash plaque, it had yet to be studied before any question would arise as to its authenticity. At this point, neither Naveh nor the Israel Museum was prepared to declare the Yehoash inscription a forgery and the Geological Survey scientists had declared it authentic.

What changed the focus to forgery? The most important thing was that the James ossuary and the Yehoash plaque were both traced to the same source at the same time—Oded Golan. Ganor suspected that Golan badly needed money and that he desperately forged two mind-boggling artifacts, one after the other, to relieve his financial situation. "In the pressure to get money quickly, he made a mistake. He put out the [James] ossuary and the [Yehoash] stone at the same time," Ganor is quoted as saying.[50]

And of course the IAA and Ganor were delighted to pursue Golan for a more serious crime than buying looted antiquities or lying to investigators. They were already irate because Golan had squirreled the ossuary out of the country without telling them. Similarly with the Yehoash plaque: Golan had passionately resisted divulging the fact that he was in possession of it.

And there was something else. In the course of their searches of Golan's apartment and his warehouses, the IAA found what it took to be forger's tools and accessories: a dentist's drill, bags of soil labeled by the archaeological site from which they came, wax, chemicals. There was more to come: In another box, the police found drawings of seals and half-completed archaeological artifacts. One of the drawings was for a seal of Jotham, a Judahite king who had ruled during the second half of the eighth century B.C.E. Ganor felt he had discovered a forgery factory. Director Shuka Dorfman announced that the IAA had discovered a forgery factory that had been operating for 15 years.[51]

Finally, when the police came to seize the James ossuary from Golan's apartment after it had returned from Canada, they discovered that Golan had been keeping it on the roof of his apartment building in an old unused toilet room that had been illegally constructed long ago. The ossuary was wrapped in layers of bubble wrap and sealed in a cardboard box, which had been placed on the toilet. The police tore open the box, unwrapped the ossuary and placed it back on the toilet. They then took photographs of it and released them to the media. Here was clear proof that Golan knew that it was a forgery: If it had been authentic and valuable, he would surely not have stored it up there on a toilet. That he did so demonstrated that he knew it was not a valuable artifact. So the police reasoned. Golan, on the other hand, claimed that he was fearful that his now-famous ossuary might be stolen from his apartment by robbers. The locked room on the roof, he said, was the safest place in the apartment building.

Paradoxically, the seizure of the Yehoash plaque provided an argument for its authenticity. When the police transported the plaque from Tel Aviv to Jerusalem, they broke it! Just how is not clear. Did they drop it? Did it occur as a result of the rumble or bump of the police vehicle? The plaque previously had a crack that ran through four lines of the inscription and when the plaque broke, it broke through this crack. This provided an opportunity to view the inscription from the side.

As the crime changed from looting to forgery, the identification of the forger or forgers became the new focus. Of course, Oded Golan was the prime suspect. The ossuary was admittedly his and the Yehoash plaque had been found in his possession. Besides, he appeared to have materials and equipment that would support his guilt.

But who else was involved?

It seemed unlikely that one person could possess all the skills necessary to forge either of these artifacts—and surely not Oded Golan. It was even more unlikely that one person could have forged both of them. Clearly the IAA was focusing on Golan. But if there had to have been more than one forger, who else was involved?

Rochelle Altman, the hitherto unknown expert in scripts who quickly obtained publicity for her comments, used her expertise to identify the forger of the ossuary inscription: none other than Shlomo Moussaieff, the 80-year-old multimillionaire with the world's greatest collection of biblically centered antiquities. Moussaieff made much of his fortune from a jewelry store he owned in the International Hilton in London, so he would have all the tools he needed to forge the inscription.

In Jerusalem the most commonly mentioned suspect was Robert Deutsch, a leading antiquities dealer who had also become a scholar. Studying for two Ph.D.s, one at Tel Aviv University and the other at Haifa University, Deutsch had written numerous books on antiquities in private collections. Some of them were coauthored with Professor Michael Helzer of Haifa University; others with André Lemaire.

At a conference at Harvard, deputy director of the IAA Uzi Dahari told me in front of others that the conspiracy of forgers included "an honored Israeli archaeologist."[52] To this day, Dahari has not identified him (or her), however.

André Lemaire was also a suspect in the rumor mill, something that hurt him deeply.

A mysterious Egyptian named Marko was another suspect. Marko was a jeweler who had worked on and off for Golan for 15 years, sometimes staying in his apartment. Marko eventually got himself an Israeli girlfriend. He apparently helped Golan with his pottery restorations. The big question was whether he forged the ossuary inscription and the Yehoash inscription. The Israeli police sent a team to Cairo to interview Marko (apparently illegally because a foreign government needs Egyptian permission to conduct a criminal investigation in Egypt). Marko flatly denied that he had ever inscribed something on an ossuary, but the police interview was about the inscription on the Yehoash plaque. Later the CBS program *60 Minutes* interviewed Marko with a hidden microphone and camera. In the broadcast transcript, Marko again denied that he had made the ossuary inscription. When he was shown a picture of the Yehoash inscription, he said he had made things "just like that." I wondered just what that meant—"just like that." So I asked *60 Minutes* for the complete transcript of their interview with Marco. They turned me down. "*60 Minutes* knows how to ask questions," I wrote, "But it is not as good at answering them ... The only basis for *60 Minutes* to deny [us this transcript is that it] might show that the producers produced a biased report." Marko has refused to return to Israel. I obtained his telephone numbers in Egypt, but the numbers had been disconnected.

There was also another suspect. Contributing BAR editor Suzanne Singer and I had gone to London for a conference at the British Museum and decided to pay a visit to Shlomo Moussaieff in his mammoth apartment on Grosvenor Square. When we arrived, Moussaieff introduced us to a guest who had preceded us—Amir Ganor, head of the IAA's fraud unit. He had come to London to interview Moussaieff as part of the IAA's investigation in the burgeoning forgery crisis. I had not met Ganor before, although I of course knew of him. Moussaieff immediately informed me that I was "under suspicion" of being part of the forgery conspiracy. André Lemaire was also "under suspicion," Moussaieff added. I broke out laughing. But Ganor quickly confirmed that I was indeed under suspicion and that when I would next come to Israel, I would become part of the investigation and could be called in for questioning.

I didn't know whether to go on laughing or to become enraged. So I decided to "confess": I told Ganor that I had originally received a call from Oded Golan in which he offered me a thousand dollars a month for ten years if I would publish an article about the ossuary inscription. I replied to Golan that that was not enough money. I then received a call from Lemaire urging me to accept the offer because he, too, had been offered a thousand dollars a month for ten years and he would not get his money if I refused to take Golan's money and publish the article. I told Lemaire that I would publish the article only if, in addition to the money I was to receive from Golan, Lemaire would give me half of the money he was to receive. Lemaire agreed—and that's how the article was published in BAR.

It was clear, even to Ganor, that I was joking. It was time for lunch, and Moussaieff took us all out to an elegant London restaurant, where we had a pleasant conversation.

As late as 2006, Ganor told a journalist that Shanks "is connected. I don't know how."[53] By 2007, however, Ganor confirmed that I was no longer under investigation, adding that "He is a very good journalist."[54]

Uzi Dahari, who had chaired the IAA committee that found the ossuary inscription to be a forgery, had a very different view. I invited him to participate in a scholarly session at an SBL conference in San Antonio. He took the occasion to castigate me:

"I accuse (publicly, not legally) the magazine BAR and its editor Hershel Shanks with being the catalyst for [a] series of forgeries ... Mr. Shanks, you are playing with fire when you continually publish finds of this nature."[55]

More recently (September 2008), Yuval Goren, a Tel Aviv University clay petrologist and the principal scholar who supposedly has uncovered proof that the inscriptions are forgeries, wrote that it is "crystal clear" that

I have played a "pivotal role" in the forgery, as he "always suspected, but now became evident."[56]

One thing seems clear: No single person could possess all the skills, both physical and academic, required to forge these inscriptions, and if there were a conspiracy, there would have been at least one "leaker" (a point made by both Gaby Barkay and Ronny Reich at our forgery conference). To induce a leak, we offered in BAR a reward of $50,000 for information leading to the arrest and conviction of the forger of the Yehoash inscription.[57] There have been no takers.

As the list of suspects grew, so did the list of suspected forgeries. I called it a "forgery frenzy."[58] According to a *New Yorker* article, between 100 and 200 artifacts from the biblical period to the Roman destruction of the Temple are "currently suspected by the Antiquities Authority to be forgeries."[59] Eric Meyers, with no expertise whatever in detecting forgeries and with no basis whatever, estimated that between 30 and 40 percent of the inscriptions in the Israel Museum are fakes.[60]

The IAA had no doubt about either the Yehoash plaque inscription or the James ossuary inscription. Both were forgeries in its view. It early on organized a committee of experts under the direction of deputy IAA director Uzi Dahari to study the two objects and determine whether they were authentic or forgeries. In less than three months, the committee completed its work. On June 15, 2004, the committee met "in order to arrive at a collective conclusion." On June 20, that conclusion was announced at a press conference: Both the James ossuary inscription and the Yehoash inscription were forgeries.

CHAPTER XIII

"The Forgery Trial of the Century" and Beyond

IT WAS NOT LONG BEFORE THE AUTHENTICITY of the ivory pomegranate inscription also became an IAA target, although it had been prominently displayed in the Israel Museum for 16 years. Instead of a formal accusation, it began with rumors. These rumors were so persistent, as I previously noted, that in March 2004 they were finally reported in the press.

I called James Snyder, the director of the Israel Museum, to find out what he knew. "I only know what I read in the newspapers," he told me. "Nothing has been presented to us. We are always willing to look at evidence that one of our pieces is a forgery, but in this case there is nothing to look at. We had it carefully examined before purchasing it by independent experts outside the museum and they raised no question about its authenticity."

Snyder's statement meant that the pomegranate had not been out of the vitrine in which it was exhibited. The rumors about its being a forgery could not have been based on an examination of the pomegranate itself. No one could conclude anything about whether it was authentic or a fake only by looking at it through the glass enclosure. Snyder attributed the rumors to a less-than-honorable motive: "It is too bad that it [the rumor] has just been presented to the media as a platform for publicity," he told me.

· Of course, there might be bases for the pomegranate rumors other than an examination of the inscription. For instance, someone involved in making the forgery might have confessed or something might have been found relating to the fashioning of the forgery. Because the rumors seemed to emanate from the IAA, at least one newspaper (*Ha'aretz*) went to the IAA for confirmation or denial. Unlike the museum, which said that it knew nothing about where the rumors had come from, the IAA fed them by simply refusing to reveal the nature or origin of the information it had regarding the forgery of the pomegranate inscription.

In September 2004, the IAA appointed a committee to determine whether the ivory pomegranate inscription was a forgery. It was supposedly a joint committee of the IAA and the Israel Museum, but the chief curator of archaeology at the museum later revealed that the committee was "determined" by the IAA; she was only an "observer" of the committee's deliberations. The curator's name was listed as one of the authors of the published committee report, however, although she had never previously seen it.[61]

The committee report was published in the March 2005 issue of the *Israel Exploration Journal*. The committee concluded that the ivory pomegranate inscription is a modern forgery.

By that time, however, another major action had been taken by the IAA. Three days before the end of 2004, a criminal indictment was brought against five defendants alleging that the pomegranate inscription, the ossuary inscription, the Yehoash inscription and numerous other artifacts and inscriptions were forgeries.

Golan was the lead defendant. The next defendant was Robert Deutsch, the Tel Aviv antiquities dealer/scholar. The indictment almost immediately devastated his scholarly career. His contract to teach epigraphy at Haifa University was not renewed. His position as area supervisor of the archaeological excavation at Megiddo was terminated. He has threatened to sue the IAA and its officials for $20 million when the case is over, on the ground that it had no credible evidence whatsoever on which to base the indictment.

A third defendant, Rafi Brown (or Braun), was a former chief conservator at the Israel Museum who had retired to become an antiquities dealer with a shop across from Jerusalem's King David Hotel. It was in his shop that André Lemaire was able initially to examine the pomegranate

Oded Golan, owner of the James ossuary and the chief defendant in the "forgery trial of the century."

inscription under a microscope (although this was not where he origi-nally saw the pomegranate). Brown has since given up the shop and lives for a major part of the year in Switzerland, where he spends his time on archaeological conservation.

Two other men complete the roster of defendants: "Momi" Cohen, a dealer who worked with Brown; and a Palestinian Arab named Fayez el-Amleh.

As of this writing, more than three years after the indictment was filed, the case is still dragging on. The government has dropped the case against Brown and Cohen—for unexplained reasons. According to an article in *Ha'aretz*, they have agreed to turn state's evidence and will tes-tify against the other defendants, but this seems not to be the case since the government has now rested its case and Brown and Cohen have not been called. The Palestinian Arab is also out of the case: He pleaded guilty to a minor offense unrelated to forgery—for lying about the source of a looted artifact. He received a suspended sentence of four months. Golan and Deutsch remain in the case, the sole defendants. IAA director Shuka Dorfman once described Golan as "the tip of the iceberg,"[62] but he has not yet found the iceberg.

When the government rested its case, it had called 120 witnesses. The trial transcript extends over 8,000 pages.[63] The trial has turned into a battle of experts. The prosecution has even called to the stand what would seem to be defense witnesses—like André Lemaire. No witness has identified anyone who actually forged or participated in any of the forgeries alleged

Shuka Dorfman, director of the Israel Antiquities Authority, who won't speak to me.

in the indictment. An Israeli trial is very different from an American trial. In Israel there are no juries. So the trial is not held continuously. Testimony before the judge is taken one or two days a month. What is most striking to me is that there seems to be no objection on grounds of irrelevancy. The testimony goes on and on, seemingly without purpose.

More recently the judge himself has indicated that the government's case is falling apart. He suggested to the prosecution that it consider dropping the case.[64] The government did not take the suggestion, however.[65] As I write, the two remaining defendants are calling their witnesses. The prosecution presumably hopes to improve its case on redirect.

The judge's decision, whichever way he decides, is in a way irrelevant. It means only that the government has not proved its case beyond a reasonable doubt, the standard of proof in a criminal case. Legally, even if it is more probable than not that the ossuary inscription is a forgery, but the proof does not rise to a level "beyond a reasonable doubt," the court must acquit. Moreover, the judge will make no decision regarding the pomegranate inscription. Although it was alleged to be a forgery in the indictment, it was not listed in any of the specific counts. Therefore the judge will make no finding with respect to it.

My own view is that both the ossuary inscription and the pomegranate inscription are authentic.

I am deeply affected by the fact that two of the world's most distinguished paleographers, André Lemaire and Ada Yardeni, are convinced that the James ossuary inscription is authentic.

Gaby Barkay, a leading Jerusalem archaeologist who has also analyzed and published ancient inscriptions, pretty much expressed my view when, at a Jerusalem conference of scholars that I convened to consider these questions, he stated:

It is true that one has to suspect everything. But still my assumption a *priori* is that if André Lemaire, a very sharp-eyed and knowledgeable scholar, has some observations about the ossuary inscription, I accept it because of his knowledge, his expertise and his honesty. But still I'm going to check the object myself. I went to see the ossuary. I went to touch it myself. I went to the Rockefeller Museum. My impression is that the inscription is genuine. And my feeling is also that of a very well-known expert in Jewish script, Ada Yardeni.

At the same conference, Yardeni remarked:

"I am sure it [the ossuary inscription] is no fake, unless Oded [Golan] comes and tells me he did it. So he's a genius. But I don't believe it."

On the other side, no paleographer has even suggested that any paleographic aspect of the inscription might indicate it is a forgery. The sole exception is someone I have already mentioned, Rochelle Altman, who has attained a modicum of fame because of her contention that the ossuary inscription is a forgery. She reached her conclusion simply by looking at a picture of the inscription. She described the inscription as excised, while in fact it was incised. She based her judgment not on the shape and stance of the letters, as do standard paleographical experts, but on what she calls "writing systems." Her 2004 book on this subject, *Absent Voices: The Study of Writing Systems in the West*, was reviewed in *Maarav*, a scholarly journal devoted to Semitic inscriptions. It is the most damning review I have ever read.[66] A single paragraph, said the reviewer, "about exhausts Altman's treatment of the Semitic scripts." The review then refers to the author's "bizarre assertion" and her "proceed[ing] by free association," and her use of words "like no one before her."

I dwell at length on Rochelle Altman because she alone is featured in two accounts by first-class journalists who wanted to find some script expert on the other side, who would say that the ossuary inscription is a forgery.[67] Rochelle Altman is the best they could find.

How, then, do I deal with the unanimous judgment of 14 experts in a variety of fields on the IAA committee that condemned the ossuary inscription as a forgery?

It's not quite accurate to say their judgment was unanimous. As Father Joseph Fitzmyer has observed, there is no "final report" to which all committee members have subscribed. There are only individual letters to the committee chairman from individual members of the committee. Some of these letters express no opinion.

For example, Victor (Avigdor) Hurowitz and Haggai Misgav express no opinion regarding the authenticity of the ossuary inscription. Yet they are included in the "unanimous" opinion that it is a forgery.

The committee's carbon-14 expert, Elisabetta Boaretto, concluded that a carbon-14 test would be "irrelevant" to determining the authenticity of the stone ossuary inscription, but she too was counted as a forgery vote.

The conclusions of other members, as Fitzmyer notes, are quite nuanced. Indeed, committee member Orna Cohen concluded that "the end of the inscription, 'brother of Jesus,' appears authentic; in some places [in the inscription] there seems to be the remains of old [original] patina." (Oddly, in the criminal indictment, only the last part of the inscription is alleged to be forged, just the part that appeared to Orna Cohen to be "authentic.")

Still another committee member, Tal Ilan, wrote:

> I do not pretend to be an expert on ossuary production techniques or carved inscriptions or paleography ... Therefore, regarding the question of authenticity and the inscriptions, I will rely on what the experts have determined ... My main claim in this report is that even if the ossuary [inscription] is authentic, there is no reason to assume that the deceased is actually the brother of Jesus [of Nazareth].

Yet she was counted in the unanimous vote concluding the inscription was a forgery.

Shmuel Ahituv expressed himself similarly:

I do not see myself qualified to decide in this area of Second Temple period paleography. The conclusions should come from the colleagues engaged in the physical aspects of the [ossuary] inscription: patina in the letters, etc.

Each of the foregoing members of the committee was counted as an affirmative vote for the forgery of the ossuary inscription.

Other infirmities in the "committee report" abound. The IAA's introduction to the "report" admits that it chose members "even if they had, in the past, expressed an opinion on the subject." Yet, as Fitzmyer points out, the committee members who had previously expressed an opinion all expressed a negative opinion. Lemaire, for example, was not invited to be a member. Neither were people like Ada Yardeni, Bezlel Porten, Gaby Barkay, to name only Israelis. Lemaire's views were not considered in any of the separate papers that comprised the report. Indeed his name was not mentioned. The IAA obviously chose the committee members with an eye to how it wanted the result to come out. Fitzmyer accuses the IAA of engaging in "politicized archaeology."

Another major problem with the committee's "unanimous" decision is that many members based their conclusion on the expertise of others (as we have seen in the case of Tal Ilan), rather than their own expertise. This is perhaps most glaring in the decision of Ronny Reich, a prominent Jerusalem archaeologist, who, on his own, would have found the ossuary inscription to be authentic. After carefully examining the inscription and analyzing the various paleographical issues, he concluded that, "It appears that each of the characteristics of the inscription, as detailed above, and all of them together, with no exception, indicate an authentic late Second Temple period (mainly first century C.E.) inscription." In the end, however, he changed his mind. "I am forced to change my opinion," he wrote, not because of his own expertise, but because of the scientific arguments advanced by Yuval Goren. (More recently, Reich told a BAR banquet that he now believes the ossuary inscription to be authentic.)

Which brings us to the central character in the committee's conclusion: Yuval Goren. A fair reading of the report and the individual letters of

Tel Aviv University scientist Yuval Goren, who insists that the James ossuary inscription, the ivory pomegranate inscription and the Yehoash inscription are all modern forgeries.

the committee members leaves the distinct impression that the committee's decision was driven by a single scientist with whom none of the humanistic members could argue. His very position commands attention, if not assent. He was the chairman of Tel Aviv University's department of archaeology. His conclusion is supposedly based on a scientific analysis that would be difficult for anyone other than another scientist to understand, let alone refute.

Goren enlisted a colleague named Avner Ayalon, a specialist from the Geological Survey (the same government agency that had previously found no reason to question the authenticity of the ossuary inscription), to perform an oxygen isotope analysis on the patina-like covering that Goren says he found on the inscription (ever the smart aleck, Goren called this covering the "James Bond"). The oxygen isotope analysis revealed that the patina-like covering on the inscription had been compounded with water at 50 degrees centigrade (about 120 degrees Fahrenheit). Water at this temperature is not found naturally in the Jerusalem area. Therefore it must be an artificial compound, Goren and Ayalon concluded. The compound consisted, according to their analysis, of crushed stone ("perhaps the powder from the newly engraved inscription") mixed with hot water to form a paste. "Heated water was used to insure good adhesion of the [fake] patina. Another possibility is grinding carbonate, spreading it over the surface and warming inside an oven [to make it adhere]." (Even with this, Goren noted the James Bond could be removed with a wooden toothpick.) Using this method, the forger was able "to blur the freshly engraved signs [of the inscription]."

The initial problem is that Yuval Goren is out of his specialty. He is a clay petrologist, not a stone petrologist. His résumé lists his specialties, but none of them involves stone. Of the hundreds of articles on his 13-page résumé, only five appear to involve only stone artifacts. That he is not a stone petrologist was exposed most embarrassingly in his analysis of the plaque on which the Yehoash inscription was written. He found that the stone is greywacke, which is "not native to Israel and the adjacent areas." According to Goren, it probably came from "the Troodos Massif in Cyprus." This was later shown to be absurd. The stone is simple arkosic sandstone, very common in Israel, near the Dead Sea and in the Sinai Peninsula.[68]

Moreover, Goren himself admits that this "James Bond" on the ossuary could have been formed either by the method described above "or" as a result of cleaning the inscription. It is well known that antiquities dealers clean inscriptions to make them stand out. According to the ossuary's owner, Oded Golan, his mother also cleaned the ossuary regularly while it was on the balcony of his parents' apartment.

But the weakest part of Goren and Ayalon's argument was expressed by James Harrell, whom I enlisted to help me understand Goren's scientific arguments. Jim, a professor at the University of Toledo, is an officer and prominent member of ASMOSIA, the Association for the Study of Marble and Other Stones in Antiquity. To paraphrase Jim's characterization of the Goren and Ayalon contention: IT JUST WON'T STICK. Goren and Ayalon had argued that hot water was used to make the paste so that it would adhere to the newly engraved inscription. But, as Harrell pointed out in an article in BAR,[69] it still won't stick, even when made with hot water.

But Goren and Ayalon had an alternative argument: The forger used cold water to make the paste, but after applying it to the inscription, he placed the ossuary in a hot oven. But it still won't stick, Harrell explains.

This is not the worst of it, however. You can't *make* a paste of crushed stone and water, even if you heat the water or heat the whole thing; crushed stone will not dissolve in hot water. For this, as Harrell wrote, you need hot acid in the mix, but if you do this, there would be an acid residue in the paste, giving it away.

Neither Goren nor Ayalon has ever attempted to refute this argument. And no other geologist or related expert has come to their defense. On the contrary, all the other scientists who have opined on the matter have come out on the other side. The geologists from the Geological Survey (Amnon Rosenfeld and Shimon Ilani) who originally authenticated the inscription continue to maintain their position. The scientists at the Royal Ontario Museum did their own tests, especially when they could examine the ossuary inscription on the side (when the ossuary had broken), and came to the same conclusion. A distinguished German geologist, Wolfgang Krumbein, testified for the defense that the inscription was genuine. And James Harrell, whom I mentioned earlier, found no impediment to the authenticity of the inscription.

Moreover, five scientists have recently reported in a peer-reviewed scholarly journal that the isotope analysis Goren and Ayalon used to detect the forgery is "unreliable," adding that "to our knowledge, this method is not used in any lab in the world."[70]

Yuval Goren stumbled on still another even more important point. He had been unable to see any original patina in the inscription when he first looked at it with his stereoscopic microscope, even though another member of the committee (Orna Cohen), as noted above, found old patina in the end of the inscription, in the word "Jesus." When Goren got on the stand to testify at the trial, he repeated his previous conclusion that there was no original patina in the inscription. However, this time he was subject to cross-examination. When shown photographs of this part of the inscription taken by another expert (Wolfgang Krumbein), Goren was flummoxed; it looked like there was original patina in the end of the inscription, the very part that the indictment alleged was a forgery. In desperation, he asked the judge if he could be excused to come back the next day after he had taken another look at the inscription through his microscope. When he came back, he revised his earlier testimony. There was indeed original patina in the last letter of the Aramaic word for Jesus.

Goren explained that his microscope "has an oblique illumination," so some parts can be in shadow. What he thought was a shadow was actually patina.

Moreover, in the course of the police examination, Goren explained, the police had put some silicone putty into the inscription to take an impression; this, Goren said, "pulled out the 'James Bond', you know, the soft patina-like material coating the letters." Only after the James Bond was pulled off could the original patina be seen underneath. And there underneath the coating was original patina. "And this of course caused some problems," said Goren with considerable understatement.[71] "Problems," indeed! There was original ancient patina in the word "Jesus."

I had a three-hour dinner with Goren when we were both in San Diego in November 2007 for the ASOR/SBL annual meetings. There he gave me his new explanation of how there happened to be original patina in the last letter of "Jesus." The last letter is an *ayin*, composed of two or three strokes. Maybe the left stroke, Goren told me, was an ancient scratch that had acquired patina; perhaps the forger decided to use this ancient scratch with the ancient patina as part of the *ayin* and simply engraved the other curving line to connect to it.

If you believe this, I have a bridge I'd like to sell you. I didn't say this to Goren, but listened politely.

As this undermining of the IAA committee report unfolded, we organized a protest petition that 1,500 people signed, asking the IAA to appoint an international panel of experts to take a second look at the James ossuary inscription. Committee chairman and deputy IAA director Uzi Dahari sarcastically dismissed our petition, congratulating us on obtaining "1,500 names out of five billion people in the world ... I don't need this list." Dahari told a *Washington Post* reporter that I was "pathetic" and "totally crazy."[72]

I mentioned a three-day conference that the Biblical Archaeology Society convened in Jerusalem in January 2007 to consider the whole issue of forgeries. Scholars came from the United States, England, France, Germany and of course Israel. Yuval Goren, although he lives in Jerusalem, declined even to respond to our invitation.

During the discussion, the question came up as to whether we should look primarily to the hard sciences or to the humanistic sciences in making a decision concerning the authenticity of an inscription. Some thought the answer was the material sciences, the so-called exact sciences. But the geologist Wolfgang Krumbein, the major representative of the hard sciences at the conference, thought otherwise. This only emphasized the view from within that there are subjective elements even in scientific demonstrations.

My own view is also to some extent subjective. Yes, I do have regard for the opinions of people like André Lemaire and Ada Yardeni and for the findings of scientists like Wolf Krumbein, but I'm also affected by what I call human factors.

For example, Golan located an old photograph of some ancient arti-facts on a wooden shelf in his apartment. The amateur photographer took the picture vertically, instead of horizontally. As a result the photograph gives a glimpse of what is on the shelf above and on the shelf below. On the shelf below we see the James ossuary. Only the end of the inscription is there, but that is enough to identify it. On the shelf above are some books. One is a 1974 Tel Aviv telephone book. Another book contains marks indicating it was borrowed from the Technion library, where Golan was studying at the time.

For the trial, Golan retained Gerald Richards, a former FBI agent in the United States who had served as the chief of its Special Photographic Unit, to analyze the photograph. On the back of the photographic paper was a date: "EXP[ires] 3/[19]76." That is, the paper expires in March 1976. Richards found that Kodak no longer made this paper after the late 1970s or early 1980s. All this indicates that the photograph was taken in the late 1970s, as Golan claims.

It is of course possible that this picture is itself forged, that Golan went online and found some old photographic paper that would still print, that he forged the markings on the book from the Technion, that he some-how obtained a 1974 Tel Aviv telephone book—and, voila, we're tricked again. Actually, there is even a picture of his old girlfriend on the shelf. She is willing to testify that that is how she looked some 30 years ago and that she was indeed his girlfriend. But maybe Golan had an old picture of her which he put on the shelf for the post-2000 shooting. All this is possible but does seem highly unlikely. At some point, when piling up far-fetched scenarios to justify a finding of forgery, the process must stop and it is time to conclude that the inscription is authentic. And if Golan owned the ossuary with its inscription since the late 1970s, it is almost surely authentic. If that is a subjective conclusion, then make the most of it.

It is impossible to prove with 100 percent certainty, however, that an inscription is authentic. There is always one, perhaps yet-unknown, test that you failed to apply, which, if you had applied, would have demonstrated that it is a forgery. The same thing is true even of inscriptions uncovered in professional excavations. You can never be 100 percent sure that a find has not been salted, perhaps with the connivance of someone on the excavation staff.

* * * *

What about the ivory pomegranate inscription from the First Temple period? I have already described how the supposedly joint committee of the IAA and the Israel Museum was in fact "determined" by the IAA. The Israel Museum observer did not participate in the deliberations.

And the critical member of this committee was the same Yuval Goren who had dominated the IAA committee that had previously found the ossuary inscription to be a forgery. Avner Ayalon, who did the oxygen isotope studies on that inscription, was also on the pomegranate committee. Added to them was a third member of the Geological Survey, Miryam Bar-Matthews, who for years had worked with Goren and Ayalon on numerous projects and papers. That it was Goren who led the troops, however, is plain from the fact that in the publication of their report all eight members of the pomegranate committee are listed in alphabetical order—except for Goren. Like Abou ben Adhem, his name leads all the rest.[73]

The other five members of the committee included two Israeli epigraphers, Shmuel Ahituv and Aaron Demsky, who had no experience in detecting forgeries. In addition, the committee consisted of the deputy director of the IAA (Uzi Dahari, who brought no relevant expertise to the committee) and someone from the Israel Police (Nadav Levin). The pomegranate committee was, in a word, Yuval Goren's show.

Goren's scenario of the forger's drama is little short of bizarre. About a third of the ball (or grenade) of the pomegranate had broken off. On close examination, it is clear that one break, in the middle, is an ancient break. On either side of this ancient break are two other breaks which, from their light coloration, appear to be modern breaks. On this, all agree. Goren argues that the forger began with a genuinely old ivory pomegranate that had an ancient break. When the forger began to inscribe it, he accidentally broke off another piece of the pomegranate, creating one of the new breaks. He then did this again, creating the second new break.

Now comes the critical part: The forger then completed the inscription, but he was so fearful of causing still another break in carving subsequent letters that *he stopped short of the breaks*, fearing to go over the edge lest he break off more of the pomegranate.

Otherwise, the committee's arguments to support a finding of forgery were flimsy at best. For example, paleographically all the committee could say was that one letter, a *mem*, was "problematic." The committee acknowledged, however, that this "might have been caused by a slip of the engraving tool on the hard surface of the pomegranate's shoulder, as well as by its small dimensions." To this might have been added the fact that the engraving surface at this point is curved and slanted.

Moreover, on the issue of paleography, the inscription not only passed Lemaire's examination, but also that of Nahman Avigad, Israel's leading paleographer before his death in 1992. Avigad was quite conscious of the possibility that the inscription could be a forgery. After his careful examination, however, Avigad declared, "I am fully convinced of ... the authenticity of the inscription ... [T]he epigraphic evidence alone, in my opinion, is absolutely convincing."[74]

When I heard of the committee's finding that the inscription was a forgery, I wrote to museum director Snyder and offered to buy the pomegranate for the same amount that the museum had paid for it ($550,000), confident that Snyder was no more convinced than I was that the inscription was forged. As expected, Snyder turned down my offer. Although "the ivory pomegranate no longer carries the historical significance which it was previously thought to have," he wrote me, "it remains for us an important story of museological process." Whatever that means, it is obviously a valuable thing to have.

In light of the committee's now-published conclusion in September 2005, André Lemaire traveled to Jerusalem to reexamine the pomegranate under a microscope. Based on this reexamination, he wrote a devastating response to the committee report, which, like the initial committee report, was published in the *Israel Exploration Journal*.[75] He dedicated his response to the memory of Nahman Avigad. Geologists Amnon Rosenfeld and Shimon Ilani, who were the principal authors of the original study of the pomegranate inscription by the Geological Survey, wrote an appendix to Lemaire's article responding to the geological aspects of the committee report that had found the inscription to be a forgery.

Lemaire's article was careful and detailed; it considered each of the several alleged indications of forgery, either demolishing it or neutralizing it. For example, the committee's contention that the new breaks in the pomegranate were created by the forger as he forged letters too close to the old break is described by Lemaire as "clearly pure conjecture ... New breaks are often made when an ancient object is dug up during excavations. [This] is very well known in field archaeology." Lemaire calls the committee's explanation of how the new breaks occurred "strained."

Lemaire recognized that "the principal argument advanced by the [committee] authors ... is that the engraving of certain fragmentary letters stops before reaching the old or new breaks." Lemaire concedes that "If true, this would be a clear indication that the engraving of the letters was made after the old and new breaks. Consequently the inscription would be a modern forgery." Lemaire expressed agreement with this principle. Indeed, it was a principle "well-known to experienced epigraphers." But, Lemaire wondered, "Why was this not noticed by" Avigad and himself in their original microscopic examinations of the inscription? It was not noticed because it did not occur! If it had occurred, Lemaire and Avigad would have noticed it.

At our Jerusalem forgery conference, we discussed the authenticity of the pomegranate inscription. It was generally recognized that the only question—the issue on which authenticity/forgery turned—was whether the partial engraved letters stopped short of the breaks. The other issues raised by the committee report pretty much faded away. Thus, for example,

Aaron Demsky, one of the two epigraphers on the committee, remarked at our forgery conference that the pomegranate inscription "is perfectly fine from a paleographical point of view."[76]

The discussion centered on whether the partial letters stopped short of the edge of the breaks. All agreed on the principle: If they did, the inscription was a modern forgery; if, on the other hand, partial letters went into the old break, they preceded the old break and the inscription was authentic.

This was recognized not only by Lemaire and IAA committee members Demsky and Ahituv, but also by the other epigraphers and paleographers at the conference. It thus seemed sensible to take another look at the pomegranate to see whether, in fact, the letters stopped short of the breaks or went into the breaks. Shmuel Ahituv and Aaron Demsky agreed to take a second look with "an open mind."

With this, I set out to organize a viewing of the pomegranate at the museum with all interested parties on hand. The big question was whether we could get Yuval Goren to attend. He was obviously the key man on the pomegranate committee (as he had been on the committee that declared the ossuary inscription to be a forgery). He had refused even to respond to my invitation to attend our forgery conference. And he had refused to discuss the matter with Lemaire privately. Nor had he responded to Lemaire's powerful "dissenting" opinion in the *Israel Exploration Journal*.[77]

After consultations with the Israel Museum, we set May 3, 2007, as the date for a meeting to reexamine the pomegranate at the museum. In my invitation to Goren, I recounted the discussions at our January conference and the decision to take another look at the object itself and that everyone "very much wanted you [to attend our May meeting] ... We would very much like to have the benefit of your expertise at this session."

This time Goren replied to my invitation. He said that the members of the committee had:

already discussed in the past the possibility of re-examining the pomegranate under the microscope in light of Prof. Lemair's [sic] paper ... The only thing that I fail to understand is how you fit into all this ...

As we ... have already ... decided to do it anyway in the near future, it is clear that we don't need any coordinators. One more thing that we don't need is more archaeological pulp fiction ... I don't think that you should be involved in it, nor your journal.

I replied in as conciliatory manner as I could, explaining that the May 3 meeting grew out of the January conference I had organized, and that "I had taken the lead in trying to arrange the [May 3] session." I concluded by saying that "I would be delighted to work with you in assuring that the proper procedures were followed and in providing a congenial and collegial atmosphere for the discussion."

In a later email I outlined the format for the discussion saying that "I will serve as moderator only as needed." Goren quickly responded: "We do not need coordinators and we can manage the discussion very well without anyone setting for us the agenda in advance."

Goren had not yet agreed to attend. Ahituv felt Goren's attendance was essential. So he sided with Goren: "No need to arrange for us the schedule," Ahituv wrote me. "We can manage for ourselves." Ahituv in effect took charge of the meeting. From that point on, I was simply allowed to attend the session. I had previously invited the American paleographer Kyle McCarter to attend, and Ahituv allowed him to attend. But I wanted Ahituv to invite Israeli paleographer Ada Yardeni to attend as well. He refused to allow her to attend, probably because she had defended the authenticity of the ossuary inscription. I was not privy to the discussions between Ahituv and Goren, but the final decision was that Goren would attend; and that, although I was permitted to attend, I would not be a moderator.

Having now agreed to attend, Goren brought his own stereoscopic microscope to the session, which was superior to the one at the museum.

The museum brought the pomegranate. There it was—in all its glory without even the glass of a vitrine to intervene between the eye and the object. The little prince, as it were. If authentic, it was the only surviving relic from Solomon's Temple. I kept my awe to myself. No one remarked on it. Was I the only one excited by this? I don't know.

Another thing: The museum did not tell us that it could be handled only with rubber or plastic hand-coverings, as I had expected. We handled the object with our bare hands.

In attendance were Goren, Avituv, Demsky, Lemaire, Michal Dayagi-Mendels from the Israel Museum, Kyle McCarter and me. In contrast to his behavior prior to the meeting, Goren was cordial, collegial and helpful in his operation of the microscope. He acceded to all requests to adjust the angle, direction or focus of the pomegranate and its inscription. He took all the photographs that we asked for. We ate lunch together in the museum and engaged in friendly, if irrelevant, conversation. The only thing that was strange about Goren's behavior was that he had almost nothing to say about the images of the inscription that he was flashing on the wall. He acted as a kind of willing technician who was there solely to work the microscope, not to participate in the discussion of whether the partially engraved letters did or did not stop short of the breaks.

Only three partial letters were involved and the simple (ha!) question was whether they stopped short of the breaks or were cut by the breaks. At the end of the day, it was clear to Lemaire that indeed the breaks cut these three partial letters; these three partial letters went into the breaks. Goren thought otherwise, but barely expressed himself. Both Ahituv and Demsky stuck to their guns, although they admitted that they had rarely, if ever, looked through a microscope for any reason, let alone to determine whether an inscription was a forgery. Lemaire had vast experience, as did Kyle McCarter. McCarter wanted to study the photographs, however, before coming to a conclusion. I, of course, was a novice at looking through a microscope and could give no opinion.

At the end of the meeting, we agreed that we would wait for the photographs and further study before making a decision.

The entire inscription consists of 15 letters. Seven of these letters form the phrase *qodesh kohanim* (קדש כהנם), "holy (or sacred) to the priests." All of the letters are there. The other eight letters, as reconstructed, form the phrase *l'beyt* [Yahwe]*h* (לבית[יהו]ה), "(Belonging) to the House (or Temple) of [Yahwe]h." Of these eight letters, only two are complete and three (the first three letters of Yahweh) are completely missing. The remaining three letters are partly there but clearly identifiable, which allows the reconstruction of this half of the inscription. It is these three partial letters that were the focus of the reexamination of the inscription under the microscope. One of them (*yod*) is adjacent to a new break. A second partial letter (*tov*) had two strokes, one adjacent to a new break and one adjacent to the old break. The third partial letter (*heh*) is adjacent to the old break. If a letter stopped short of a new break, this meant the inscription was a forgery. But the reverse was not true (if it went into a new break, this would not necessarily indicate authenticity; this would only show that the inscription was engraved prior to the new, modern break). On the other hand, if a letter goes into the *old* break, this would indicate authenticity.

Goren's photographs, which he later distributed to everyone at the session, were excellent. You don't have to be an expert to read them. And you can see the partial letters both from the top down and from the side— and from all angles in between. From the side, the letter would form a "v" if it extended into the break, but not if it stopped short of the break.

The *yod* was the easiest of the three. Even during the session, Demsky and Ahituv readily admitted they had erred with respect to the *yod*. The committee, they conceded, had been "mistaken" in concluding that the *yod* stopped artificially short of the break. In the language of the grudging concession that Ahituv, Demsky and Goren published in the *Israel Exploration Journal* following the session at the Israel Museum, "We accepted Lemaire's observation ... The shallow v-like indentation seen on the section *might* support Lemaire's contention that the tip arrives at the *new* break below this letter" (emphasis supplied).[78] Because it went into a new break, however, the *yod* wouldn't indicate authenticity. All it would show is that the *yod* was engraved prior to the *new* break.

Although the *yod* could not establish authenticity, it was instructive as to how the IAA committee functioned. It indicated how easy it was for this committee to err. It also indicated that the other members of the committee simply followed the lead of Goren and the two epigraphers (Ahituv and Demsky) on the committees. And Ahituv and Demsky simply followed Goren's lead. Moreover, Goren is not an epigrapher. The error with regard to the *yod* demonstrated how easy it is for this combination of "experts" in different fields to reach a flawed conclusion.

The second partial letter is a *tov*, which in the paleo-Hebrew script of the inscription looks like an "x." The upper tip of each of the two strokes has survived. One (the right one) goes into a new break. The left one, however, goes into the old break.

Next to the right stroke of the *tov* is a bulge in the ivory of the pomegranate. When viewed from an oblique angle it can appear that this stroke stops behind the bulge. To Lemaire, Kyle McCarter and even to me, it appeared that this stroke went directly into the new break, both when photographed from above and when photographed straight on from the side. But Goren, Ahituv and Demsky were of the view that it stopped behind the bulge. This then—one stroke of one letter about which there is great controversy—is the basis of their conclusion that the inscription is a forgery. As they state in their *Israel Exploration Journal* report: "The main reason for this conclusion [that the inscription is a forgery] is the apparent caution of the engraver not to access the *old* break" (emphasis supplied). They probably mean *new* break, because the *only* stroke that even arguably stops short of a break is the right tip of the *tov*—and that goes into a new break. As we will see, in the only two instances where partial letters are adjacent to the old break, they do go into the old break, indicating authenticity.

The left tip of the partial *tov* is adjacent to the old break. Although the "v" in the section is clear, Goren, Ahituv and Demsky had a difficult time admitting this. All they could say in their report in the *Israel Exploration Journal* is that "it is difficult to determine whether the left stroke [of the *tov*] arrived at the old break, creating a v-like indentation on the section."[79] Why it is difficult to determine is not explained. As Lemaire wrote, "I do not see any reason to doubt that the left stroke [of the *tov*] arrives at the OLD break since it creates a v-like indentation in the section."

The last partial letter was the *heh*. The trio's treatment of this letter is even worse: The short surviving vertical stroke of the *heh* clearly goes into the old break. Here there is no bulge to use as a forced observation that the *heh* stopped short of the break. At the session, we extensively discussed the vertical stem of the *heh*, which formed a "v" in the section. I wondered what the trio would write regarding the *heh* in their report of the session for the *Israel Exploration Journal*. I didn't have long to wait. Somewhat astonishingly, they simply ignored it! Not a single mention of the *heh*. No discussion whatever of whether the *heh* did or did not go into the break. I wrote a letter to the editor on this blatant omission. Ahituv is editor of the journal, however. I received a reply from the editorial office saying that the "policy [of the journal was] not to publish Letters to the Editor."

Aaron Demsky had written in his abstract at our earlier forgery conference that "*Some* of the letters were engraved after the pomegranate was initially damaged in antiquity!" (The italics are mine; the exclamation point is Demsky's!) In fact, only one stroke of one letter is even argued to stop before a break, while two letters clearly go into the old break.

As with the IAA committee that found the ossuary inscription to be a forgery, the committee that found the pomegranate inscription to be a forgery seems to have been largely driven by a preordained conclusion. The failure even to mention the partial *heh* seems inexplicable except as a determination to confirm the earlier finding that the pomegranate inscription is a forgery.

Kyle McCarter, the independent (and universally respected) observer at the museum session felt he could not make a decision at the conclusion of the session; he wanted to see the photographs. After seeing the photographs, he too concluded that the three partial letters did go into the breaks. He was still not ready to judge the inscription authentic, however. He was concerned at something else. In its original report, the committee found on stylistic grounds that the admittedly genuine ancient ivory pomegranate dated from the Late Bronze Age (14th–13th century B.C.E.); the inscription, however, dated by paleography, was from Iron Age II, more specifically about the eighth century B.C.E. To the committee, this was one indication that the inscription had been forged. Lemaire never accepted this argument. Even if the pomegranate was created in the Late Bronze Age, it could have been a rare relic that had survived and was inscribed in Iron Age II. He pointed to examples of Late Bronze artifacts that had been excavated in Iron Age II contexts.

McCarter agreed that this was possible, but it also seemed unlikely. He concluded that an extra measure of caution would lead us to have the pomegranate tested by carbon-14 analysis to determine its date. Indeed, in his original response to the committee report, Lemaire himself had proposed that a carbon-14 test be performed on the pomegranate: "A carbon-14 test could perhaps clearly decide between the two possible dates [of the pomegranate]."[80] When the museum's Michal Dayagi-Mendels proved unavailable to McCarter in his efforts to urge a carbon-14 test, I decided to call Dayagi-Mendels myself. She was cordial but said she feared that taking the sample might shatter the object. I had already been in contact with Tom Higham at the Oxford Radiocarbon Laboratory, who had assured me this would not be a problem; the new AMS technique required only a minute sample, barely the head of a pin. When I told this to Dayagi-Mendels, she said that if the test was to be done, she wanted it done by the Weizmann Institute in Israel. I replied that this was of course satisfactory. She said she would contact Weizmann. When she failed to do so, I called Elisabetta Boaretto, who heads Weizmann's radiocarbon lab. Boaretto confirmed that only a minute sample would be needed (that could be taken from the bottom of the object). She agreed to contact Dayagi-Mendels. After Boaretto had done so, she reported back to me that Dayagi-Mendels had told her that the museum was not interested in having a carbon-14 test performed on the pomegranate.

* * * *

What about the Yehoash inscription, which, if authentic, would be the first royal Israelite inscription ever discovered?

BAR has never taken a position with regard to the authenticity of the Yehoash inscription. Some of the most eminent paleographers and linguists feel certain that it is a forgery. Among them is Joseph Naveh, although when he first saw the inscription years before, he was not sure. Others include John Hopkins' Kyle McCarter, who has characterized some of the forger's errors as "real howlers." Harvard's Frank Cross agrees. Add to this leading Semitic linguists like Avigdor Hurowitz and Edward

Greenstein. We extensively published all of their negative analyses, giving prominence to the forgery argument.[81]

There is another side, however. There are scholars, like the late David Noel Freedman, who contend that we simply don't know enough about the Hebrew of this period to declare the Yehoash inscription a forgery.[82] History has shown how often we have been surprised, said Freedman. He cited as an example, in personal conversation, the famous Mesha Stela or Moabite Stone: If it were to come on the market today with the limited knowledge of Hebrew that we had at the time it was discovered in the 19th century, it would be judged a forgery.

Chaim Cohen, a leading Hebrew and Semitic linguist from Ben-Gurion University in Beer Sheba, has written extensively (some might say exhaustively) about the text of the Yehoash inscription. (His latest paper on it is 80 pages long.) Cohen finds numerous Hebrew usages in the text that reflect an intimate knowledge of 8th-century B.C.E. Hebrew— even beyond what the most sophisticated researchers have yet observed or written about. Cohen is not ready to say that the Yehoash inscription is authentic, but he does say that if it is a forgery, the forger was an extraordinarily brilliant and insightful Hebrew linguist, seeing usages never before understood by scholars.

Another factor that suggests to me that it might well be authentic is the length of the inscription. As I frequently put it in my conversations with scholars, "The first thing they teach you in forgery school is, 'Make it short.'" I don't know of another forged Semitic inscription, even alleg-edly forged inscription, that is anywhere near as long as this one (15 lines).

Recently the strongest case for the authenticity of the Yehoash inscription has been made in a scientific article that appeared in the highly regarded, peer-reviewed *Journal of Archaeological Science*, which I have already briefly mentioned.[83] Two of the authors are associated with the Geological Survey of Israel, another with Tel Aviv University, another with a leading German university and the last with the American Museum of Natural History.

As I have already mentioned, the Yehoash tablet had a crack in it that ran through four lines of the inscription. The forger—if it was forged—would have had to inscribe the text across the crack, which would have been not only extremely difficult (if not impossible) but also dangerous. If the forger chose a tablet to work on with such a crack, it might break, ruining all his previous work. It is highly unlikely that a forger would choose such a tablet with which to create his forgery. Why would he be so foolish when it was so unnecessary? Why start with a stone in which one more tap might ruin all your work? As the journal authors express it more scientifically: "The presence of the crack favors the authenticity of the inscription since a modern engraver would have known that incising across this line of weakness would have jeopardized the structural integrity of the tablet."

After the Yehoash tablet was seized from Oden Golan's Tel Aviv apartment, the police took it to Jerusalem. On the way, the tablet broke in two along the crack. Whether it was dropped and then broke is not known. But that is unlikely. Probably it was simply fragile and broke from the rumbling or bumping of the truck. This only emphasizes how unlikely it is that a forger forged the inscription across the crack.

In any event, when it broke, the inscription could be seen from the side. As reported in the *Journal of Archaeological Science*, the upper (outer) part of the crack had developed a patina, indicating the crack was there in ancient times. The new part of the crack, where it broke, was clean. In the words of the scientific article: "The sudden breakage of the tablet revealed that the top half of the fissure exhibits some natural bleaching and incipient patina formation due to weathering whereas the lower part of the table exhibits a clearly fresh line of breakage." This indicates that the inscription was very likely ancient, having been inscribed before the tablet developed its crack.

But this is not all.

The patina on the plaque contains miniscule globules of gold so small (1 micron, a millionth of a meter) that they are unavailable on the commercial market. The smallest size available on the commercial market is 500 millimeters in diameter. Both the size and the scatter pattern of the minute gold globules indicate that they were created by an intense conflagration. According to the authors, "The occurrence of pure gold globules

(1–2 micrometers) is evidence of the melting of gold artifacts or gold-gilded items (above 1000 degrees Celsius)." Moreover, as the authors state, "One would expect many gold globules of various sizes to occur in clustered aggregates in the patina if it were of recent origin, but this is clearly not the case. The small amounts detected and its distribution would be difficult to produce within an artificial patina."

The authors suggest that "the source of the gold globules may have been gold artifacts or gold-gilded items that existed in Jerusalem at that time. As Jerusalem was burned (2 Kings 25:9), some of the gold could have been melted in the conflagration, been injected into the air and re-solidified there, to settle later as minute globules on the ground. These globules were later incorporated within the patina that developed on the buried tablet ... Our analyses altogether support the authenticity of the YI tablet and the tablet inscription."

What Lies Behind the Forgery Crisis?

IT IS ALMOST AS IF ISRAELI OFFICIALS, and particularly the Israel Antiquities Authority, are determined by hook or by crook to confirm their suspicions of forgery and to trash significant objects that provide a direct link to the ancient Jewish and Christian world. It is difficult to explain.

My best guess, suggested by many, is that the IAA is out to destroy the antiquities market.[84] Israel is the only country in the Middle East where antiquities dealers are legal. Not that outlawing antiquities dealers has reduced looting in the slightest in those countries; it hasn't. These laws simply send the market underground, often into the hands of criminal elements. As in other antiquities-rich Mediterranean countries where antiquities dealers are illegal, looting in Israel and the West Bank is rampant. There is no difference between Israel and the countries that have outlawed antiquities dealers.

All the defendants in the Israeli forgery case are, in one way or another, involved in the antiquities trade, suggesting that that may be the target of the case. The original defendants included two of the most prominent and knowledgeable dealers in Israel (Deutsch and Brown); a third is a less-well-known dealer (Cohen). One of the others is a prominent Israeli collector (Golan). The last one is a Palestinian who pretended to know where the looted objects came from.

In the end, the steadfast belief of so many that these inscriptions are forgeries is based on the "smell" test. There is always some subjective element in the decision as to whether an inscription is a forgery. A prevalent reason for a finding of forgery is the claim "It's too good to be true." As Ronny Reich noted in his initial report on the ossuary inscription, if the inscription had read "Joseph, son of James, brother of Jesus," instead of "James, son of Joseph, brother of Jesus," "no one would have raised an eyebrow" regarding authenticity. Only because of the possible importance of the inscriptions is the question even raised. Another form of this argument was expressed at our forgery conference by Aaron Demsky: Because the inscription came from the antiquities market, he said, "The onus of proof is on the inscription." In other words, until authenticity is proven (which can never be proved beyond any uncertainty), the inscription is assumed to be a forgery.

Perhaps naturally, considering the positions I have taken, my own subjective predilections lean in the other direction. I am, first of all, impressed with the enormous scholarly and technical knowledge that the forger(s) must have had—if they are forgeries. For example, in the case of the pomegranate, the forger had to find an uninscribed ancient pomegranate; he had to know how to engrave an inscription on the pomegranate; he had to know enough about the language of the time to make up a plausible inscription; he had to know the paleo-Hebrew alphabet and the shape and form of the letters so well that he could fool the world's greatest paleographers; he had to be able to carve letters into an old break in the pomegranate with no tell-tale marks; he had to be enough of a psychologist to know to leave out the three most significant letters in God's name. As Ronny Reich said in one of his earlier reports when he still felt the Yehoash inscription might be authentic (contrary to his later vote, "forced" on him by Yuval Goren's scientific argument), "It is difficult for me to believe that a forger (or group of forgers) should be so knowledgeable of all aspects of the inscription—the physical, paleographic, linguistic and biblical—to produce such an object."

It is hard enough to imagine a forger skilled enough in all the knowledge and skills required to produce one of these forgeries. But the requirements are multiplied when we consider the enormous variations in these alleged forgeries. The pomegranate inscription and the Yehoash inscription must use the First Temple-period Hebrew script; the ossuary inscription must be engraved in an entirely different Second Temple-period Aramaic script. Still other skills and other knowledge would be required in forging the numerous other artifacts alleged to be forgeries in the 18 counts of the indictment in the forgery case.

As Ronny Reich has elsewhere remarked, if these are forgeries, no one person could possess all the skills required. It must be a conspiracy. Deputy IAA director Uzi Dahari agrees; he claims that the conspiracy includes experts in Bible, history, archaeology and epigraphy. He even knows who they are, but "I won't tell you at this time."[85] That was nearly five years ago, and he still won't tell us.

And if it is a conspiracy, it's hard to imagine that there wouldn't be at least one leaker (a point make by both Gaby Barkay and Ronny Reich). True, what was found in Oded Golan's apartment and warehouses may be interpreted as forger's tools, but none of these can be related to the artifacts alleged to be forgeries in the forgery case. We seem to have a forgery case without a forger.

As many have suggested, perhaps the best way to resolve the forgery question is by free scholarly discussion over time, rather than by a committee appointed to make a definitive decision—let alone a decision by a court of law. "Allow the scholarly discussion to play out," as Father Joseph Fitzmyer has recommended.[86] Over the years, a consensus might gradually be reached. In the meantime, as Reich has said, "Let each one remain with his [or her] degree of conviction about its authenticity."

Unfortunately, the effect of the actions taken by the Israel Antiquities Authority is to stifle the scholarly discussion.

CHAPTER XIV

My Credo

BAR CONTINUES TO ABSORB ME AS I approach my 35th anniversary as editor. I find it more exciting than ever. And I am working harder at it than ever.

As I write, we are developing a story on fragments of a secret gospel of Mark discovered in a Judean desert monastery by an eminent American scholar named Morton Smith. Smith has died and he is now being charged by several leading scholars with having forged the document from the monastery. (We believe the charge is false.)

Another article we are working on involves the eruption of Mt. Vesuvius in 79 C.E., almost nine years to the day after the Romans destroyed God's house in Jerusalem. Was this destruction of the watering hole of Rome's elite somehow seen as God's revenge? As the pumice and debris were settling on Pompeii, someone picked up a piece of charcoal and wrote on the wall of a Pompeii house the words "Sodom" and "Gomorrah"!

Another article on the boards is by a prominent Israeli archaeologist who proposes a new account of Israel's ethnogenesis—how and why Israel first distinguished itself from other peoples. Still another article we are preparing looks at the siege of Masada from the Roman point of view.

We have just put the finishing touches on a double issue of BAR that we have created to mark our 200th issue. We think it will become a collector's item.

As I approach my 80th birthday, life is good. My wife of nearly 44 years and I are in good health. Our younger daughter Julia is building a career as a restaurant and food consultant, while teaching accounting at Babson College in Wellesley, Massachusetts. Our elder daughter Elizabeth is happily married to Drew. They have two lovely children, Charlie and

Nancy. And Elizabeth has recently received tenure at the University of Virginia where she teaches rabbinics.

So with all of this, I turn to my own faith commitments. What of my own struggle with faith and spirituality? How do I relate to the Bible?

While I sense that this has long been a matter of discussion among BAR devotees, it has recently been raised in print. "I understand the editor [of BAR] is not himself particularly religious," Bible scholar Lester Grabbe wrote in a new book, "yet he seems at times to pursue an almost fundamentalist agenda ... But as time has gone by I have wondered if there is not something much more personal to it all."[87]

I am often asked about these things. Except to make it clear that I am Jewish (I don't want to be accused of hiding the fact), I have always regarded my faith as personal and irrelevant to judging BAR. Let me be me. And let BAR (and me—they are often considered to be synonymous) be BAR, judged by what appears in its pages.

However, in an autobiography it is appropriate to address these matters.

Not long ago, I interviewed four Bible and religion scholars simultaneously—two who had lost their faith and two who hadn't.[88] Oddly enough, the two who hadn't—a Baptist minister and an Orthodox Jew— had much in common. They both admitted that it was a continuing struggle to maintain their faith in God. Indeed, Judaism has a commandment to have faith. As Lawrence Schiffman explained, "It wouldn't be a commandment if it were so easy."

My faith is rather simple; some may say it is simplistic. My relationship to the Bible is more subtle and complicated.

As for my faith in a deity, I recognize more than the two categories of yes and no. The third is uncertainty. That's where I am. I simply don't know.

Of one thing, I'm pretty sure: If there is a God, he is not as he is described in the Hebrew Bible (or the New Testament). If you ask me how I know this, I can't defend the statement, except to point to all the horrifying undeserved suffering in the world. The God of the Hebrew Bible (or the New Testament) wouldn't allow this.

On the other hand, I cannot avoid the conviction that there must be something behind all this, something I cannot conceive of.

To illustrate why I cannot conceive of the deity or its nature, I summon some analogs: Try to teach a dog to speak. Or try to teach a five-year-old, even one as bright as my granddaughter, the principles of algebra or plane geometry. It can't be done. Some things are simply beyond our ken.

I recently heard a lecture by a theoretical physicist (Lawrence Krauss) who has extended the idea of black holes (negative matter) to negative energy. There were many questions even he couldn't answer, but he seemed quite sure that an enormous number of constellations (or universes) similar to the one that includes the earth are out there. Moreover, in 14 billion years the earth will inevitably be destroyed. Neither he nor I can really contemplate this. It is only a mathematical construct. But the bottom line is that we know enough to know that there is much we do not and cannot know.

To my limited brain, it does seem that there must be something behind it all. But what that is, I don't and cannot know. Perhaps this is what I think of as the deity—the *mysterium*.

"We never see, save through a glass, darkly" (1 Corinthians 13:12). Learned Hand, a great American judge whose judicial opinions were the subject of my first book,[89] spoke of "humility before the vast unknown."[90]

The good judge also taught me to doubt—even some of his own wisdom, as when he wrote, "A sparrow cannot fall without God's will."[91] For me, the world is too random to see God's will in every atom or falling sparrow, except in some vague, unimaginable fashion. In any event, I am resigned to living in doubt. In truth, it is not so uncomfortable.

Faith is not propositional, as the scholars say. It does not depend on the truth of propositions. It cannot be proved—or falsified. It is—or it is not. Or it's an attempt.

For this reason, I do not regard one religion as truer or better than another. The questions about life—and death—remain the same. So too questions of evil—and good.

Judaism and Christianity represent man's struggle to address these issues—to understand, to explain why. All inevitably fall short.

Different religious traditions give strength and comfort with different content. We tend to find the most comfortable anchor in the tradition in which we were raised. I was raised as a Jew, so I feel most comfortable facing life's limitations within this tradition. But I understand that others raised in different traditions would find that same kind of comfort in the traditions in which they were raised. I do not feel that mine is better—except for me (and with all its faults). Yet I take pride in it.

As a general rule, however, I would not encourage conversion. You are most likely to find comfort in the religious tradition in which you were raised. But conditions vary. Today, it is very common to change religious traditions. And most religious traditions welcome this.

A recent op-ed piece in the *New York Times* documents the recent movement of the unchurched to churches.[92] Their choice was not determined by doctrine. For most of these newly churched people, "the most-cited reason for settling on their current religion was that they simply enjoyed the services and style of worship." What did they want to know about their new church/religion? "When does the choir sing? And when is the picnic? And is my child going to get a part in the holiday play?"

Let me give an example of the pull of tradition from within my Judaism. Lighting candles at the onset of the Sabbath, or Shabbat (Friday evening), is part of the Jewish tradition. The candles are lit and the blessing is said by the wife. This custom was not observed in my wife's family. But when we married, she agreed to adopt the tradition. I once had occasion to study the tradition and concluded that it was kind of silly. Why light candles? What was the significance? It seemed to have none. You just light candles! Moreover, the short prayer you say (or chant) when you light them makes no sense: "Blessed art thou O God, ruler of the universe, who commands us to light the lights of Shabbat." Nowhere in the Bible are we commanded to light candles for Shabbat. The rabbis invented the custom! So why say, "God commanded." It is even worse than this; nowhere do the rabbis specifically command this. It has to be inferred.

When my wife began lighting Shabbat candles, she did it to please me. But gradually, she did it for herself. She is certainly not into religious observance. Nevertheless, there is some strange meaning—undefined and unarticulated—with which the custom has infused our household. It lends a serenity and specialness to our Friday evening meal. It marks the beginning of a day of peacefulness (most of the time) and a day different from the hurly-burly of the other days.

The lighting of candles gradually became the first of a growing list of traditional Jewish customs we have adopted on Friday evenings—the recitation of Proverbs 31 (a tribute of the husband to his wife), the *Kiddush* (or sanctification of the Sabbath meal), including the blessing over wine (something else that God commanded!), the ritual washing of the hands, the blessing over the bread, and, yes, the blessing of the children.

What does all of this have to do with faith, the problem of evil in God's world (theodicy) and the really big issues? Seemingly, nothing. Yet, in some strange way, we somehow—"understand" is not the right word— "imbibe" our place in the universe, even with all its limitations.

This is hardly the only Jewish tradition that has this subtle effect. And for many Jews, it does not. And for other religious traditions, the same effect is reached through other traditions. We are not in a rational world here of proof or disproof. What is right for one person does not necessarily work for another.

All of which brings me to the sacred writings, specifically the Bible, to which I have devoted the past 35 years.

The Bible makes historic claims. Are they true?

An Orthodox Jew named James Kugel, who taught a popular course on the Bible at Harvard (when his course became more popular even than Economics 101, the *Harvard Crimson* headlined its story "God Beats Mammon"), recently wrote a bestselling book that asked whether modern critical scholarship on the Bible can be reconciled with traditional rabbinic learning about the text.[93] His answer, after nearly 700 pages, is "No." The two ways of looking at the Bible are irreconcilable.

Yet both are valuable. Each teaches truths about the text. The one tells us how the book came to be, what the world of the Bible was like, what in it is likely to be historically accurate and what is not. The other teaches its meaning—subtle and complicated with unplumbable depths. Simple as that. Both are rich treasures.

Both ways of looking at the biblical text represent, for me, my ancestors' struggle to understand the same mysteries that continue to mystify me. We are on the same journey, Abraham and I. Both ways of looking at the text make me feel this way. And so does archaeology, because it enriches my understanding of the world in which the events occurred and were written down (admittedly, mostly at a different time). My biblical studies—both traditional and historical—bring me closer to these ancestors and the world they lived in. And archaeology is an exciting additional tool.

If I do not fully understand, I am not alone. The Bible is *their* record of *their* struggle to understand. It is a never ending venture—it is mine as well. We—they and I—are in the same struggle. It is ultimately invigorating and life affirming. I love it.

NOTES

1   S.v. "Kishinev," in *Encyclopedia Judaica*, vol. 10, p. 1066.

2   S.v. "Odessa," in *Encyclopedia Judaica*, vol. 12, p. 1323.

3   Edward Davison, *Collected Poems, 1917–1939* (New York and London: Harper and Brothers, 1940).

4   "'State Action' and the Girard Estate Case," 105 *Univ. Pa. L. Rev.* 213 (1956).

5   Hershel Shanks, "An Incised Handle from Hazor Depicting a Syro-Hittite Deity," *Israel Exploration Journal* 23.4 (1973), p. 234.

6   Mendel Kaplan, "Teddy Kollek, In Memoriam," in *Eretz Israel, Teddy Kollek Volume*, vol. 28 (Jerusalem: Israel Exploration Society, 2007), p. ix at p. x.

7   This offer was also published in a note on p. 17 in BAR's fourth issue. See Queries and Comments, *Biblical Archaeology Review*, December 1975.

8   See Hershel Shanks, "Tom Crotser Has Found the Ark of the Covenant—Or Has He?" *Biblical Archaeology Review*, May/June 1983.

9   Hershel Shanks, "Memorandum—Re: Restoring Gezer," *Biblical Archaeology Review*, May/June 1994.

10 See Aren Maeir, "Did Captured Ark Afflict Philistines With E.D.?" *Biblical Archaeology Review*, May/June 2008.

11 Michael O. Wise, et al., eds., *Methods of Investigation of the Dead Sea Scrolls and the Khirbet Qumran Site* (New York: New York Academy of Sciences, 1994), p.154.

12 See Hershel Shanks, *The Copper Scroll and the Search for the Temple Treasure* (Washington, D.C.: Biblical Archaeology Society, 2007).

13 Frank Moore Cross, Jr., *The Ancient Library of Qumran and Modern Biblical Studies*, rev. ed. (Grand Rapids, MI: Baker Book House, 1961, reprinted 1980), pp. 35, 37.

14 Apparently, Israel's Archaeological Council and the Shrine of the Book Foundation made a decision that "The rights of the scholars previously given by the board of directors of the Rockefeller Museum were to be respected and ensured by the Israeli authorities." See Hershel Shanks, "BAR Interviews Avraham Eitan: Antiquities director confronts problems and controversies," *Biblical Archaeology Review*, July/August 1986.

15 See BARview, "Israeli Authorities Now Responsible for Delay in Publication of Dead Sea Scrolls," *Biblical Archaeology Review*, September/October 1985.

16 See "Scroll Publication" in Lawrence H. Schiffman and James C. VanderKam, eds., *Encyclopedia of the Dead Sea Scrolls* (Oxford: Oxford University Press, 2000).

17 See John Strugnell, "The Original Team of Editors," in Timothy H. Lim, Hector L. MacQueen and Calum M. Carmichael, eds., *On Scrolls, Artefacts and Intellectual Property* (Sheffield, U.K.: Sheffield Academic Press, 2001).

18 See Queries and Comments, *Biblical Archaeology Review*, January/February 1990, pp. 16, 18.

19 *Biblical Archaeology Review*, May/June 1989.

20 See Queries and Comments, "Are the Dead Sea Scrolls Being Suppressed for Doctrinal Reasons?" *Biblical Archaeology Review*, November/December 1989, p. 18.

21 Eugene R. Fisher, "The Church's Teaching on Supersessionism," *Biblical Archaeology Review*, March/April 1991.

22 Hershel Shanks, "Will Marty Abegg Ever Find a Job?" *Biblical Archaeology Review*, January/February 2003.

23 Robert Alter, "How Important Are the Dead Sea Scrolls?" *Commentary*, February 1992, p. 35.

24 In the official publication of MMT, the editors preferred to call it a "treatise." Elisha Qimron and John Strugnell, Qumran Cave IV, Vol. V, *Miqsat Ma'aseh Ha-Torah*, Discoveries in the Judaean Desert, Vol. 10 (Oxford: Clarendon Press, 1994), p. 121. But on p. 204 of the book, Strugnell withdraws the suggestion.

25 Martin Abegg, "Paul, 'Works of the Law' and MMT," *Biblical Archaeology Review*, November/December 1994.

26 Niva Elkin-Koren, "Of Scientific Claims and Proprietary Rights: Lessons from the Dead Sea Scrolls Case," *Houston Law Review* 38.2 (Summer 2001), at p. 449.

27 David Nimmer, "Copyright in the Dead Sea Scrolls," *Houston Law Review* 38.1 (Spring 2001), at p. 50.

28 "MMT as the Maltese Falcon," *Biblical Archaeology Review*, November/December 1994.

29 Elisha Qimron and John Strugnell, Qumran Cave IV, Vol. V, *Miqsat Ma'aseh Ha-Torah*, Discoveries in the Judaean Desert, Vol. 10 (Oxford: Clarendon Press, 1994), p. 201.

30 See, for example, Jeffrey M. Dine, "Authors' Moral Rights in Non-European Nations," *Michigan Journal of International Law* 16 (1995), p. 545; Cindy Alberts Carson, "Raiders of the Lost Scrolls: The Right of Scholarly Access to the Content of Historic Documents," *Michigan Journal of International Law* 16 (1995), p. 299; Lisa M. Weinstein, "Ancient Works, Modern Dilemmas: The Dead Sea Scroll Copyright Case," *American University Law Review* 43 (1994), p. 1637; Dennis S. Karjala, "Copyright and Misappropriation," *University of Dayton Law Review* 17 (1992), p. 885; "Who Owns Religious Information?" in Ann Wells Branscomb, *Who Owns Information?* (New York: Basic Books, 1994).

31 Jeffrey M. Dine, "Authors Moral Rights in Non-European Nations," *Michigan Journal of International Law* 16 (1995), p. 545 at p. 566.

32 David Nimmer, "Copyright in the Dead Sea Scrolls," *Houston Law Review* 38.1 (Spring 2001), p.1 at p. 50.

33 Hershel Shanks, "For This You Waited 35 Years," *Biblical Archaeology Review*, November/December 1994.

34 Elisha Qimron, "The Nature of the Reconstructed Composite Text of 4QMMT," in John Kampen and Moshe Berstein, eds., *Reading 4QMMT: New Perspectives on Qumran Law and History*, SBL Symposium Series 2 (Atlanta: Scholars Press, 1996), pp. 9–13.

35 The Israel Supreme Court's opinion, as well as that of Judge Dorner in the trial court, can be found in English translation.

36 David Nimmer, "Copyright in the Dead Sea Scrolls," *Houston Law Review* 38.1 (Spring 2001), p. 1 at p. 75.

37 John Strugnell, "The Original Team of Editors," in Timothy H. Lim, Hector L. MacQueen and Calum M. Carmichael, eds., *On Scrolls, Artefacts and Intellectual Property* (Sheffield, U.K.: Sheffield Academic Press, 2001), p. 190.

38 Israel Knohl, "The Messiah Son of Joseph," *Biblical Archaeology Review*, September/October 2008.

39 Hershel Shanks, "Background to Hanukkah—Inscription Reveals Roots of Maccabean Revolt," *Biblical Archaeology Review*, November/December 2008.

40 "Is the New Moabite Inscription a Forgery?" *Biblical Archaeology Review*, July/August 2005.

41 Hershel Shanks, "Magic Incantation Bowls," *Biblical Archaeology Review*, January/February 2007.

42 See Update: Finds or Fakes?, "An Interview With Othmar Keel," *Biblical Archaeology Review*, July/August 2005.

43 William G. Dever, "A Temple Built for Two," *Biblical Archaeology Review*, March/April 2008.

44 See Edward J. Keall, "New Tests Bolster Case for Authenticity," *Biblical Archaeology Review*, July/August 2003.

45 Hershel Shanks and Ben Witherington, *The Brother of Jesus: The Dramatic Story & Meaning of the First Archaeological Link to Jesus & His Family* (San Francisco: Harper, 2003).

46 Suzanne Singer, "Jerusalem Update: More Temple Mount Antiquities Destroyed," *Biblical Archaeology Review*, September/October 2000.

47 Nina Burleigh, *Unholy Business: A True Tale of Faith, Greed, and Forgery in the Holy Land* (New York: HarperCollins, 2008), p. 54.

48 Burleigh, p. 168.

49 Much of this account in taken from Burleigh, pp. 171–177.

50 Quoted in David Samuel, "Written in Stone," *The New Yorker*, April 12, 2004, p. 59.

51 Reported in *Ha'aretz*, March 24, 2004; see also Update: Finds or Fakes?, "Fakes Everywhere? The Plot Thickens—and Widens," *Biblical Archaeology Review*, July/August 2004, p. 52.

52 Hershel Shanks, "The Trial of Oded Golan," *Biblical Archaeology Review*, May/June 2004, note 12; see also Update: Finds or Fakes?, "All Bogus: Three New Rumors," *Biblical Archaeology Review*, July/August 2004, p. 59.

53 Burleigh, p. 200.

54 Ibid.

55 "Dahari: J'Accuse, Mr. Shanks," *Biblical Archaeology Review*, March/April 2005, p. 46.

56 See Strata, "BAR Editor Charged With Pivotal Role in Fraud and Forgery," *Biblical Archaeology Review*, January/February 2009, p. 13.

57 See Strata, "BAR Offers $50,000 Reward," *Biblical Archaeology Review*, May/June 2007, p. 18.

58 See First Person, "Needed: A Protocol Needed to Test Authenticity," *Biblical Archaeology Review*, July/August 2004.

59 Samuel, p. 59.

60 Ann Byle, "Duke University Professor Claims: A Third of Israel Museum's Inscriptions Are Forgeries," *Biblical Archaeology Review*, September/October 2004.

61 See Strata, "How an Israeli Forgery Committee Operates," *Biblical Archaeology Review*, March/April 2009, p. 10.

62 Matthew Kalman, "'James Ossuary Trial' Stalls After More Than Three Years," *Jerusalem Post*, April 1, 2009.

63 Ibid.

64 See Strata, "Forgery Case Collapses," *Biblical Archaeology Review*, January/February 2009, p. 12.

65 See Strata, "Trial to Continue," *Biblical Archaeology Review*, March/April 2009, p. 11.

66 Peter T. Daniels, *Maarav* 11 (2004), p. 103.

67 See especially David Samuel, "Written in Stone," *The New Yorker*, April 12, 2004; and Nina Burleigh's book *Unholy Business: A True Tale of Faith, Greed, and Forgery in the Holy Land* (New York: HarperCollins, 2008).

68 See Hershel Shanks, "Ossuary Update," *Biblical Archaeology Review*, March/April 2004.

69 See James A. Harrell, "Final Blow to IAA Report: Flawed Geochemistry Used to Condemn James Inscription," *Biblical Archaeology Review*, January/February 2004.

70 Shimon Ilani, Amnon Rosenfeld, Howard R. Feldman, Wolfgang E. Krumbein and Joel Kronfeld, "Archaeometric Analysis of the 'Jehoash Inscription' Tablet," *Journal of Archaeological Science* 35 (2008), pp. 2966–2972.

71 Burleigh, p. 249.

72 Guy Gugliotta and Samuel Sockol, "Find or Forgery, Burial Box is Open to Debate," *Washington Post*, February 21, 2005.

73 Yuval Goren et al., "A Re-Examination of the Inscribed Ivory Pomegranate From the Israel Museum," *Israel Exploration Journal* 55 (2005), p. 3.

74 Nahman Avigad, "The Inscribed Pomegranate From the 'House of the Lord,'" in Hillel Geva, ed., *Ancient Jerusalem Revealed* (Jerusalem: Israel Exploration Society, 1994), p. 137.

75 André Lemaire, "A re-examination of the Inscribed Pomegranate: A Rejoinder," *Israel Exploration Journal* 56 (2006), p. 167.

76 Hershel Shanks, Jerusalem Forgery Conference, p. 14. Published in a limited edition by the Biblical Archaeology Society. The report is also available at the Society's website: www.biblicalarchaeology.org

77 André Lemaire, "A Re-examination of the Pomegranate: A Rejoinder," *Israel Exploration Journal* 56 (2006), p. 167.

78 Shmuel Ahituv, Aaron Demsky, Yuval Goren and André Lemaire, "The Inscribed

Pomegranate from the Israel Museum Examined Again," *Israel Exploration Journal* 57 (2007), p. 87.

79 Ibid., p. 91.

80 André Lemaire, "A Re-examination of the Pomegranate: A Rejoinder," *Israel Exploration Journal* 56 (2006), p. 167.

81 See Hershel Shanks, "The Paleographer: Demonstrably a Forgery," *Biblical Archaeology Review*, May/June 2003; Edward L. Greenstein, "Hebrew Philology Spells Fake," *Biblical Archaeology Review*, May/June 2003.

82 David Noel Friedman, "Don't Rush to Judgment," *Biblical Archaeology Review*, March/April 2004.

83 Shimon Ilani, Amnon Rosenfeld, H.R. Feldman, Wolfgang E. Krumbein and Joel Kronfeld, "Archaeometric Analysis of the 'Jehoash Inscription' Tablet" *Journal of Archaeological Science* 35 (2008), pp. 2966–2972.

84 See Updates: Finds or Fakes, "Is the IAA Out to Shut Down the Legal Antiquities Market?" *Biblical Archaeology Review*, March/April 2005.

85 Ann Byle, "Israel Antiquities Authority: Too Much Booze Nabs Golan as Forger," *Biblical Archaeology Review*, September/October 2004.

86 See Strata, "Leading Scholar Lambastes IAA Committee," *Biblical Archaeology Review*, November/December 2007, p. 16.

87 Lester L. Grabbe, "Some Recent Issues in the Study of the History of Israel," in H.G.M. Williamson, ed., *Understanding the History of Ancient Israel* (Oxford: Oxford University Press, 2007), pp. 60–63.

88 "Losing Faith—Two Who Did and Two Who Didn't," *Biblical Archaeology Review*, March/April 2007.

89 Hershel Shanks, ed., *The Art and Craft of Judging, The Decisions of Judge Learned Hand* (New York: Macmillan, 1968).

90 Learned Hand, "Foreword to Williston's Life and Law," in Irving Dillard, ed., *The Spirit of Liberty, Papers and Addresses of Learned Hand* (New York: Knopf, 1959), p. 108.

91 Learned Hand, "At the Harvard Tercentenary Observance," in Irving Dillard, ed., *The Spirit of Liberty, Papers and Addresses of Learned Hand* (New York: Knopf, 1959), p. 93.

92 Charles M. Blow, "Defecting to Faith," *The New York Times*, May 2, 2009.

93 James L. Kugel, *How to Read the Bible: A Guide to Scripture, Then and Now* (New York: Free Press, 2007).

ILLUSTRATION CREDITS

Index

White, Gilbert Fowler 27
Wiesel, Elie 118, 119
Wolf, Block, Schorr and
    Solis-Cohen 35
Wolf, Robert 35
Wright, G. Earnest 84, 106
  Biblical Archaeology 61

Yadin, Yigael 67, 70, 72, 73, 74, 78,
    104, 129, 130, 137

Yale Law School 32
Yardeni, Ada 185, 206, 207, 209,
    214, 219
Yediot Achronot 74
Yehoash inscription 193–202, 224,
    225–6, 228

Zeitlin, Solomon 63
Zhitomir 7
Zionism 87